GENDER INEQUALITY

Feminist Theories and Politics

Second Edition

Judith Lorber

*Brooklyn College and
Graduate School, CUNY*

Roxbury Publishing Company
Los Angeles, California

Library of Congress Cataloging-in-Publication Data

Gender inequality: feminist theories and politics/Judith Lorber.—2nd ed.
p. cm.
Includes bibliographical references.
ISBN 1-891487-60-4
1. Sex discrimination against women. 2. Sex role. 3. Women—Social
conditions. 4. Equality. 5. Feminist theory. I. Title.
HQ1237.L67   2001
305.42'01—dc21   00-039012
                                                           CIP

Gender Inequality:
Feminist Theories and Politics (Second Edition)

Publisher and Editor: Claude Teweles
Copyeditors: Michelle N. MimLitsch, Jackie Estrada, Pauline Piekarz
Production Editors: Michelle N. MimLitsch, Jim Ballinger
Assistant Editor: Casey Haymes
Production Assistant: Kathryn Croom
Typography: Synergistic Data Systems
Cover Design: Marnie Deacon Kenney

Printed on acid-free paper in the United States of America.

This paper meets the standards for recycling of the Environmental Protection
Agency.

ISBN: 1-891487-60-4

Roxbury Publishing Company
P.O. Box 491044
Los Angeles, California 90049-9044
Tel: (310) 473-3312
E-mail: roxbury@roxbury.net
Website: www.roxbury.net

In Memory of Zina Segre
May 8, 1933 – April 27, 1997

"Her wounds came from the
same source as her power."
—Adrienne Rich

Table of Contents

Preface to the First Edition

Despite an enormous output of scholarly and popular books and articles, what feminists have actually thought and fought for in the last 35 to 40 years is being forgotten. Popular books criticizing feminism and women's studies have jumbled and caricatured complex ideas and portrayed feminists as man-hating, puritanical "women's libbers". Feminist activism has been coopted to sell Nikes.

What I have tried to do in this account of current feminism is, first, to show that there is a variety of feminist theories, and how the various theories diverge and converge. Second, I describe feminism's significant contributions to redressing gender inequality in order to give credit for its accomplishments, to document on-going political activism, and to indicate the work still to be done.

As my ideas coalesced, I have given talks around the world on the topic, and some of these talks were published. In September 1995, I spoke on "The Variety of Feminisms in the U.S. Women's Movement" at the Non-Governmental Organizations Forum at the United Nations Fourth World Conference on Women, held in Beijing, China. An excerpt was published in the *Status of Women Journal* of the British Columbia Teachers' Federation (Vancouver, Canada, March 1996).

In April 1996, I presented "The Variety of Feminisms and Their Contributions to Gender Equality" at the Eastern Sociological Society Annual Meetings held in Boston. During May and June of 1997, in conjunction with the Marie Jahoda International Visiting Professorship in Feminist Studies at Ruhr University, Bochum, Germany, I gave longer versions of that talk at the Workshop on Feminism and Social Change, and at the University of Bielefeld; Wolfgang Goethe University, Frankfurt; Humboldt University, Berlin; and Carl von Ossietzky University, Oldenburg. That talk has been published in English by the Universitätsreden BIS (Bibliotheks-und-Information System), CVO University, Oldenburg, and in German in *Feministische Studien*, as "Kontinuitäten, Diskontinuitäten und Konvergenten in Neueren Feministischen Theorium und in Feministischer Politik" ("Continuities, Discontinuities, and Convergences in Recent Feminist Theories and Politics").

Some sections of this text have been adapted from my book *Paradoxes of Gender* (New Haven, CT: Yale University Press, 1994).

The input I got from students and faculty at all these presentations was enormously helpful, as were the comments of the reviewers of the book manuscript. Throughout, the discussions and critique of Maren Carden, Susan Farrell, Eileen Moran, and Barbara Katz Rothman, my multi-feminist writing group, have made my thinking clearer. I particularly thank Susan Farrell for her information on women ethicists and feminist religions.

I also thank Claude Teweles for getting me started on this book and Carla Max-Ryan for her work and patience during the writing and production of the First Edition.

—Judith Lorber
New York City

Preface to the Second Edition

In the few years since the First Edition of *Gender Inequality: Feminist Theories and Politics,* two sets of debates have erupted—the "nature-nurture" or biology-versus-culture controversy, and the equality-versus-equity controversy. Neither are new topics to feminism; indeed, both are almost bedrock controversies. The biology-versus-culture controversy was, in fact, the starting point of the current feminist movement, with feminists arguing that women as social beings are not born, but made. (Men, too.) At that time, about 35 years ago, feminists started to split *sex* from *gender,* and to argue that *sexuality* (especially sexual behavior) was also socially constructed.

Today, the debate is much more complicated. Biology has become a shorthand term for genes, hormones, the body, the brain, and long-standing evolutionary adaptation. Culture is more than childhood learning and adult reinforcement. It involves the constant production and maintenance of the attributes, attitudes, emotions, and behavior patterns a society associates with and deems appropriate for boys and girls, women and men. Biology and culture are conceptualized today by most feminists not as antithetical, but as reciprocal elements in individual development and in social patterns, intertwining and looping back on each other.

A related topic in feminism is whether the culturally constructed side of people—their *gender*—or the biological side—*sex*—should be the focus of feminist theories and politics. These two perspectives show up as a theoretical debate between *gender feminists* and *difference feminists.* Gender feminists tend to look at social structures as the source of gender inequality and favor policies that treat everyone *equally.* Difference feminists tend to focus on differences in experiences and bodily vulnerabilities as the source of women's oppression and exploitation. They don't think that equal treatment is enough to redress major differences and favor *equitable* social remedies.

The first controversy is the subject of the new part V, "Feminist Theories of the Body." (A related issue, radical feminist perspectives on women's bodies, is discussed in part III, chapter 4. Feminist critiques of the male biases in science and medicine are summarized in part III, chapter 7, Standpoint Feminism.) The second debate is discussed in part I, in the new section, "Current Controversies and Convergences." Also new to the Second Edition is "Feminist Politics for the 21st Century." Both of these are adapted from Judith Lorber, "Using Gender to Undo Gender: A Feminist Degendering Movement," *Feminist Theory* 1:101–18, 2000.

Some of the types of feminisms have new excerpts, and all have additions to the reading list at the end of the chapters. Most of the suggested readings are books, but I have included some articles that have become classics in feminist theory. Another new feature is the list of websites for research on women, men, and gender, the last item in the book.

—Judith Lorber
New York City

About the Contributors

Edna Acosta-Belén is Distinguished Service Professor of Latin American and Caribbean Studies and Women's Studies, and Director of the Center for Latino, Latin American and Caribbean Studies (CELAC) at the University at Albany, SUNY. She is the founder and co-editor of the *Latino Review of Books* and co-editor (with Christine E. Bose) of *Women in the Latin American Development Process*.

Christine E. Bose is Associate Professor of Sociology, Women's Studies, and Latin American and Caribbean Studies at the University at Albany, SUNY. She was the founding Director of the Institute for Research on Women (IROW). She is the co-editor (with Edna Acosta-Belén) of *Women in the Latin American Development Process* and author of a forthcoming book, *Women in 1900: Gateway to the Political Economy of the 20th Century*.

Lynn S. Chancer is Associate Professor of Sociology at Fordham University in New York City. She is the author of *Sadomasochism in Everyday Life* (1992); *Reconcilable Differences: Confronting Beauty, Pornography and the Future of Feminism* (1998); and *Provoking Assaults: When High Profile Crimes Become Impassioned Social Causes* (forthcoming). She has written numerous articles and book chapters about gender and crime, feminist theory, American culture, and psychoanalysis and sociology.

Nancy J. Chodorow is Professor of Sociology at the University of California, Berkeley, a faculty member of the San Francisco Psychoanalytic Institute, and a psychoanalyst in private practice. She is the author of *The Reproduction of Mothering, Feminism and Psychoanalytic Theory*, and *Femininities, Masculinities, Sexualities: Freud and Beyond*. Her most recent book is *The Power of Feelings: Personal Meaning in Psychoanalysis, Gender and Culture*.

Patricia Hill Collins is Charles Phelps Taft Professor of Sociology in the Department of African-American Studies at the University of Cincinnati. She is the author of *Black Feminist Thought: Knowledge, Consciousness, and the Politics of Empowerment,* which has won many awards and has just been reissued in a tenth-anniversary edition. She is co-editor of *Race, Class, and Gender: An Anthology* (with Margaret

Andersen), which is now in its third edition. Her latest book, *Fighting Words: Black Women, Critical Social Theory, and the Search for Justice*, was published in 1998.

R. W. Connell is Professor of Education at the University of Sydney. He was Professor of Sociology at the University of California, Santa Cruz; Professor of Australian Studies at Harvard University; and Professor of Sociology, Marquarie University, Sydney. He is the author or co-author of 15 books, including *Class Structure in Australian History, Making the Difference, Gender and Power, Schools and Social Justice,* and *Masculinities*. He is a past president of the Sociological Association of Australia and New Zealand.

Kathy Davis is Associate Professor of Women's Studies at the Institute of Media and Representation at Utrecht University in the Netherlands. She is the author of *Reshaping The Female Body* (1995) and *Power Under the Microscope* (1988), editor of *Embodied Practices* (1997), and co-editor of *Negotiating at the Margins* (1993) and *The Gender of Power* (1991).

Bonnie Thornton Dill is Professor of Women's Studies and Affiliate Professor of Sociology at the University of Maryland. Her research focuses on African American women, work, and families. She is currently conducting a research project on coping and survival strategies of low-income single mothers in rural Southern communities.

Cynthia Fuchs Epstein is Distinguished Professor of Sociology at the Graduate Center of the City University of New York. She has been a fellow of the Institute for Advanced Study in the Behavioral Sciences, a Guggenheim Fellow, and winner of awards of the American Bar Association and the American Sociological Association. Her books include *Woman's Place: Options and Limits in Professional Careers, Women in Law, Access to Power: Cross National Studies on Women and Elites,* and *Deceptive Distinctions: Sex, Gender and the Social Order.*

Lillian Faderman is Professor of English at California State University, Fresno. She is the author of *Surpassing the Love of Men: Romantic Friendship and Love Between Women from the Renaissance to the Present* and *Odd Girls and Twilight Lovers: A History of Lesbian Life in Twentieth-Century America,* as well as two books on ethnic minorities.

Roslyn L. Feldberg is a sociologist committed to improving women's conditions of employment. She has written on social and technical changes in clerical work and on comparable worth. Now she is working to improve the conditions of work for nurses from her position as Associate Director in Labor Relations at the Massachusetts Nurses Association.

Jane Flax teaches political theory at Howard University and is a psychotherapist in private practice. Her publications include *Thinking Fragments, Disputed Subjects,* and *Hearts of Whiteness: The Clarence Thomas Hearings and Contemporary American Dilemmas of Race and Gender.*

Anne Fausto-Sterling is Professor of Biology and Women's Studies at Brown University. She is the author of numerous articles and of two extremely influential books: *Myths of Gender: Biological Theories about Women and Men* (originally published in 1985; 2nd edition, 1992) and *Sexing the Body: Gender Politics and the Construction of Sexuality* (2000). She is a Fellow of the American Association for the Advancement of Science and has been the recipient of grants and fellowships in both the sciences and the humanities.

Heidi Hartmann is Director of the Washington-based Institute for Women's Policy Research, which she founded in 1987. An economist, she has co-authored *Unnecessary Losses: Costs to Americans of the Lack of Family and Medical Leave; Women's Access to Health Insurance;* and *Combining Work and Welfare: An Alternative Anti-Poverty Strategy.* In 1994, she was the recipient of a MacArthur fellowship award to recognize her pioneering work in the field of women and economics.

Nancy C. M. Hartsock is Professor of Political Science at the University of Washington in Seattle, where she teaches graduate courses on the philosophy of social science and twentieth century Marxism and contemporary feminist theory. She is the author of *Money, Sex, and Power: Toward a Feminist Historical Materialism* and co-editor of *Building Feminist Theory* (with Charlotte Bunch, Jane Flax, Alexa Freeman, and Mary Ellen Mautner). Her newest book is *Post-Modernism and Political Change: Issues for Feminist Theory.*

Sarah Blaffer Hrdy is an independent scholar affiliated with the Anthropology Department at the University of California–Davis. She is the author of *The Langurs of Abu: Female and Male Strategies of Reproduction* and *The Woman That Never Evolved.* In both, she stressed the extent to which female primates were sexually assertive and competitive "strategists." Her most recent book, *Mother Nature,* was chosen by *Publishers Weekly* and *Library Journal* as one of the Best Books of 1999. Hrdy has been elected to the National Academy of Sciences and to the American Academy of Arts and Sciences.

Nhlanhla Jordan lectures in sociology at the University of the Transkei in South Africa, where she focuses on rural and gender sociology. She is also one of the editors of the journal *Women's Studies.*

Rosabeth Moss Kanter holds the class of 1960 Chair as Professor of Business Administration at the Harvard Business School. She is the author of 12 books and over 150 articles on organization, management, and social change, most recently, *Frontiers of Management. When Giants Learn to Dance* received the Johnson, Smith & Knisely Award for New Perspectives on Executive Leadership and was translated into 10 languages. *Men and Women of the Corporation* was the winner of the Society for the Study of Social Problems C. Wright Mills Award for the year's best book on social issues.

Suzanne J. Kessler is Professor of Psychology at Purchase College, SUNY. Her interests include the psychology of gender, categories that violate gender assumptions (transsexuality, intersexuality), and women, and AIDS. Her awards include Purchase College Students' Union Award for Outstanding Faculty Member and the SUNY Chancellor's Award for Excellence in Teaching. She is the co-author of *Gender: An Ethnomethodological Approach* and author of *Lessons from the Intersexed.*

Judith Lorber is Professor Emerita of Sociology at Brooklyn College and the Graduate School, City University of New York. She is the author of *Breaking the Bowls: Gender Theory and Social Change* (forthcoming), *Gender and the Social Construction of Illness* (1997), and *Paradoxes of Gender* (1994). She is co-editor of *Revisioning Gender* and *The Social Construction of Gender.* She was founding editor of *Gender & Society,* official publication of Sociologists for Women in Society.

Catharine A. MacKinnon is Professor of Law at the University of Michigan and the University of Chicago. She is the author of *Sexual Harassment of Working Women,* which advocated making sexual harassment illegal as sex discrimination, as well as *Feminism Unmodified: Discourses on Life and Law* and *Toward a Feminist Theory of the State.* She and Andrea Dworkin wrote ordinances making pornography a violation of civil rights, and they are the co-authors of *Pornography and Civil Rights: A New Day for Women's Equality* and co-editors of *In Harm's Way: The Pornography Civil Rights Hearings.*

Michael A. Messner is Associate Professor of Sociology and Gender Studies at the University of Southern California. He is author of *Power at Play: Sports and the Problem of Masculinity* and co-author of *Sex, Violence, and Power in Sports: Rethinking Masculinity* (with Donald F. Sabo). His latest book is *Politics of Masculinities: Men in Movements* in the Sage Gender Lens series.

Maria Mies is Professor of Sociology in Cologne, Germany. From 1979 to 1981 she worked at the Institute of Social Studies, The Hague,

Holland, where she initiated the Women and Development program. Her main areas of work are feminist theory and methodology; patriarchy, colonialism, and capitalism; and ecofeminism. She is author of many books, including *Patriarchy and Accumulation, Ecofeminism* (co-authored with Vandana Shiva), and *The Lace Makers of Narsapur*. Her latest book is *The Subsistence Perspective: Beyond the Globalized Economy* (co-authored with Veronika Bennholdt-Thomsen).

Barbara Katz Rothman is Professor of Sociology at Baruch College and the Graduate School, City University of New York. Her latest book is *Genetic Maps and Human Imaginations: The Limits of Science in Understanding Who We Are* (1998), to be reissued as *The Book of Life* (2001). She is also the author of *Recreating Motherhood: Ideology and Technology in a Patriarchal Society* (2000; 1989), which won the American Sociological Association Jessie Bernard Award; *The Tentative Pregnancy: Prenatal Diagnosis and the Future of Motherhood* (1986); and *In Labor: Women and Power in the Birthplace* (1982).

Sara Ruddick teaches at the Eugene Lang College of The New School for Social Research. She is the author of *Maternal Thinking: Toward a Politics of Peace*.

Paula C. Rust is Associate Professor at the State University of New York, Geneseo. She is a sociologist who specializes in the study of sexual identities and politics, with emphasis on bisexuality. Her newest book is *Bisexuality in the United States: A Social Science Reader*. She reached political consciousness during the height of lesbian feminism in the 1970s, and lives with her partner, Lorna, and their three children in an interracial, bicultural family.

Eve Kosofsky Sedgwick is Distinguished Professor of English at the Graduate Center of the City University of New York. She is the author of *The Coherence of Gothic Conventions, Between Men: English Literature and Male Homosocial Desire, Epistemology of the Closet,* and *Tendencies.* Her latest book, *A Dialogue on Love,* is autobiographical.

Barrie Thorne is Professor of Sociology and Women's Studies and Co-Director of the Center for Working Families at the University of California, Berkeley. She is the author of *Gender Play: Girls and Boys in School* and co-editor of *Feminist Sociology: Life Histories of a Movement,* and of *Rethinking the Family: Some Feminist Questions.* She is now working on an ethnography of childhoods in contemporary California.

Candace West is Professor of Sociology at the University of California–Santa Cruz. She is the author of *Routine Complications: Troubles with Talk Between Doctors and Patients,* as well as articles on language, gender, and conversational analysis and on the interactional basis for social structure.

Don H. Zimmerman is Professor of Sociology at the University of California–Santa Barbara. Other articles on gender co-authored with Candace West include "Sex Roles, Interruptions, and Silences," "Women's Place in Everyday Talk," and "Gender, Language, and Discourse."

Maxine Baca Zinn is Professor of Sociology at Michigan State University, where she is also Senior Research Associate at the Julian Samora Research Institute. Her publications include *Women of Color in U.S. Society* (co-edited with Bonnie Thornton Dill), *Through the Prism of Difference: A Sex and Gender Reader* (co-edited with Pierrette Hondagneu-Sotelo and Michael A. Messner), and *Diversity in Families* (co-edited with D. Stanley Eitzen). ✦

Part I

The Variety of Feminisms and Their Contributions to Gender Equality

Feminism is a social movement whose goal is raising the status of women. In many times and places in the past, men and women have proclaimed women's capabilities and have tried to better women's social position. As an organized movement, however, feminism rose in the nineteenth century in Europe and America.

A Brief History of Organized Feminism

The *first-wave* feminists of the nineteenth and early twentieth centuries fought for rights we take for granted today. It is hard to believe these rights were among those once denied to women of every social class, racial category, ethnicity, and religion—the right to vote (suffrage), to own property and capital, to inherit, to keep money earned, to go to college, to become a professionally certified physician, to argue cases in court.

1

The theory of equality that feminists of the nineteenth century used in their fight for women's rights came out of liberal political philosophy, which said that all men should be equal under the law, that no one should have special privileges or rights. Of course, when the United States of America was founded, that concept of equality excluded enslaved men and indentured menservants because they were not free citizens, as well as all women, no matter what their social status, because they were not really free either. Their legal status was the same as that of children—economically dependent and borrowing their social status from their father or husband. In Ibsen's famous play *A Doll's House*, Nora forged her dead father's signature because she could not legally sign her own name to the loan she needed to save her sick husband's life.

First-wave feminism's goal was to get equal rights for women, especially the vote, or suffrage. (Feminists were often called *suffragists*.) In the United States, women did not get the right to vote until 1919. Many European countries also gave women the right to vote after World War I, in repayment for their war efforts. French women, however, did not get suffrage until after World War II, when a grateful Charles de Gaulle enfranchised them for their work in the underground fight against the Nazis and the collaborationist government of occupied France.

The Russian and Chinese revolutions of the early twentieth century gave women equal rights, even though they criticized the individualism of "bourgeois feminism." Their emphasis was on work in the collective economy, with prenatal care and child care provided by the state so women could be both workers and mothers.

As the countries of Africa, Asia, and Central and South America broke free of colonial control after World War II and set up independent governments, they, too, gave their women citizens the right to vote. In some Muslim countries, however, women still cannot vote, leave the house without their husband's permission, drive cars, or appear in public unveiled.

Suffrage was the main goal of women's liberation in the first wave of feminism, but rights concerning property, earnings, and higher education—many of which were granted by the end of the nineteenth century—gave women a chance for economic independence. These rights were vital for raising married women's status from childlike dependence on a husband and for giving widows and single women some way of living on their own instead of as a poor relation in their father's or brother's or son's household. Liberated women in the first part of the twentieth century included independent factory girls who worked all day and went dancing at night, and middle- and upper-class educated women who had "Boston marriages" (were housemates for life).

There was another branch of nineteenth-century feminism that did not focus on equal rights but on a woman's right to "own" her body and to plan her pregnancies. A twentieth-century feminist struggle that was as hard fought as that for suffrage was the fight for legal means of contraception that could be controlled by the woman. Women could not be free to be good mothers and wives, especially if they were poor, if they had one child after another. But doctors were forbidden to fit women with diaphragms or cervical caps (the precursors of the coil and the pill). Even mailing information across state lines was illegal. The widespread use of contraception by married women was feared by traditionalists, who saw the downfall of the family. Feminists feared that men would sexually exploit unmarried women who were protected against pregnancy. For women themselves, the positive outcome of this long battle for legalized woman-controlled contraception has been both greater sexual freedom before marriage and planned parenthood after marriage.

As is evident from this brief overview, the first-wave feminist movement had many of the theoretical and political differences of the feminist movement that succeeded it. The question of differences between women and men, and whether they should be treated *equally* because they are essentially the same or *equitably* because they are essentially different, is still under debate. The question of where feminist politics should put the most effort—the public sphere (work and government) or the private sphere (family and sexuality)—is also still with us.

The current feminist movement is called the *second wave*. A post–World War II movement, it began with the publication in France in 1949 of Simone de Beauvoir's *The Second Sex*. This sweeping account of the historical and current status of women in the Western World argues that men set the standards and values and that women are the Other, those who lack the qualities the dominants exhibit. Men are the actors, women the reactors. Men thus are the first sex, women always the second sex. Men's dominance and women's subordination is not a biological phenomenon, de Beauvoir insisted, but a social creation:

> One is not born, but rather becomes, a woman ...; it is civilization as a whole that produces this creature ... which is described as feminine. (1953, 267)

Although *The Second Sex* was widely read, the second wave of feminism did not take shape as an organized political movement until the 1960s, when young people were publicly criticizing many aspects of Western society. In the years since, feminism has made many contributions to social change by focusing attention on the continued ways women are more socially disadvantaged than men, by analyzing the sexual oppressions women suffer, and by proposing interpersonal as well as political and legal solutions. However, the feminist view of what makes women and men unequal is less unified today than in first-wave feminism, and there is a myriad of feminist solutions to gender inequality. If feminist voices seem to be much more fragmented than they were in the nineteenth century, it is the result of a deeper understanding of the sources of gender inequality. It is also the contradictory effect of uneven success. Feminists who are now members of corporations, academia, or government, who are lawyers or doctors or respected artists and writers, are well aware of the limitations of their positions, given glass ceilings and sexual harassment. But their viewpoint is different from that of the more radical anti-establishment feminist critics, who decry institutionalized sexual oppression and pervasive devaluation of women.

Although much of the feminist movement of the twentieth century has happened in industrialized countries, there have also been vital and important struggles for resources for girls and women in African and South and Central American countries, especially after these countries became independent of their colonial masters. In the Middle East, women and men have struggled to reconcile the rights of women with the traditional precepts of Islam and Judaism. In Asia, the problems of poverty and overpopulation, even though they more often adversely affect women and girls, need remedies that affect everyone. Women's political movements in these countries may not be called "feminist," but they are gender-based battles nevertheless.

Further from the mainstream are feminisms that challenge "what everyone knows" about sex, sexuality, and gender—the duality and oppositeness of female and male, homosexual and heterosexual, women and men. These feminist theories are now being called the feminist *third wave;* they argue that there are many sexes, sexualities, and genders. If these ideas seem farfetched or outlandish, remember that at the beginning of the second wave, when feminists used "he or she" for the generic "he," "Ms." instead of "Miss" or "Mrs.," and "worker in the home" for "housewife," they were called radical troublemakers. Social change does not come without confrontation, and it is important to know what feminists who are not heard in the mass media are saying about gender inequality and how it can be eradicated.

Gender Inequality

The goal of feminism as a political movement is to make women and men more equal. *Gender inequality* takes many different forms, depending on the economic structure and social organization of a particular society and on the culture of any particular group within that society. Although we speak of *gender* inequality, it is usually women who are disadvantaged relative to similarly situated men. Women often receive lower pay for the same or comparable work, and they are frequently blocked in their chances for advancement, especially to top positions. There is usually an imbalance in the amount of housework and child care a wife does compared to her husband, even when both spend the same amount of time in paid work outside the home. When women professionals are matched with men of comparable productiveness, men still get greater recognition for their work and move up career ladders faster. On an overall basis, gender inequality means that work most often done by women, such as teaching small children and nursing, is paid less than work most often done by men, such as construction and mining. Gender inequality can also take the form of girls getting less education than boys of the same social class. Nearly two-thirds of the world's illiterates are women, but the gender gap in education is closing at all levels of schooling. In many countries, men get priority over women in the distribution of health care services and in the emphasis on research of men's diseases over women's. Contraceptive use has risen in industrial countries, but in developing countries, death in childbirth is still a leading cause of death for young women. AIDS takes an even more terrible toll on women than men globally, since women's risk of becoming infected with HIV during unprotected sex is two to four times higher than in men. In 1999, 52 percent of the 2.1 million adults who died from AIDS were women, and they are almost half of the 32.4 million adults living with HIV/AIDS; in sub-Saharan Africa, they are 55 percent.[1]

Gender inequality takes even more oppressive and exploitative forms. Women are vulnerable to beatings, rape, and murder—often by their husbands or boyfriends, and especially when they try to leave an abusive relationship. The bodies of girls and women are used in sex work—pornography and prostitution. They are on display in movies, television, and advertising in Western cultures. In some African and Middle Eastern cultures their genitals are mutilated and their bodies are covered from head to toe in the name of chastity. They may be forced to bear children they do not want or to have abortions or be sterilized against their will. In some countries with overpopulation, infant girls are much more often abandoned in orphanages than infant boys. In other countries, if the sex of the fetus can be determined, it is girls who are aborted.

Gender inequality can also disadvantage men. In many countries, only men serve in the armed forces, and in most countries, only men are sent into direct combat. It is mostly men who do the more dangerous work, such as firefighting and policing. Although women have fought in wars and are entering police forces and fire departments, the gender arrangements of most societies assume that women will do the work of bearing and caring for children while men will do the work of protecting and supporting them economically.

This gendered division of labor is rooted in the survival of small groups living at subsistence level, where babies are breastfed and food is obtained for older children and adults by foraging and hunting. The child-carers (mostly women) gathered fruits and vegetables, and hunted small animals—babies were carried in slings and older children were helpers. Those not caring for children (mostly men, but also unmarried women) could travel further in tracking large animals, more dangerous work. Hunters who came back with meat and hides were highly praised, but if the hunt was unsuccessful, they still had something to eat when they returned to the home camp, thanks to the child-minders' more reliable foraging.

Most women in industrial and post-industrial societies do not spend their lives having and caring for babies, and most women throughout the world do paid and unpaid work to supply their families with food, clothing, and shelter, even while they are taking care of children. The modern forms of gender inequality are not a complementary exchange of responsibilities but an elaborate system within which, it was estimated by a United Nations report in 1980, women do two-thirds of the world's work, receive 10 percent of the world's income, and own 1 percent of the world's property. The gender gap in paid work is narrowing, but women still do most of the domestic work and child care, and at the same time do agricultural labor, run small businesses, and do a great deal of home-based paid work, all of which is low-waged labor.

The major social and cultural institutions support this system of gender inequality. Religions legitimate the social arrangements that produce inequality, justifying them as right and proper. Laws support the status quo and also often make it impossible to redress the outcomes—to prosecute husbands for beating their wives, or boyfriends for raping their girlfriends. In the arts, women's productions are so often ignored that they are virtually invisible, leading Virginia Woolf to conclude that Anonymous must have been a woman. Sciences have been accused of asking biased questions and ignoring findings that do not support conventional beliefs about sex differences.

Except for the Scandinavian countries, which have the greatest participation of women in government and the most gender-equal laws and state policies, most governments are run by socially dominant men, and their policies reflect their interests. In every period of change, including those of revolutionary upheaval, men's interests, not women's, have prevailed, and many men, but few women, have benefited from progressive social policies. Equality and justice for all usually means for men only. Women have never had their revolution because the structure of gender as a social institution has never been seriously challenged. Therefore, all men benefit from the "patriarchal dividend"—women's unpaid work maintaining homes and bringing up children; women's low-paid work servicing hospitals, schools, and myriad other workplaces; and women's emotional nurturing and caretaking.

The main point recent feminisms have stressed about gender inequality is that it is not an individual matter but is deeply ingrained in the structure of societies. Gender inequality is built into the organization of marriage and families, work and the economy, politics, religions, the arts and other cultural productions, and the very language we speak. Making women and men equal, therefore, necessitates social and not individual solutions.

Feminist Theories

The foregoing portrait of a gender-unequal world is a summation of the work of generations of feminist researchers and scholars. Feminist theories were developed to explain the reasons for this pervasive gender inequality. Feminists are not satisfied with the explanation that it is natural, God-given, or necessary because women get pregnant and give birth and men do not. With deeper probing into the pervasiveness of gender inequality, feminists have produced more complex views about gender, sex, and sexuality. Although there is considerable overlap among them, it is useful to separate the concepts of gender, sex, and sexuality in order to illustrate how gendering modifies bodies and sexual behavior. This book uses the following definitions and vocabulary:

Gender: a social status and a personal identity, as enacted in parental and work roles and in relationships between women and men. Through the social processes of gendering, gender divisions and roles are built into the major social institutions of society, such as the economy, the family, the state, culture, religion, and the law—the gendered social order. *Woman* and *man* are used when referring to gender.

Sex: a complex interplay of genes, hormones, environment, and behavior, with loop-back effects between bodies and society. *Male, female,* and *intersex* are used when referring to sex.

Sexuality: lustful desire, emotional involvement, and fantasy, as enacted in a variety of long- and short-term intimate relationships. *Homosexuality, heterosexuality*, and *bisexuality* are used when referring to sexuality.

Third-wave feminism has concentrated on examining the complex interplay of sex, sexuality, and gender. These feminists speak of genders, sexes, and sexualities. The two "opposites" in each case—women and men, female and male, homosexual and heterosexual—have become multiple. These feminists point to recent research that has shown female and male physiology to be produced and maintained by both female and male hormones. They argue that sex is more of a continuum than a sharp dichotomy. Similarly, studies of sexual orientation have shown that neither homosexuality nor heterosexuality is always fixed for life, and that bisexuality, in feelings and in sexual relationships, is widespread. When it comes to gender, many third-wave feminist social researchers prefer to speak of genders, since men's and women's social statuses, personal identities, and life chances are intricately tied up with their racial, ethnic, and religious groups, their social class, their family background, and their place of residence.

Nonetheless, these widely differing groups of people have to fit into two and only two socially recognized genders in Western societies—"men" and "women." The members of these two major status categories are supposed to be different from each other, and the members of the same category are supposed to have essential similarities. Work and family roles, as well as practically all other aspects of social life, are built on these two major divisions of people. This gendering produces the *gendered social order.* Gender inequality is built into the structure of the gendered social order because the two statuses—women and men—are treated differently and have significantly different life chances. How and why these social processes have come about and continue to operate is the subject of feminist theories. What to do about them is the aim of feminist politics.

Feminist politics does not refer only to the arena of government or the law; it can be confrontational protests, such as Take Back the Night marches, or work through organizations with a broad base, such as the National Organization of Women (NOW) and the National Organization for Men Against Sexism (NOMAS). It can be service centers, such as battered women's shelters, and service activities, such as gender-sensitivity and anti-rape sessions for college men. Changing language and media presentations to remove sexist put-downs that denigrate men as well as women is also feminist politics. Other remedies for redressing gender inequality, such as creating culture and knowledge from a woman's point of view, may not look political, but to feminists, they are deeply political because their intent is to change the way people look at the world.

Types of Feminisms

In this book, current feminisms are categorized according to their *theory or theories of gender inequality*—what they consider the main reason for women having a lesser social status and fewer advantages than men of similar education, class background, religion, racial category, and ethnic group. From these theories follow the feminism's proposed solutions or remedies—its *politics.*

Given the variety of feminist theories about the main sources of gender inequality, it would be better to speak of *feminisms,* rather than feminism. The feminisms of the last half-century can be grouped into three broad categories that reflect their solutions to gender inequality. These are *gender reform feminisms, gender resistance feminisms,* and *gender rebellion feminisms. Gender reform feminisms* fight to equalize the status of women and men within the existing structure of the gendered social order; for example, they want to see more women as presidents of major corporations. *Gender resistance feminisms* struggle against the oppression and exploitation of women in the gendered social order, particularly in sexuality, violence, and cultural representations. *Gender rebellion* feminisms challenge the very structure of the gendered social order by questioning its basis—the division of people into two genders.

In an overall sense, the politics of each group of feminisms takes its emphasis from the feminism's theoretical focus. *Gender reform feminisms* focus on women's work in the family and the economy as the source of gender inequality. *Gender resistance feminisms* blame violence and sexual oppression against women, and the invisibility of women's experiences in the production of knowledge and culture. *Gender rebellion feminisms* deconstruct the processes and symbols that build and maintain the unequal gender order.

Gender reform feminisms (liberal, marxist and socialist, and postcolonial) have made visible the pervasiveness of overt discriminatory practices, both formal and informal, in the work world and in the distribution of economic resources. The 1960s and 1970s brought dissatisfaction with conventional ideas about women and men, their bodies, sexualities, psyches, and behavior. The beliefs prevalent at that time about women and men tended to stress differences between them and to denigrate women in comparison with men, who were seen as stronger, smarter, and generally more capable than women—except for taking care of children. Mothering was women's strength and responsibility, and so women were seen as mothers before, during, and after they were anything else. The extent of the work women do—in the family, in kinship networks, as volunteers and as "off-the-books" workers, and in family enterprises—was virtually invisible and uncounted in national economic statistics.

Gender reform feminisms want women to be valued as much as men and to be free to live their lives according to their *human* potential. People should be able to work, parent, produce culture and science, govern, and otherwise engage in social life as they choose, whether they are women or men. The goal of gender reform feminisms is equal participation of women and men in all walks of life and equal recognition and reward for the work they do.

Gender resistance feminisms (radical, lesbian, psychoanalytic, and standpoint) claim that the gender order cannot be made gender-neutral because men's dominance is too strong. Gender equality, they argue, ends up with women becoming just like men—career-oriented and unemotional. They stress the importance of a perspective based on women's experience. By examining the gender order from the standpoint of women, they make visible the hidden relationships among organizations, institutions, and daily practices that allow men to control women's lives. They call it *patriarchy,* a concept referring to men's pervasive domination introduced by marxist feminism and expanded by radical feminism to encompass the entire gender order.

In the 1970s and 1980s, gender resistance feminisms developed an important theoretical insight—the power of *gender ideology,* the values and beliefs that justify the gendered social order. Gender resistance feminisms argue that gender inequality has been legitimated by major religions that say men's dominance is a reflection of God's will, by sciences that claim that dominance is a result of genetic or hormonal differences, and by legal systems that deny women redress in the courts. The mass media, sports, and pornography encourage the excesses of men's power—violence, rape, and sexual exploitation.

Some feminists feel that men's oppression of women is so universal that the best way to resist is to form a woman-centered society and create a women-oriented culture, ethics, and even religion. This strategy is called *cultural feminism.* It is not really a separate feminism but a trend within radical and lesbian feminism. Other gender resistance feminists say that the systemic violence against women and exploitation of women's sexuality needs continued political engagement with the larger society, at the same time as woman-only spaces are created for refuge and recreation. All the gender resistance feminisms stress the importance of countering the negative evaluations of women by valorizing their nurturance, emotional supportiveness, and mothering capacities, by encouraging pride in women's bodies, and teaching women how to protect themselves against sexual violence.

Gender rebellion feminisms (multicultural, men, social construction, postmodern, and queer theory) attack the gender order directly by multiplying the categories of and undermining the boundaries between women and men, female and male, heterosexual and homosexual. Since the 1980s, feminist deconstruction of the categories of sex, sexuality, and gender has shown how their taken-for-grantedness maintains the gender order. By questioning the dualities of male and female, heterosexual and homosexual, masculine and feminine, man and woman, gender rebellion feminisms undermine the legitimacy of favoring one group over its opposite.

Gender rebellion feminisms trace the connections among gender, racial category, ethnicity, religion, social class, and sexual orientation to show how people become advantaged or disadvantaged in complex stratification systems. The gendered social order, they argue, sets men against men as well as men against women. Men and women of the same racial and ethnic group or in the same economic stratum have much in common with each other, more than men may have with men or women with women in other groups. Sexual orientation also divides groups of women and men, with gay men and lesbian women splitting off and forming their own communities. But gays and lesbians together also form homosexual-rights coalitions and work together in AIDS service organizations.

Thus, according to gender rebellion feminism, both personal identities and the identity politics of groups are constantly shifting. There is room in life for individual and social change, for new kinds of relationships, and for new ways of organizing work and family.

Gender reform feminisms laid the theoretical groundwork for second-wave feminism. Their politics are practical and perhaps the best way to redress gender inequality at the present time. The fight for equal legal status and political representation for women and men, and for autonomy for women in making procreative, sexual, and marital choices, still has not been won in most countries of the world. Gender segregation in the workplace and lower pay for women's work is pervasive in capitalist and socialist economies. The global economy exploits poor women and men as cheap labor, and economic restructuring in industrializing and postindustrial economies has reduced social-service benefits to mothers and children. These economic problems are another arena for feminist gender politics.

Although the politics of gender reform feminisms spill over into a politics for every disadvantaged person, the battles of gender resistance feminisms are for women alone. Fighting to protect women's bodies against unwanted pregnancies and sterilizations, abortions of female fetuses, genital mutilation, rape, beatings, and murder has been an enormous and never-ending struggle. The sexual integrity of women and girls needs protection from forced prostitution, exploitative sex work in pornographic productions and nightclubs, and loveless marriages. Both lesbians and gay men need to be able to live free of discrimination and violent attacks, but many lesbian women also want their own physical space and cultural communities, where they can live free of sexual harassment and men's domination, nourish their loves and friendships, and produce books, music, art, and drama that reflect their different ways of thinking and feeling. Standpoint feminists argue that women's experiences and distinctive outlooks on life have to be included in the production of knowledge, especially in science and social science research. It is not enough to just add women subjects to research designs; questions have to be asked from a critical feminist perspective, data have to include women's voices, and analysis has to reflect the points of view of those who have been marginalized and silenced.

Picking up on the importance of social position, gender rebellion feminisms exploded the categories of women and men into all sorts of multiples. Multicultural, multiracial, and multiethnic feminisms are part of a powerful political movement to redress past and present legal and social discrimination of disadvantaged groups in so many societies, and to preserve their cultures. Men's feminism follows in the footsteps of working-class social research and politics but expands their political arena to include gay men. Condemnation of the price paid for the rewards of professional sports and the physical and sexual violence they foster is their particular political agenda. In conjunction with the radical feminist fight against rape and pornography, men's feminism has gone directly to men in college workshops, seminars, and conferences to make them aware of how their behavior can be so harmful to women.

Social construction and postmodern feminisms have only begun to translate their theoretical and linguistic destabilization of the gender order into politics or praxis. Degendering needs to be translated into everyday interaction, which could be revolutionary enough. But to fulfill their political potential, the gender rebellion feminisms need to spell out what precisely has to be done in all the institutions and organizations of a society—family, workplace, government, the arts, religion, law, and so on—to ensure equal participation and opportunity for every person in every group. Gender rebellion feminists have said that there are multiple voices in this world; now, they have to figure out how to ensure that every voice can be heard in the production of knowledge and culture and in the power systems of their societies.

Current Controversies and Convergences[2]

All the feminisms have made important contributions to improving women's status, but each also has limitations. Indeed, feminist theories have changed as the limitations of one set of ideas were critiqued and addressed by what was felt to be a better explanation about why women and men were so unequal in status and power. But it has not been a clear progression by any means, because many of the debates went on simultaneously. As a matter of fact, many are still going on. And because all of the feminisms have insight into the problems of gender inequality, and all have come up with good strategies for remedying these problems, all the feminisms are still very much with us. There are continuities and convergences, as well as sharp debates, among the different feminisms. One current debate—over the concept of gender itself—cuts across the different types of feminisms.

Feminists want a social order in which gender does not privilege men as a category nor give them power over women as a category. As with feminists of the past, feminists today are faced with the dilemma of opting for gender-neutral *equality* or gender-marked *equity*. Feminists who argue for gender equality claim that women and men are virtually interchangeable, so they should be treated the same. Feminists who take the perspective of gender equity focus on the physiological and procreative sex differences between females and males and look for ways to make them socially equivalent. These two perspectives have produced a debate over whether to talk about *gender* or *women*.

At the beginning of the second wave of feminism, the use of *gender* in place of *sex* by English speakers was a deliberate strategy to counter prevailing ideas about the universality and immutability of sex differences. What we now call gender was originally conceptualized as "sex roles"— the social and cultural overlay that exaggerates and builds on the biological differences between males and females, with procreative functions the most obvious and universal. "Sex roles" encompassed behavior and attitudes learned in growing up and applied to adult work and family situations. As the concept of gender has developed in the social sciences, it has moved from an attribute of individuals that produces effects in the phenomenon under study (e.g., women and men have different crime rates, voting patterns, labor force participation) to a major building block in the social order and an integral element in every aspect of social life (e.g., how crime is conceptualized and categorized is gendered, political processes are gendered, the economy and the labor force are gender-segregated and gender-stratified).

Gender feminists contend that sex, sexuality, and gender are constructed in everyday interaction within the constraints of social norms. The intertwining of sex, sexuality, and gender with each other and with other socially produced categories, such as social class, racial groups, and ethnicity, results in multiple and fluid social identities. *Difference feminists* argue that the experience of female bodies and sexuality produces a common and stable identity—woman. In this perspective, women's procreative potential enhances their nurturing capacities; their emotional openness makes them good mothers and bonds them to other women. Their sexuality, however, makes them vulnerable to violence and exploitation. Conversely, the social encouragement of male aggression and their patriarchal entitlement encourages the violent potentialities of men's control of women's bodies, sexuality, and emotions.

Gender reform and *gender rebellion* feminists tend to be comfortable with the concept of gender as a social status that is produced and maintained through social processes. *Gender resistance* feminists are uncomfortable with a concept that downplays the distinctive qualities of women—their relationship to their bodies and sexuality, their emotional and nurturing capabilities, their special viewpoint in male-dominated societies and cultures.

These two perspectives in feminism have polarized because difference feminists have contended that a focus on gender erases the category "woman" on which so much of feminist theory, research, and politics is based. However, non-White, non-European feminists have already critiqued the global conceptualization of "woman" and insisted on racial, ethnic, and cultural multiplicities. Feminists writing about men have described the differences among them—bodily, sexual, racial, ethnic, and social class. In addition, a large body of theory and research from gay, lesbian, and transgender studies has provided extensive data on the variety in gendered sexualities.

These perspectives are not as far apart as they may seem. A gender perspective locates the source of women's oppression in the organization of the social world, so that biology and sexuality are socially constructed *as* gendered. Therefore, biological and sexual sources of oppression are symptoms of the underlying pathology—the gendered social order. Menstruation, menopause, hormonal fluctuations, pregnancy, eating disorders, and propensities to different illnesses are biological phenomena that are mediated by social experiences. Feminists who would not be considered gender feminists have described the social constraints on childbirth and motherhood. Others have laid out the politics of the social formation and control of sexual practices. They all argue that bodies do matter and the way they matter is a social phenomenon. Gender theory adds another layer, claiming that the body is always gendered, therefore female and male bodies are made feminine or masculine by family and peer approval, through mass media representations, and through sports and other physical activity.

Gender feminism and difference feminism both argue that emotions are gendered as well. Empathy and ability to nurture emerge from responsibility for care of others, so men as well as women who do intensive parenting become good at it. Rape, battering, and other forms of sexual aggression are encouraged and discouraged in different situations. Gang rape, for instance, has occurred at fraternity parties where there is heavy drinking and sexual showing off. "Take back the night" movements on campuses and sexual harassment guidelines have raised awareness of women students' vulnerability and have resulted in protective policies and practices.

Gender feminism and difference feminism merge in analyses of how psyches get structured in girls and boys. *Psychoanalytic feminism* links the division of parenting in the heterogendered Western nuclear family to emotional repression in men and emotional openness and nurturance in women. Both emerge from the primacy of women in parenting. Boys' separation from their mothers and identification with their fathers leads to becoming part of the dominant world of men but also necessitates continuous repression of their emotional longings for their mother and fear of castration by their father. Girls' continued identification with their mothers makes them available for intimacy, but the men they fall in love with have been taught to repress their emotions. So women put their emotions into their children, which reproduces the family structure from which gendered psyches emerge. Difference feminists focus on the divergent emotions of women and men, gender feminists on the family structure that makes them so at odds with each other.

Ideas about patriarchy and the dominance of men over women have become more nuanced. Difference feminists have used the concept of *patriarchy* as a shorthand way of referring to men's control of economic resources, entitlement to sexual services, domination of political processes and positions of authority, and sense of superiority. *Multicultural and post-colonial feminists* claim that systems of dominance and subordination are complex—some men are subordinate to other men, and to some women as well. All men may have a "patriarchal dividend" of privilege and entitlement to women's labor, sexuality, and emotions, but some men additionally have the privileges of whiteness, education, and property ownership. A gender analysis sees gender hierarchies as inextricable from other hierarchies, such as economic class, racial categorization, and educational achievement.

In all these ways, *difference* has been expanded from men versus women to the multiplicities of sameness and difference among women and among men and within individuals as well, differences that arise from similar and different social locations. Thus, both equality and equity are needed for a complete feminist politics. It sounds paradoxical, but people have to be treated under the law as equals, and at the same time, the advantages and disadvantages that come from the different social positions of groups and individuals have to be attended to as well. To make them equitable, they may need to be treated differently. These seemingly contradictory goals of feminist politics may result in conflicting strategies of action, but the long-term goal of all the feminisms is a social world where gender means interesting diversities rather than discrimination and disadvantage.

Organization of the Book

The focus of this book is the continuities, discontinuities, and convergences in recent feminist theories and politics. I will be combining ideas from different feminist writers, and usually will not be talking about any specific writers, except for the excerpted authors. A list of suggested readings can be found at the end of each chapter.

Because I am not examining the ideas of particular feminists but speaking of ideas that have emerged from many theorists, I will talk of feminisms rather than feminists. Any feminist may incorporate ideas and politics from several feminisms, and many feminists have shifted their views over the years. I myself was originally a liberal feminist, then a socialist feminist, and now consider myself to be primarily a gender rebellion feminist.

What I am looking at first is *feminist theories* about why women and men are unequal, and second, *feminist politics*, the activities and strategies for remedying gender inequality. Feminist theories and feminist politics are the result of personal experiences shared among friends and in consciousness-raising groups. They are developed in classes and conferences on all kinds of topics. They are refined in journals and books. And they are translated into political action through large and small feminist organizations, in marches and voting booths, in the marble halls of the United Nations and in grassroots efforts in urban racial ethnic ghettos and developing countries of Africa, South and Central America, and Asia.

In Parts Two through Four, the theories and politics of *gender reform, gender resistance*, and *gender rebellion feminisms* are first described in a general way, followed by more detailed descriptions of the feminisms within the larger grouping. Each discussion of a particular feminism begins with an outline of its attribution of the main causes of gender inequality, its recommendations for remedies, and its contributions to social change. The discussion of each type of feminism includes two excerpts from feminist theorists who use that viewpoint, one more theoretical, the other more focused on politics. Each chapter ends with a discussion of the feminism's theoretical and political limitations.

Part Five, "Feminist Theories of the Body," presents current feminist ideas on the "nature-nurture" debates—whether differences between women and men are biological or social. These debates have proliferated as scientific research and media reports have focused on the search for the source of gendered behavior in brain structure, genes, hormones, and pre-historical evolutionary adaptations. The source of gendered behavior has political implications. If it is biological, differences between women and men are natural and not amenable to change through social practices. The current feminist perspective on biology, the body, and evolution is that they do not shape human behavior without significant social input. In this social input lies the potential for change. Six readings illustrate varied aspects of these debates.

In the final section, "Feminist Politics for the Twenty-First Century," I present my own ideas about fruitful theoretical and political directions for feminism.

Notes

1. United Nations. 2000. *The World's Women 2000: Trends and Statistics.* New York: Department of Economic and Social Affairs.

2. Adapted from Judith Lorber, "Using Gender to Undo Gender: A Feminist Degendering Movement." *Feminist Theory* 1:101–18, 2000.

Suggested Readings–Overviews and History

Bem, Sandra Lipsitz. 1993. *The Lenses of Gender: Transforming the Debate on Sexual Inequality.* New Haven, CT: Yale University Press.

Bernard, Jessie. 1981. *The Female World.* New York: Free Press.

Braidotti, Rosi. 1994. *Nomadic Subjects: Embodiment and Sexual Difference in Feminist Theory.* New York: Columbia University Press.

Chafetz, Janet Saltzman. 1990. *Gender Equity: An Integrated Theory of Stability and Change.* Thousand Oaks, CA: Sage.

Chafetz, Janet Saltzman, and Anthony Gary Dworkin. 1986. *Female Revolt: Women's Movements in World and Historical Perspective.* Totowa, NJ: Rowman & Allanheld.

Clough, Patricia Ticineto. 1994. *Feminist Thought: Desire, Power, and Academic Discourse.* Cambridge, MA: Blackwell.

Connell, R. W. 1987. *Gender and Power.* Stanford, CA: Stanford University Press.

Cott, Nancy F. 1987. *The Grounding of Modern Feminism.* New Haven, CT: Yale University Press.

de Beauvoir, Simone. [1949] 1953. *The Second Sex.* (Trans. by H. M. Parshley). New York: Knopf.

De Lauretis, Teresa. 1987. *Technologies of Gender.* Bloomington: Indiana University Press.

Epstein, Cynthia Fuchs. 1988. *Deceptive Distinctions: Sex, Gender and the Social Order.* New Haven, CT: Yale University Press.

Evans, Judith. 1995. *Feminist Theory Today: An Introduction to Second-Wave Feminism.* Thousand Oaks, CA: Sage.

Ferree, Myra Marx, Judith Lorber, and Beth B. Hess (eds.). 1999. *Revisioning Gender.* Thousand Oaks, CA: Sage.

Firestone, Shulamith. 1970. *The Dialectic of Sex: The Case for Feminist Revolution.* New York: William Morrow.

Foster, Johanna. 1999. "An Invitation to Dialogue: Clarifying the Position of Feminist Gender Theory in Relation to Sexual Difference Theory." *Gender & Society* 13:431–456.

Fraser, Nancy. 1989. *Unruly Practices: Power, Discourse and Gender in Contemporary Social Theory.* Minneapolis: University of Minnesota Press.

Gordon, Linda. 1990. *Woman's Body, Woman's Right: Birth Control in America.* (Rev. ed.). Baltimore, MD: Penguin.

Jaggar, Alison M. 1983. *Feminist Politics and Human Nature.* Totowa, NJ: Rowman & Allanheld.

Kraditor, Aileen S. 1981. *The Ideas of the Woman Suffrage Movement/1890–1920.* New York: Norton.

Lerner, Gerda. 1986. *The Creation of Patriarchy.* New York: Oxford University Press.

Lorber, Judith. 1994. *Paradoxes of Gender.* New Haven, CT: Yale University Press.

Marks, Elaine, and Isabelle de Courtivron (eds.). 1981. *New French Feminisms.* New York: Schocken.

Mernissi, Fatima. 1987. *Beyond the Veil: Male-Female Dynamics in Muslim Society.* Bloomington: Indiana University Press.

Millett, Kate. 1970. *Sexual Politics.* Garden City, NY: Doubleday.

Mohanty, Chandra Talpade, Ann Russo, and Lourdes Torres (eds.). 1991. *Third World Women and the Politics of Feminism*. Bloomington: Indiana University Press.

Moi, Toril. 1985. *Sexual/Textual Politics: Feminist Literary Theory*. New York: Methuen.

Oyě wùmí, Oyèrónké. 1997. *The Invention of Women: Making an African Sense of Western Gender Discourses*. Minneapolis, MN: University of Minnesota Press.

Rhode, Deborah L. (ed.). 1990. *Theoretical Perspectives on Sexual Difference*. New Haven, CT: Yale University Press.

Riley, Denise. 1988. *Am I That Name? Feminism and the Category of Women in History*. Minneapolis, MN: University of Minnesota Press.

Rossi, Alice S. (ed.). 1973. *The Feminist Papers: From Adams to de Beauvoir*. New York: Columbia University Press.

Rowbotham, Sheila. 1973. *Women's Consciousness, Man's World*. New York: Penguin.

———. 1974. *Women, Resistance and Revolution: A History of Women and Revolution in the Modern World*. New York: Vintage.

———. 1976. *Hidden from History: Rediscovering Women in History from the 17th Century to the Present*. New York: Vintage.

———. 1989. *The Past Is Before Us: Feminism in Action Since the 1960s*. Boston: Beacon Press.

Scott, Joan Wallach. 1988. *Gender and the Politics of History*. New York: Columbia University Press.

Showalter, Elaine (ed.). 1985. *The New Feminist Criticism: Essays on Women, Literature, and Theory*. New York: Pantheon.

Tong, Rosemarie. 1989. *Feminist Thought: A Comprehensive Introduction*. Boulder, CO: Westview Press.

Warhol, Robyn R., and Diane Price Herndl (eds.). 1991. *Feminisms: An Anthology of Literary Theory and Criticism*. New Brunswick, NJ: Rutgers University Press.

Woolf, Virginia. 1929 [1957]. *A Room of One's Own*. New York: Harcourt, Brace & World.

Young, Iris Marion. 1990. *Throwing Like a Girl and Other Essays in Feminist Philosophy and Social Theory*. Bloomington: Indiana University Press. ✦

Part II

Gender Reform Feminisms

The feminisms of the 1960s and 1970s were the beginning of the *second wave* of feminism. (Part One gives a brief history of the first wave.) Liberal feminism's roots are in eighteenth and nineteenth century liberal political philosophies that developed the idea of individual rights; marxist and socialist feminisms' base is Marx's nineteenth-century critique of capitalism and his concept of class consciousness; post-colonial feminism uses twentieth-century anticolonial politics and ideas of national development. These earlier works were mostly about men. Gender reform feminisms put women into these perspectives.

Liberal feminism claims that gender differences are not based in biology and therefore that women and men are not all that different: their common humanity supersedes their procreative differences. If women and men are not so different, then they should not be treated differently under the law. Women should have the same legal rights as men and the same educational and work opportunities.

Marxist and socialist feminisms argue that the source of women's oppression is their economic dependence on a husband and their exploitation as cheap labor in the capitalist workforce because they are seen primarily as wives and mothers. The solution is full-time jobs for women, with the state providing paid maternity leave and child care. These feminisms recognize that what the state gives, the state can take away. State policies reflect state interests, not women's. Women are worker-mothers or just mothers, depending on the state's economic and procreative needs.

Women's work for the family and men's production work give each of them different consciousnesses. Women are grounded in everyday life and in emotional relationships; men are detached and inexpressive. These diametrically opposed ways of thinking and feeling, plus women's and men's different interests as wife-mother or breadwinner, make the family a terrain for conflict and power struggles.

For *post-colonial feminism*, the theoretical emphasis on universal human rights is reflected in developing countries in political pressure for the education of girls, maternity and child health care, and economic resources for women who contribute heavily to the support of their families. However, when feminist gender politics calls for wives and husbands to be equal, and for women to have sexual autonomy, post-colonial feminism frequently has to confront traditional cultural values and practices that give men power over their daughters and wives. The women's own solution to this dilemma is community organizing around their family roles.

All of the gender reform feminisms have revolutionary potential because they address the basic structure of the gendered social order—the division of labor between women and men. They all see men as advantaged in the sphere of paid work, in that they usually have better jobs and are paid more than women. Theoretically, men's work should allow them to support a wife and children, but throughout the world and throughout history, women have taken care of children and also produced food, clothing, and other material necessities as part of their work for their family.

When the industrial revolution moved the production of commodities outside of the home into the factory, not only men, but women and children, went out to work for wages. The men who could support their families completely were the factory owners and those who had inherited wealth, and their wives were expected to be hostesses and supervisors of the household servants. By the middle of the twentieth century, working-class women were still juggling family work and paid work to supplement the family income, and middle-class, college-educated women were languishing in the suburbs, feeling useless once their children were in school.

It is this historically intertwined structure of work and family and women's roles within it that gender reform feminisms tackle. But their political solutions leave the gendered structure of family work intact and concentrate on raising women's low economic status through paid work and state-provided children's benefits. Such reforms have to be tailored to a society's economic development. Even within the same country, what works for the women of one class or racial ethnic group is not necessarily going to work for another. Women of disadvantaged racial and ethnic groups who have to work at low-level factory or service jobs to keep food on the table may see being "just a housewife" as utopia. Similarly, women in the former communist countries envied the stable marriages of women in capitalist countries, who, in turn, envied the state supports for child care and encouragement to hold full-time jobs. However, as women in countries at all different stages of industrial development have seen, the success of their fight for gender equality in the paid workplace depends enormously on a high level of economic prosperity. ✦

Chapter One

Liberal Feminism

Sources of Gender Inequality

- Gender stereotyping and devaluation of women.
- Division of work into women's jobs and men's jobs.
- Low pay for women's jobs.
- Restricted entry into top positions (*glass ceiling*).
- Lack of affordable child care for mothers who work outside the home.
- Limitations on reproductive choice.

Remedies

- Gender-neutral child-rearing and education.
- Bringing women into occupations and professions dominated by men and breaking through the glass ceiling to positions of authority (*affirmative action*).
- More women in politics.
- Shared parenting and employer-financed child care.
- Legal, accessible, and affordable reproductive services.

Contributions

- Calling attention to gender discrimination and gender stereotyping in workplaces and in education.

- Making language more gender-neutral.
- Working with civil rights organizations to frame affirmative action guidelines and to bring lawsuits for women and disadvantaged men.
- Encouraging employers to provide workplace childcare and paid parental leave.
- Getting more women elected and appointed to governmental positions.
- Getting abortion legalized in the United States.

In the 1960s and 1970s, the feminist focus in the United States was on women as individuals and the narrowness of their lives. Liberal feminism's complaint that women were confined to a main "job" of wife-mother, with anything else they did having to take a backseat to child care and housework, was the theme of Betty Friedan's best-selling book *The Feminine Mystique*. Women who wanted careers or who were ambitious to make a mark in the arts or in politics were suspect unless they were also "good" wives and mothers (especially mothers). Another problem that kept women down was men's devaluation of them as not too bright, clothes-conscious, and overly emotional. Of course, these impressions were exactly what a woman was taught to convey to a man if she wanted to get a husband.

In many ways, the early appeals of liberal feminism to men were open and straightforward—stop calling a wife "the little woman," recognize women' past achievements and capabilities in many fields, let women do the kind of work they want outside the home, share some of the housework and childcare, legalize abortion. It does not sound very earth-shaking today because so many of these goals have been achieved. Women have entered every field, from mining to space travel. Women in the police force and the military are no longer an oddity, and women in high positions, including leaders of countries, are no longer a rarity.

Other liberal feminist goals are still being debated. One is the question of whether men can be as good at parenting as women. Liberal feminism argues that gendered characteristics, such as women's parenting abilities, may seem biological but are really social products. Their proof that mothering skills are learned and not inborn, for example, is that men learn them, too, when they end up with responsibility for raising children alone. But when there is a woman around, the assumption is that she is better at childcare than any man, and so women end up doing most of the physically and emotionally intensive work of bringing up children.

A second continuing problem is that families, teachers, picture books, school books, and the mass media still encourage boys to be "masculine" and girls to be "feminine," even when they show adult women and men acting in more gender-neutral ways. Gender inequality is built into this socialization because supposedly masculine characteristics, such as assertiveness, are more highly valued than supposedly feminine characteristics, such as emotional supportiveness. Liberal feminism promotes nonsexist socialization and education of children as well as media presentations of men and women in nontraditional roles, especially men as caring and competent fathers. These areas still need constant monitoring—computer software programs for girls feature sexy Barbie dolls and kissing skills, while boys' computer games feature violent adventure fantasies.

The workplace is another area where liberal feminism has made important contributions, but where women are still a long way from gender equality. Thanks to feminist pressure, more and more women have entered fields formerly dominated by men, such as the sciences, and women in positions of authority are not the big news they once were. However, sexist patterns of hiring and promotion still produce workplaces where men and women work at different jobs and where most of the top positions are held by men. Liberal feminism has developed important theories to explain the persistence of the *gender segregation* of jobs (men work with men and women work with women) and the *gender stratification* of organizational hierarchies (the top of the pyramid is invariably almost all men).

The theory of *gendered job queues* argues that the best jobs are kept for men of the dominant racial ethnic group. When a job no longer pays well or has deteriorating working conditions, dominant men leave for other work, and men of disadvantaged racial ethnic groups and all women can move into them. Occupations stay segregated, but who does the job changes. Some jobs have shifted from men's work to women's work within a decade. A typical case is bank teller in the United States.

Disadvantaged groups of workers continue to get lower pay and have poorer working conditions than the dominant group because the new crop of "best jobs" again goes to the most advantaged group of workers. Thus, in the United States, White men monopolize the most lucrative financial and computer jobs.

The strategy of *affirmative action* was developed to redress the gender, racial category, and ethnic imbalance in workplaces, schools, and job-training programs. Affirmative action programs develop a diversified pool of qualified people by encouraging men to train for such jobs as nurse, elementary school teacher, and secretary, and women to go into fields like engineering, construction, and police work. Employers are legally mandated to hire enough workers of different racial categories and genders to achieve a reasonable balance in their workforce. The law also requires employers to pay the workers the same and to give them an equal chance to advance in their careers.

With regard to gender, this change in numbers of women in a workplace was supposed to have a psychological effect on both men and women. Earlier theories had argued that women were not aggressive about competing with men on the job or at school because they feared that success would make them so disliked that they would never have a social life. Rosabeth Moss Kanter, a sociologist and management researcher, said that it was token status as the lone woman among men, visible and vulnerable, that created women's fears. The *Kanter hypothesis* predicted that as workplaces became more gender-balanced, men would become more accepting of women colleagues, and women would have other women to bond with instead of having to go it alone as the single token woman. The following excerpt from her influential book, *Men and Women of the Corporation,* lays out Moss Kanter's hypothesis about the effect of numbers of women on the culture and social structure of a workplace.

Numbers: Minorities and Majorities

Rosabeth Moss Kanter

. . . **Y**et questions of how many and how few confound any statements about the organizational behavior of special kinds of people. For example, certain popular conclusions and research findings about male-female relations or role potentials may turn critically on the issue of proportions. One study of mock jury deliberations found that men played proactive, task-oriented leadership roles, whereas women in the same groups tended to take reactive, emotional, and nurturant postures—supposed proof that traditional stereotypes reflect behavior realities. But, strikingly, *men far outnumbered women in all of the groups studied.* Perhaps it was the women's scarcity that pushed them into classical positions and the men's numerical superiority that encouraged them to assert task superiority. Similarly, the early kibbutzim, collective villages in Israel that theoretically espoused equality of the sexes but were unable to fully implement it, could push women into traditional service positions because there were *more than twice as many men as women.* Again, relative numbers interfered with a fair test of what men or women can "naturally" do, as it did in the case of the relatively few women in the upper levels of Indsco (the company in this example). Indeed, recently Marcia Guttentag has found sex ratios in the population in general to be so important that they predict a large number of behavioral phenomena, from the degree of power women and men feel to the ways they cope with the economic and sexual aspects of their lives.

To understand the dramas of the many and the few in the organization requires a theory and a vocabulary. Four group types can be identified on the basis of different proportional representations of kinds of people. . . . *Uniform* groups have only one kind of person, one significant social type. The group may develop its own differentiations, of course, but groups called uniform can be considered homogeneous with respect to salient external master statuses such as sex, race, or ethnicity. Uniform groups have a typological ratio of 100:0. *Skewed* groups are those in which there is a large preponderance of one type over another, up to a ratio of perhaps 85:15. The numerically dominant types also control the group and its culture in enough ways to be labeled "dominants." The few of another type in a skewed group can appropriately be called "tokens," for . . . they are often treated as representatives of their category, as symbols rather than individuals. If the absolute size of the skewed group is small, tokens can also be solos, the only one of their kind present; but even if there are two tokens in a skewed group, it is difficult for them to generate an alliance that can become powerful in the group. . . . Next, *tilted* groups begin to move toward less extreme distributions and less exaggerated effects. In this situation, with ratios of perhaps 65:35, dominants are just a "majority" and tokens become a "minority." Minority members have potential allies among each other, can form coalitions, and can affect the culture of the group. They begin to become individuals differentiated from each other as well as a type differentiated from the majority. Finally, at about 60:40 and down to 50:50, the group becomes *balanced.* Culture and interaction reflect this balance. Majority and minority turn into potential subgroups that may or may not generate actual type-based identifications. Outcomes for individuals in such a balanced peer group, regardless of type, will depend more on other structural and personal factors, including formation of subgroups or differentiated roles and abilities.

It is the characteristics of the second type, the skewed group, that underlay the behavior and treatment of professional and managerial women observed at Indsco. If the ratio of women to men in various parts of the organization begins to shift, as affirmative action and new hiring and promotion policies promised, forms of relationships and peer culture should also change. But as of the mid-1970s, the dynamics of tokenism predominated in Indsco's . . . ranks, and women and men were in the positions of token and dominant. Tokenism, like low opportunity and low power, set in motion self-perpetuating cycles that served to reinforce the low numbers of women and, in the absence of external intervention, to keep women in the position of token.

The recognition that a token or two did not make for a truly diversified workplace provided the impetus for affirmative action. The goal is not perfect balance but a workplace where different kinds of people are fully integrated and respected colleagues. The Kanter hypothesis predicts a positive attitude change when a formerly imbalanced workplace becomes more gender-balanced. However, later research found that as more women enter, there is often a backlash in the form of increasing sexual harassment and denigration of women's capabilities—a defense against what is felt to be the encroachment of women on men's territory. Men's stonewalling is particularly likely when women are competing with them for jobs on the fast track up the career ladder.

The concept of *gatekeeping* explains how most women are kept from getting to the top in occupations and professions dominated by men. Gatekeeping used to keep women out of male-dominated fields entirely. Now gatekeeping keeps women out of the line for promotion to the top positions. The ways that most people move up in their careers are through *networking* (finding out about job and promotion opportunities through word-of-mouth and being recommended by someone already there) and *mentoring* (being coached by a protective senior to understand the informal norms of the workplace). Becoming part of a network and getting a mentor are made much easier if you become a *protégé* of a senior colleague.

In many fields, hiring and promotion decisions are not made strictly on the basis of merit but through the help and support of "godfathers" or "rabbis," who take younger people under their wing as protégés and invite them into the "inner circles," where information is traded and deals are cut. Because senior members of an organization are looking for people to eventually succeed them, they usually choose as protégés those who are similar to themselves in racial category, ethnicity, religion, and gender. The exclusivity of the protégé system and its discriminatory role in sorting out people who "don't belong" has for years come under attack by liberal feminism.

Cynthia Fuchs Epstein, a sociologist who has done extensive research on women lawyers, has documented the difficulties even well-trained professional women have in making careers because they are excluded from the informal protégé system and from men's clubs.

The Protégé System

Cynthia Fuchs Epstein

The protégé system is typical of many professions, especially in their upper reaches. It operates both to train personnel in certain specialties and to assure continuity of leadership. The fields in which it exists are marked by interplay between the formal and informal relationships of the practitioners. At certain levels one must be "in" to learn the job. . . .

The sponsor-protégé, or master-apprentice, relationship may inhibit feminine advancement in the professions. The sponsor is most likely to be a man and will tend to have mixed feelings, among them a nagging sense of impending trouble, about accepting a woman as a protégé. Although the professional man might not object to a female assistant—he might even prefer her—he cannot identify her (as he might a male assistant) as someone who will eventually be his successor. He will usually prefer a male candidate in the belief that the woman has less commitment and will easily be deflected from her career by marriage and children. This presumed lack of commitment is troublesome in the relationship even if the woman is accepted as an apprentice or a protégé. She may be under considerable strain because the sponsor may be oblivious of her other role demands. In addition, her other role partners—husband, father, child—may be suspicious or resentful of her loyalty to and dependence on the sponsor. The sponsor's wife may also be suspicious of the ties between the sponsor and his female protégé. Many professional men feel it is wiser to avoid this kind of domestic trouble.

Even if she serves an apprenticeship, the woman faces serious problems at the next step in her career if she does not get the sponsor's support for entrée to the inner circles of the profession—support that a male apprentice would expect as a matter of course. The sponsor may exert less effort in promoting a woman for a career-line job. He may feel less responsibility for her career because he assumes she is not as dependent on a career as a man might be. . . .

Because of the woman's presumed lack of commitment and drive, the sponsor may be reluctant to present her to colleagues as a reliable candidate for their long-term enterprises. It is true, however, that if a woman can enter into a protégé relationship it may be more important for her than for a man, and that a male sponsor may make an extra effort to promote the female protégée because he is aware of the difficulties she is apt to face. In fact, she may be able to rise or gain notice in a field only because she is a protégée, although this form of entrée is not typical or necessary for men.

We cannot specify the conditions under which one or the other pattern will prevail. It is probably highly contingent on the social structure of the discipline or specialty in which the relationship arises, the personalities of the sponsor and protégée, and, of course, the quality of the woman's talent as well as her personality and physical attractiveness. . . .

In many professions, men have chosen to conduct their business in men's faculty and university clubs, men's bars, golf and athletic clubs, and during poker games. In addition, many once informal traditions have developed into rigidly formalized male cults, as, for example, the academic "high table" in the colleges of Cambridge and Oxford. Obstacles abound not only for females aspiring to membership in such groups, but also for males from an alien social class or social tradition. Informal systems of introduction and support abound in the job markets of many countries (Mexico and Israel are two), but not in the United States and other nations where technical skills count most. In the United States, ability and achievement alone may only occasionally suffice to insure a good career; the talented but retiring and the promising but nonconforming may simply fall by the wayside.

The only possible antidote for the familiarity and lineage which oil the wheels in professional environments is power through rank, seniority, money, or charisma; women do not often have any of these defenses. . . .

Eminence also often correlates with age, which may further reduce the focus placed on sex status. Many of the feminine role components attached to the female sex status become less intrusive in interactions between men and women as the woman grows older; it is probably accurate to suppose that in most cases as the woman ages, her sexual appeal becomes less an object of focus. Since a woman is apt to encounter resistance if her professional status requires the exercise of authority over others, she may find that she can depend on deriving a certain amount of authority from her age. While a man might resent "taking orders" from a woman, he probably would be less resistant if the woman is older. Thus, the woman needs not only the rank which derives from her status as an expert, but also that from her age status. Correlatively, when the woman is younger than the man, or the same age, she is more apt to encounter resistance to her authority. . . .

In professions and in managerial positions, where jobs pay the best, have the most prestige, and command the most authority, few senior men take on women as their protégées. As a result, there has been a *glass ceiling* on the advancement of women in every field they have entered in the last 25 years. The concept of the glass ceiling assumes that women have the motivation, ambition, and capacity for positions of power and prestige, but hidden barriers keep them from reaching the top. They can see their way to their goal, but they bump their heads on a ceiling that is both invisible and impenetrable. Similar processes of informal discrimination hinder the careers of men of disadvantaged groups as well; women of color have had to face both racism and sexism.

Critique. There is an internal theoretical contradiction in liberal feminism that centers on the question of whether women and men have to be the same to be equal. The campaign to bring up children in a gender-neutral way has meant encouraging a mixture of existing masculine and feminine characteristics and traits (*androgyny*), so that boys and girls will be similar in personalities and behavior. The corollary campaign to integrate women into all parts of public life, especially the workplace, and for men to share parenting and other roles in private life, means that women and men can be interchangeable.

The logical outcome of liberal feminism is a genderless society, one not based on women and men as socially meaningful categories. But because of men's social domination, the actual thrust of both gender-neutrality and integration is often the continued predominance of masculine traits and values, such as devotion to a career, with the consequence that women become like men. For this reason, liberal feminism has been accused of denigrating *womanliness* (nurturance, empathy, an ethics of care) and pregnancy and childbirth in their fight to advance the social status of women.

The goal of liberal feminism in the United States was embodied in the Equal Rights Amendment to the U.S. Constitution, which was never ratified. It said, "Equality of rights under the law shall not be denied or abridged by the United States or any state on account of sex." The negative response of the American public to the Equal Rights Amendment may have been a gut reaction to the genderless possibilities of an absolutely even-handed legal status for women and men. When laws speak of "pregnant persons," as did a Supreme Court decision equating pregnancy with disability or illness, many people, including feminists, feel that androgyny has gone too far.

Summary

The main contribution of liberal feminism has been to show how much modern society discriminates against women by insisting that women and men must be treated differently. Liberal feminist theory says that biological differences should be ignored in order to achieve gender equality. Women and men should be treated in a gender-neutral manner, especially under the law.

In the United States, liberal feminism has been successful in breaking down many barriers to women's entry into formerly male-dominated jobs and professions, in helping to equalize wage scales, and in legalizing abortion. But liberal feminism has not been able to overcome the prevailing belief that women and men are intrinsically different. Although gender differences can co-exist with equitable or even-handed treatment, the way women are treated in modern society, especially in the workplace, still produces large gaps in salaries, job opportunities, and advancement.

Politically, liberal feminism's focus has been on visible sources of gender discrimination, such as gendered job markets and inequitable wage scales, and with getting women into positions of authority in the professions, government, and cultural institutions. Liberal feminist politics takes important weapons of the civil rights movement—anti-discrimination legislation and affirmative action programs—and uses them to fight gender inequality, especially in the job market. Liberal feminism has been less successful in fighting the informal processes of discrimination and exclusion that have produced the glass ceiling that so many women face in their career advancement.

The great strides that women of the last generation have made have led many young people to think that feminism is passé. But the gender equality in the workplace and the home that liberal feminism achieved is concentrated in the United States in the middle and upper classes, where people are more likely to have good jobs, enjoy steady incomes, and live in two-parent households. The Scandinavian countries have achieved gender equality through welfare-state benefits to everyone, and also have many more women in government and in policy-making positions than the rest of the world, including North America and much of the rest of Europe.

Most of the world's women, however, live in countries where only a very small group of people have a high standard of living. Their economic and social problems produce a level of gender inequality that needs quite different feminist theories and politics.

Suggested Readings in Liberal Feminism

Bartlett, Katharine T., and Rosanne Kennedy (eds.). 1991. *Feminist Legal Theory: Readings in Law and Gender.* Boulder, CO: Westview Press.

Daniels, Arlene Kaplan. 1988. *Invisible Careers: Women Civic Leaders from the Volunteer World.* Chicago: University of Chicago Press.

Eisenstein, Zillah. 1981. *The Radical Future of Liberal Feminism.* New York: Longman.

———. 1984. *Feminism and Sexual Equality: Crisis in Liberal America.* New York: Monthly Review Press.

———. 1988. *The Female Body and the Law.* Berkeley: University of California Press.

Epstein, Cynthia Fuchs. 1971. *Women's Place: Options and Limits in Professional Careers*. Berkeley: University of California Press.

——. 1981. *Women in Law*. New York: Basic Books.

Friedan, Betty. 1963. *The Feminine Mystique*. New York: Norton.

Gelb, Joyce. 1989. *Feminism and Politics: A Comparative Perspective*. Berkeley: University of California Press.

Hertz, Rosanna. 1986. *More Equal Than Others: Women and Men in Dual-Career Marriages*. Berkeley: University of California Press.

Hochschild, Arlie, with Anne Machung. 1989. *The Second Shift: Working Parents and the Revolution at Home*. New York: Viking.

Holmstrom, Lynda Lytle. 1972. *The Two-Career Family*. Cambridge, MA: Schenkman.

Hood, Jane C. 1983. *Becoming a Two-Job Family*. New York: Praeger.

Huber, Joan and Glenna Spitze. 1983. *Sex Stratification: Children, Housework, and Jobs*. New York: Academic Press.

Jacobs, Jerry A. 1989. *Revolving Doors: Sex Segregation and Women's Careers*. Stanford, CA: Stanford University Press.

Kanter, Rosabeth Moss. 1977. *Men and Women of the Corporation*. New York: Basic Books.

Kaufman, Debra R. and Barbara L. Richardson. 1982. *Achievement and Women: Challenging he Assumptions*. New York: Free Press.

Komarovsky, Mirra. 1976. *Dilemmas of Masculinity: A Study of College Youth*. New York: Norton.

——. 1985. *Women in College: Shaping New Feminine Identities*. New York: Basic Books.

Lamb, Michael E. 1987 (ed.). *The Father's Role: Cross-cultural Perspectives*. Hillsdale, NJ: Lawrence Erlbaum.

Lopata, Helena Znaniecki. 1971. *Occupation: Housewife*. New York: Oxford University Press.

Lorber, Judith. 1984. *Women Physicians: Careers, Status, and Power*. London and New York: Tavistock.

Luker, Kristin. 1984. *Abortion and the Politics of Motherhood*. Berkeley: University of California Press.

Oakley, Ann. 1974. *The Sociology of Housework*. New York: Pantheon.

——. 1976. *Women's Work: The Housewife, Past and Present*. New York: Vintage.

——. 1980. *Becoming a Mother*. New York: Schocken.

Okin, Susan Moller. 1979. *Women in Western Political Thought*. Princeton, NJ: Princeton University Press.

Petchesky, Rosalind Pollack. 1984. *Abortion and Woman's Choice: The State, Sexuality, and Reproductive Freedom*. Boston: Northeastern University Press.

Pleck, Joseph H. 1985. *Working Wives/Working Husbands*. Thousand Oaks, CA: Sage.

Reskin, Barbara F., and Patricia A. Roos. 1990. *Job Queues, Gender Queues: Explaining Women's Inroads into Male Occupations*. Philadelphia: Temple University Press.

Rossi, Alice S. 1964. "Equality Between the Sexes: An Immodest Proposal." *Daedalus* 93:607–52.

Schwartz, Pepper. 1994. *Love Between Equals: How Peer Marriage Really Works*. New York: Free Press.

Tuchman, Gaye, Arlene Kaplan Daniels, and James Benet. 1978. *Hearth and Home: Images of Women in the Mass Media*. New York: Oxford University Press.

Valian, Virginia. 1998. *Why So Slow? The Advancement of Women*. Cambridge, MA: MIT Press.

Vannoy-Hiller, Dana and William W. Philliber. 1989. *Equal Partners: Successful Women in Marriage*. Newbury Park, CA: Sage.

Weisberg, D. Kelly (ed.). 1993. *Feminist Legal Theory: Foundations*. Philadelphia: Temple University Press.

Weitzman, Lenore J. 1985. *The Divorce Revolution: The Unexpected Social and Economic Consequences for Women and Children in America*. New York: Free Press. ✦

Chapter Two

Marxist and Socialist Feminism

Sources of Gender Inequality

- Exploitation of women in unwaged work for the family.
- Use of women workers as a *reserve army of labor*—hired when the economy needs workers, fired when it does not.
- Low pay for women's jobs.

Remedies

- Government-subsidized maternal and child health care, child care services, financial allowances for children, free education.
- Permanent waged work for women.
- Comparable worth programs to equalize salaries of men's and women's jobs.

Contributions

- Gender analysis putting women as paid and unpaid workers into capitalist and socialist economies.
- Making visible the necessity and worth of women's unpaid work in the home to the functioning of industrial economies and to the social reproduction of future workers.

- Getting government-subsidized maternal and child services in social-welfare states and in the former communist countries.

During the 1970s, marxist and socialist feminist theories identified the economic structure and the material aspects of life as the main source of gender inequality. These theories are grounded in historical materialism, which says that every major change in production—from hunting and gathering to farming to the industrial revolution—changes the social organization of work and family. In preindustrial societies, women's domestic labor not only maintained the home and brought up the children but also entailed getting or growing food, making cloth and sewing clothing, and other work that allowed the family to subsist. This work was done side by side with the men and children of the family. The industrial revolution of the nineteenth century brought a major change—the removal of production work from the home to factories, and the change from making household goods at home to their becoming mass-produced commodities. The means of production, then, were no longer owned by the worker but by capitalists, who hired workers at wages low enough to make a profit.

Marx's analysis of the social structure of capitalism was supposed to apply to people of any social characteristics. If you owned the means of production, you were a member of the capitalist class; if you sold your labor for a wage, you were a member of the proletariat. That should be true of women as well, except that until the end of the nineteenth century, married women in capitalist countries were not allowed to own property in their own name; any wages they earned and their profits from any businesses they ran belonged legally to their husband.

Although Marx and other nineteenth-century economic theorists recognized the exploitation of wives' domestic labor, it was marxist feminism that put housewives at the forefront of its analysis of the gendered structure of capitalism. Housewives are vital to capitalism, indeed to any industrial economy, because their unpaid work in the home maintains bosses and workers and reproduces the next generation of bosses and workers (and their wives). Furthermore, if a bourgeois husband falls on hard times, his wife can do genteel work in the home, such as dressmaking, to earn extra money, or can take a temporary or part-time white-collar job. And when a worker's wages fall below the level needed to feed his family, as it often does, his wife can go out to work for wages in a factory or shop or another person's home, or she can turn the home into a small factory and put everyone, sometimes including the children, to work. The housewife's labor, paid and unpaid, is for her family. Marxist feminism argues that this exploitation of women's work, both in the home and in the marketplace, is the prime source of gender inequality.

Marxist feminism analyzes the ways in which two parallel institutions—the economy (capitalism) and the family (patriarchy)—structure women's and men's lives. A man who works for wages is exploited by capitalism because he is never paid as much as the profits he produces. At home, however, he has someone to work for him—his wife. She cooks his food, washes his clothing, satisfies his sexual needs, and brings up his children. If he loses his job, or cannot earn enough to support his family, she will go out to work or take work into the home, but she will continue her domestic duties as well. She will be paid less than a man doing comparable work because her main job is supposed to be taking care of her husband and children. She is part of a *reserve army of labor;* she can be hired when the economy can use her labor and fired when she is no longer needed by her employer, even if she would like to continue to work and her family could use extra income. Housewives are thus a flexible source of cheap labor in industrial societies.

Work in the marketplace and work in the home are inextricably intertwined. Because a woman rarely makes enough money to support herself and her children in capitalist economies, marriage is an economic necessity. A wife earns her husband's economic support by doing housework and taking care of their children. Her work in the home is not only necessary to the physical and emotional well-being of her husband and children, it is also vital to the economy. Women's housework and child care make it possible for men to go to work and children to go to school, where they learn to take their future place in society—as workers, bosses, or the wives of workers or bosses. Mothers reproduce the social values of their class by passing them on to their children, teaching future bosses to be independent and take initiative and future workers and wives to be docile and obey orders.

A paper that was given at a workshop conference on occupational segregation at Wellesley College in 1975 was the start for what came to be known as *dual systems* theory in marxist feminism—an analysis of patriarchy and capitalism as twin systems of men's domination of women. The conference was mainstream and not at all marxist in its auspices—it was funded by the Carnegie Corporation and jointly sponsored by the American Economics Association Committee on the Status of

Women and the Wellesley Center for Research on Women in Higher Education and the Professions. Yet the seed of a counter-theory to the liberal feminist view of gender inequality was planted there by Heidi Hartmann, an economist.

Capitalism and Patriarchy

Heidi Hartmann

The present status of women in the labor market and the current arrangement of sex-segregated jobs is the result of a long process of interaction between patriarchy and capitalism. I have emphasized the actions of male workers throughout this process because I believe that emphasis to be correct. Men will have to be forced to give up their favored positions in the division of labor—in the labor market and at home—both if women's subordination is to end and if men are to begin to escape class oppression and exploitation. Capitalists have indeed used women as unskilled, underpaid labor to undercut male workers, yet this is only a case of the chickens coming home to roost—a case of men's cooptation by and support for patriarchal society, with its hierarchy among men, being turned back on themselves with a vengeance. Capitalism grew on top of patriarchy; patriarchal capitalism is stratified society par excellence. If nonruling-class men are to be free they will have to recognize their cooptation by patriarchal capitalism and relinquish their patriarchal benefits. If women are to be free, they must fight against both patriarchal power and capitalist organization of society.

Because both the sexual division of labor and male domination are so long standing, it will be very difficult to eradicate them and impossible to eradicate the latter without the former. The two are now so inextricably intertwined that it is necessary to eradicate the sexual division of labor itself in order to end male domination. Very basic changes at all levels of society and culture are required to liberate women. In this paper, I have argued that the maintenance of job segregation by sex is a key root of women's status, and I have relied on the operation of society-wide institutions to explain the maintenance of job segregation by sex. But the consequences of that division of labor go very deep, down to the level of the subconscious. The subconscious influences behavior patterns, which form the micro underpinnings (or complements) of social institutions and are in turn reinforced by those social institutions.

I believe we need to investigate these micro phenomena as well as the macro ones I have discussed in this paper. For example, it appears to be a very deeply ingrained behavioral rule that men cannot be subordinate to women of a similar social class. Manifestations of this rule have been noted in restaurants, where waitresses experience difficulty in giving orders to bartenders, unless the bartender can reorganize the situation to allow himself autonomy; among executives, where women executives are seen to be most successful if they have little contact with others at their level and manage small staffs; and among industrial workers, where female factory inspectors cannot successfully correct the work of male production workers. There is also a deeply ingrained fear of being identified with the other sex. As a general rule, men and women must never do anything which is not masculine or feminine (respectively). Male executives, for example, often exchange handshakes with male secretaries, a show of respect which probably works to help preserve their masculinity.

At the next deeper level, we must study the subconscious—both how these behavioral rules are internalized and how they grow out of personality structures. At this level, the formation of personality, there have been several attempts to study the production of gender, the socially imposed differentiation of humans based on biological sex differences. A materialist interpretation of reality, of course, suggests that gender production grows out of the extant division of labor between the sexes, and, in a dialectical process, reinforces that very division of labor itself. In my view, because of these deep ramifications of the sexual division of labor we will not eradicate sex-ordered task division until we eradicate the socially imposed gender differences between us and, therefore, the very sexual division of labor itself.

In attacking both patriarchy and capitalism we will have to find ways to change both society-wide institutions and our most deeply ingrained habits. It will be a long, hard struggle.

Marxist feminism once proposed that all women should get paid for housework and child care; they should not do it for love alone. If wives were waged workers, they would be part of the gross national product and could get raises and vacations and sick leave. But there is a sense in which wives *are* paid for their work for the family; husbands supposedly are paid enough to maintain their families as well as themselves—they are supposed to get what is called a *family wage*. The problem is that when a husband "pays" his wife for work in the home, either directly or indirectly, she is an economic dependent with few financial resources, a dangerous situation should her husband get sick, die, or leave her. The marxist and socialist feminist solution, like that of liberal feminism, is that women, too, should have permanent, full-time jobs. They would have independent means to fall back on in case they got a divorce or became a widow—or they did not have to get married at all, since they would be economically independent. For a mother, this solution entails affordable and accessible child care services.

And what about people living in areas where neither women nor men can get jobs? Since the men in their communities are equally poor, women do not have an economic advantage in marrying. They have to rely on government support—what we call "welfare." In the United States, government welfare benefits go only to poor women (after a means test), and so these benefits—and the women who receive them—are singled out as deviant and stigmatized. In many industrialized countries, there is government financial support for all mothers, and benefits are much more extensive than in the United States. The benefits include prenatal care, paid maternal leave, maternal and child health services, cash allowances each month for each child, free education through college (including books), and child care services. Every mother in the Scandinavian and other European countries and Israel receives some or most of these benefits. These *welfare states* recognize that producing children is work and that mothers therefore deserve state support. Their governments do not distinguish among poor and middle-class or wealthy women, or among full-time employees, part-time workers, and full-time homemakers. These services make it possible for all women to be both mothers and economically independent.

Such state welfare benefits were the norm in the former communist countries, but feminists there soon recognized that this solution to gender inequality only substitutes economic dependence on the state for dependence on a husband. Women are even more responsible for child care, since the benefits are usually for the mother and rarely for the father. (Even when it is offered to them, few fathers take advantage of paid child care leave.) Furthermore, when women take paid jobs, it is other women who still do the childcare, as paid workers in the home or in a child care facility, or as unpaid "helpers." The women who do paid domestic labor in people's homes are usually from disadvantaged social groups; under capitalism, their wages tend to be minimal, and they rarely get any sick leave or health insurance, but in socialist countries, they get what any other worker receives.

The solution to women's economic dependence on men cannot simply be work for wages, if jobs continue to be gender-segregated and women's work is paid less than men's. Socialist feminism has a different solution to the gendered workforce than liberal feminism's program of affirmative action. It is *comparable worth*.

In examining the reasons that salaries for women and men are so discrepant, proponents of comparable worth found that wage scales are not set by the market for labor, or by what a worker is worth to an employer, or by the worker's education or other credentials. Salaries are set by conventional ideas of what men's and women's work is worth, which are rooted in sexism, racism, and other forms of discrimination. Comparable worth programs compare jobs in traditional women's occupations, such as secretary, with traditional men's jobs, such as automobile mechanic. They give point values for qualifications needed, skills used, extent of responsibility and authority over other workers, and dangerousness. Salaries are then equalized for jobs with a similar number of points (which represent the "worth" of the job). Although comparable worth programs do not do away with gendered job segregation, feminist proponents argue that raising the salaries of women doing traditional women's jobs could give the majority of women economic resources that would make them less dependent on marriage or state benefits as a means of survival.

The pros and cons of comparable worth are carefully weighed in the following overview by Roslyn Feldberg, a sociologist, presented at a conference of the International Working Group on Women and the Transformation of the Welfare State, held in Italy in 1983.

Comparable Worth

Roslyn L. Feldberg

. . . Comparable worth is related to the status quo in both the overall degree of inequality in the society and the hierarchy of wages. It can have only a modest effect on the overall degree of inequality because it does not attack all forms of inequality. It does attack gender inequality in the wage system, which is, as the earnings gap shows, a major component of gender inequality in the United States. The possibility that other forms of inequality will become more visible (e.g., similar patterns of wage differentials by race or age or inequities arising from the distribution of wealth) as a result of a lessening of gender inequality is not an argument against working for comparable worth. Indeed, struggles for comparable worth may set the stage for attacks on other forms of inequity.

How comparable worth will affect the hierarchy of wages is more difficult to foresee. On the one hand, it does not directly challenge the concept of a hierarchy; in fact, its insistence that jobs be evaluated implies a hierarchy. On the other hand, its rejection of the market as an adequate basis for determining wages initiates a discussion of how value is assigned to jobs independent of the market and which job dimensions are worthy of compensation. Advocates of comparable worth have challenged prevailing standards of evaluation. They have pointed out that formal job evaluations were first developed in industrial settings and tend to give considerable weight to tasks such as heavy lifting and the operation of expensive equipment. As a corollary, the skills and knowledge more typical of women's work are often unacknowledged or less heavily weighted. . . .

While comparable-worth advocates eschew questioning the principle of a hierarchy of wages, arguing only that they seek more objective, less sex-biased measures of job worth, the issues they raise provoke a broader debate. This debate does not . . . concern the feasibility of setting and applying such standards. Employers have been engaging in that activity for centuries. Rather the debate is about social values and priorities underlying the wage hierarchy. Is the labor-intensive work of caring for people less valuable than the work of caring for buildings or cars? How large a wage difference is reasonable between positions in the hierarchy? Or, to put it differently, what ought to be the relationship between wages and position in the job-evaluation hierarchy? What is the value of labor, and what social considerations ought to guide decisions about wages? These fundamental questions reveal how priorities are embedded in the market, where historical conventions and social and political, as opposed to purely economic, forces enter the process of setting wages.

The major legal questions concern the definition of discrimination and its relationship to established employment practices. Where these practices are long-standing, they are often seen by judges as well as by employers as arising naturally from economic laws or from differences among groups of workers. This perspective masks discrimination and creates difficulties for women who bring charges of unfair wages. The conflict is highlighted in both *Christensen v. State of Iowa* and *Lemons v. City and County of Denver*. In the former, the University of Northern Iowa was paying its secretaries less than its physical plant employees, although the university's own internal job evaluation awarded both categories the same labor grades. The Eighth Circuit Court ruled that these differences in pay were not evidence of discrimination because they reflected prevailing wage rates in the local labor market. Such legal opinions imbue the operating principles of the economic system with the force of natural law.

Comparable-worth advocates argue that the market is a historic development rather than an expression of natural law. Conventions within the market, including wage-setting practices and labor market divisions, perpetuate a historic discrimination against women and women's work. Without contesting the principle of hierarchy in wages, they advance the notion that wage hierarchies for women can be categorically lower than those for men only because they are discriminatory.

If comparable worth does succeed in raising women's wages, how will it affect relationships among groups of women and between women and men? Will it further divide women, stringing them out along the same hierarchy that divides male workers? If so, will it reduce our common ground and create new barriers to collective action?

First, all women should not continue to suffer from certain inequities simply because the proposed solution will not eliminate all inequities. Second, having said that, I believe it is crucial that we guard against further divisions both as a matter of simple justice and to prevent the gains from being eroded. The whole strength of the comparable-worth approach rests on cooperation among women. As long as some areas of women's paid work are devalued, the potential exists for all women's work to be devalued; consider the way in which arguments about married women not needing a living wage have been used against all women. Third, comparable worth can further divide women where they are already divided into separate occupational categories. For example, insofar as registered nurses tend to be white women and licensed practical nurses and nurses' aides tend to be women of color, comparable-worth attacks on inequities in nurses' wages could perpetuate and exacerbate divisions. There is no abstract, general solution for this potential problem. To the extent that the occupational distribution of white women and women of color has become more similar in the post–World War II period, the possibility is lessened. However, such structural shifts cannot eliminate the problem altogether. Divisions will be contained only by careful political analysis and concerted action. In the above example, the use of comparable worth to attack inequities based on gender provides the opportunity to develop conceptual and political tools that can also be used to address racial inequities among women. If gender-based inequities are eliminated between nurses and, for example, pharmacists, the same reasoning should be useful in attacking inequities between nurses and aides. That is not to say that comparable worth will create an egalitarian wage structure, but it will provide the grounds for eliminating wage inequities between groups doing comparable work.

A related concern is that comparable worth will become a class-specific strategy—advantageous to college-educated women at the expense of their high school counterparts and the latters' husbands. Again, such outcomes are possible, but there is already evidence that they are not necessary. . . .

Women who are not members of professional associations or unions will have less access to comparable-worth strategy than will those who are. Organized workers have an advantage in using methods that require major resources. This suggests that women need to do more organizing, with the support of unions and other sympathizers, not that comparable-worth strategy should be discounted.

The last question concerns relationships between men and women. Would comparable worth be disadvantageous for men? Would attempts to implement comparable worth lead to a new form of gender politics? Comparable worth could be relatively disadvantageous to men who are paid more than the content of their jobs warrants. No one has predicted absolute reductions in wages. Instead, the wages for these men's work would rise more slowly. Any attempt to lessen inequality would involve at least this form of disadvantage for some men.

Women married to those men might feel increased pressure to enter or remain in the labor force. Yet women's economic dependence on husbands' wages has proven insufficient for a large proportion of women . . . In two-earner households, increases in women's wages would lessen the impact of a slower rise in men's wages, while they would improve the economic situation of the growing number of female-headed households.

The issue of gender politics is more problematic. There are already important divisions between men and women, which this article addresses. Economic self-sufficiency among women would radically alter the system of gender relations but would not necessarily exacerbate divisions. Materially, comparable worth is unlikely to work against the interests of most employed men. In fact, raising women's wages would probably raise the floor below men's wages, as the decline of a cheap labor supply in the past has bolstered wages. Furthermore, better-paid women workers would be in a stronger position to ally with men around common concerns. What comparable worth would threaten is the gender hierarchy in wages, which could be perceived as a threat to traditional notions of masculinity. Men's work and male workers would no longer automatically be seen as worth higher wages. Whether the new common standard would become a basis of solidarity or a loss of preeminence that men would fight depends in large part on the response of organized labor, especially at the local, grass-roots level.

Finally, I think that attempts to develop comparable worth claims would provide an opportunity for both organizing and consciousness raising. The history and dynamics of gender relations in the United States are such that women as well as men tend to devalue women's work. Many of us feel underpaid, yet few claim that we deserve men's wages. The few women who get such wages seem nervous, as if they occupy a position of privilege that is undeserved and might be taken away at any time. Given our experience of social subordination and low wages, it is not surprising that we are uncertain about the value of our work. The process of evaluating our own work and presenting claims on our own behalf might offer an opportunity to see our work more objectively, to appreciate its importance and its value.

Reprinted from: Roslyn L. Feldberg, "Comparable Worth: Toward Theory and Practice in the United States," in *Signs* 10:323–27. Copyright © 1984 by The University of Chicago Press. Reprinted by permission.

In addition to its political program of comparable worth, socialist feminism expands the marxist feminist critique of the family as the source of women's oppression. Building on Marx's concept of *class consciousness*, which says that capitalists and members of the proletariat have conflicting interests and therefore an entirely different outlook on life, socialist feminism explores the ways that a wife's work in the home shapes her consciousness to be different from that of her husband. His work is future-oriented, geared to making a product or a profit; hers is present-oriented, getting dinner on the table and the children dressed for school every day. His work is abstract, dealing with money or ideas or an object; her work is hands-on, directly involved with living people who have bodily and emotional needs. He is supposed to be cool and impersonal and rational on the job; her job as wife and mother demands sensitivity to interpersonal cues and an outpouring of affection. He works as an individual, even when he brings home his paycheck; she is first and foremost a family member. In their ways of thinking and feeling, men and women are different kinds of people, not because their brains are wired differently but because their life experiences give them diverse consciousnesses.

The socialist feminist insight into women's "class consciousness," as we shall see, became the theoretical support for gender resistance feminisms.

Critique. Marxist and socialist feminisms have been the foundation of an influential economic theory of gender inequality that links the gendered division of labor in the family and in the workplace. The political solutions based on this theory, as carried out in the former communist countries and in democratic welfare states, improve women's material lives but fall far short of freeing women from men's control.

Marxist and socialist feminisms show that women are locked into a condition of lesser economic resources whether they are wives of workers or workers themselves. If they marry economically successful men, they become dependents, and if they marry poor men or not at all, they and their children can starve. The welfare-state solution—benefits to all mothers—is rooted in this analysis. There is, however, a negative side to state payments for child care (the equivalent of wages for housework); they are important in giving mothers independent economic resources, but they can also keep women out of the paid marketplace or encourage part-time work. These policies thus have the latent function of keeping women a reserve army of cheap labor in capitalist, state-owned, and welfare-state economies.

Women's economic inequality in the family division of labor has been somewhat redressed in countries that give all mothers paid leave before and after the birth of a child and that provide affordable child care. But that solution puts the burden of children totally on the mother and encourages men to opt out of family responsibilities altogether. (To counteract that trend, feminists in the government of Norway allocated a certain portion of paid child care leave to fathers specifically.)

Women in the former communist countries had what liberal feminism in capitalist economies always wanted for women—full-time jobs with state-supported maternity leave and child care services. But as marxist and socialist feminists recognize, the state can be as paternalistic as any husband. They argue that male-dominated government policies put the state's interests before those of women: When the economy needs workers, the state pays for child care leave; with a downturn in the economy, the state reduces the benefits. Similarly, when the state needs women to have more children, it cuts back on availability of abortions and contraceptive services. Thus, the marxist and socialist feminist solution to women's economic inequality—full-time jobs and state-provided maternal and child welfare benefits—does not change women's status as primarily wives and mothers and men's status as the primary breadwinners. The gendered social order has been reformed but not significantly changed.

Summary

Marxist and socialist feminist theory emphasizes the economic and psychological differences between women and men, and men's power over women that emerges from their different statuses in the gendered division of labor. Marxist and socialist feminist theory is based on the division between work in the family (primarily women's work) and work in paid production (primarily men's work). Women are exploited because they work at production *and* reproduction in the home, and frequently at low-paying jobs outside the home as well.

In welfare-state economies that provide maternal and child care benefits, a woman with children is better off materially than under capitalism, but she is not much more economically independent. Instead of the private patriarchy of economic dependence on a husband, women are subject to the public patriarchy of a paternalistic state, which is more interested in women as paid and unpaid workers and as child producers than in furthering gender equality in the home or in the workplace.

In all industrial economies, women and men have a different "class" consciousness because they do different work. Women have prime responsibility for child care, even though they may work full time outside the home. Thus, they live a significant part of their lives in a world of reciprocity and cooperation, personal responsibility and sharing, physical contact and affection, in contrast to the impersonal and abstract world of industrial production, the world of men's work. Men's work in the marketplace is rewarded according to time spent or product made. Women's work in the home is never-ending; rewards depend on personalized standards, and others come first. It is emotional as well as intellectual and physical labor. Just as the economic positions of capitalists and the proletariat shape their class consciousness, women's daily material and socioemotional labor differentiates their consciousness from that of men.

Suggested Readings in Marxist and Socialist Feminism

Acker, Joan. 1989. *Doing Comparable Worth*. Philadelphia: Temple University Press.

Bannerji, Himani. 1995. *Thinking Through: Essays on Feminism, Marxism, and Anti-Racism*. Toronto: Women's Press.

Barrett, Michèle. 1988. *Women's Oppression Today: The Marxist/Feminist Encounter*. (Rev. ed.) London: Verso.

Blum, Linda M. 1991. *Between Feminism and Labor: The Significance of the Comparable Worth Movement*. Berkeley: University of California Press.

Brenner, Johanna. 2000. *Women and the Politics of Class*. New York: Monthly Review Press.

Collins, Jane L. and Martha E. Gimenez (eds.). 1990. *Work Without Wages: Comparative Studies of Domestic Labor and Self-Employment*. Albany: State University of New York Press.

Coontz, Stephanie, and Peta Henderson. 1986. *Women's Work, Men's Property: The Origins of Gender and Class*. London: Verso.

Croll, Elisabeth. 1978. *Feminism and Socialism in China*. New York: Schocken.

Glazer, Nona Y. 1993. *Women's Paid and Unpaid Labor: The Work Transfer in Retailing and Health Care*. Philadelphia: Temple University Press.

Hansen, Karen V., and Ilene J. Phillipson (eds.). 1990. *Women, Class and the Feminist Imagination: A Socialist-Feminist Reader*. Philadelphia: Temple University Press.

Hartsock, Nancy C. M. 1983. *Money, Sex, and Power: Toward a Feminist Historical Materialism*. New York: Longman.

Hennessy, Rosemary. 1993. *Materialist Feminism and the Politics of Discourse*. London: Routledge.

Holter, Harriet (ed.). 1984. *Patriarchy in a Welfare Society*. Oslo, Norway: Universitetsforlaget.

Johnson, Kay Ann. 1983. *Women, the Family and Peasant Revolution in China*. Chicago: University of Chicago Press.

Kruks, Sonia, Rayna Rapp, and Marilyn B. Young (eds.). 1989. *Promissory Notes: Women in the Transition to Socialism*. New York: Monthly Review Press.

Milkman, Ruth. 1987. *Gender at Work*. Urbana and Chicago: University of Illinois Press.

Redclift, Nanneke and Enzo Mingione (eds.). 1985. *Beyond Employment: Household, Gender and Subsistence*. Oxford and New York: Basil Blackwell.

Sainsbury, Diane (ed.). 1994. *Gendering Welfare States*. Newbury Park, CA: Sage.

Sargent, Lydia (ed.). 1981. *Women and Revolution: A Discussion of the Unhappy Marriage of Marxism and Feminism*. Boston: South End Press.

Sayers, Janet, Mary Evans, and Nanneke Redclift (eds.). 1987. *Engels Revisited: New Feminist Essays*. London and New York: Tavistock.

Stacey, Judith. 1983. *Patriarchy and Socialist Revolution in China*. Berkeley: University of California Press.

Stites, Richard. [1978] 1990. *The Women's Liberation Movement in Russia: Feminism, Nihilism, and Bolshevism, 1860–1930*. Princeton, NJ: Princeton University Press.

Tax, Meredith. 1980. *The Rising of the Women: Feminist Solidarity and Class Conflict, 1880–1917*. New York: Monthly Review Press.

Treiman, Donald J. and Heidi I. Hartmann (eds.). 1981. *Women, Work and Wages: Equal Pay for Jobs of Equal Value*. Washington, DC: National Academy Press.

Walby, Sylvia. 1986. *Patriarchy at Work: Patriarchal and Capitalist Relations in Employment*. Minneapolis: University of Minnesota Press.

———. 1990. *Theorizing Patriarchy*. Oxford and New York: Basil Blackwell.

———. 1997. *Gender Transformations*. New York and London: Routledge.

Ward, Kathryn (ed.). 1990. *Women Workers and Global Restructuring*. Ithaca, NY: ILR Press. ✦

Chapter Three

Post-Colonial Feminism

Sources of Gender Inequality

- Undercutting of women's traditional economic base by colonialism.
- Exploitation of women workers in the post-colonial global economy.
- Lack of education for girls.
- Inadequate maternal and child health care.
- Patriarchal family structures and cultural practices harmful to women and girls.

Remedies

- Protection of women's economic resources in modernization programs.
- Education of girls.
- Health care and family planning services.
- Community organizing of mothers.
- Eradication of such practices as female genital mutilation.[1]

Contributions

- Gender analyses of modernization and economic restructuring programs.

- Data on exploitation of women and children workers.
- Documentation of importance of economic resources to women's social status.
- Recognition of women's rights as human rights.

Economic exploitation of women in countries on the way to industrialization is even greater than in developed economies. Post-colonial feminist research has shown that women workers in developing countries in Latin America, the Caribbean, and Africa are paid less than men workers, whether they work in factories or do piece work at home. To survive in rural communities, women grow food, keep house, and earn money any way they can to supplement what their migrating husbands send them.

Post-colonial feminism uses theories of colonial underdevelopment and post-colonial development, as well as marxist and socialist feminist theories, to analyze the position of women in the global economy, with particular emphasis on newly industrializing countries. *The global economy* links countries whose economies focus on service, information, and finances with manufacturing sites and the sources of raw materials in other countries. Men and women workers all over the world supply the labor for the commodities that end up in the stores in your neighborhood. They are not paid according to their skills but according to the going wage, which varies enormously from country to country because it is dependent on the local standard of living. Women workers tend to be paid less than men workers throughout the world, whatever the wage scale, because they are supposedly supporting only themselves. However, in South Korea's economic development zone, many young single women factory workers live in crowded dormitories and eat one meal a day in order to send money home for a brother in college. In Mexico, many older married women's jobs are a significant source of their family's income. The gendered division of labor in developing countries is the outcome of centuries of European and American colonization. Under colonialism, women's traditional contributions to food production were undermined in favor of exportable crops, such as coffee, and the extraction of raw materials, such as minerals. Men workers were favored in mining and large-scale agriculture, but they were barely paid enough for

.their own subsistence. Women family members had to provide food for themselves and their children; however, good land was often confiscated for plantations, so women also lived at a bare survival level.

Since becoming independent, many developing nations have sought financial capital and business investments from wealthier European and American countries. The consequent economic restructuring and industrialization disadvantages women. Men workers, considered heads of families, are hired for the better-paying manufacturing jobs. Young single women, although they are working as much for their families as for themselves, are hired for jobs that pay much less than men's jobs. And married women, whose wages frequently go to feed their children, are paid the least of all. For example, in the *maquiladoras*, the Mexican border industries, where 85 to 90 percent of the workers are women, there is a division between the electronics industries, which offer somewhat better working conditions and higher pay but hire only young single women, and the smaller, less modern apparel factories, which employ older women supporting children. In Puerto Rico's "Operation Bootstrap," a U.S.-sponsored economic development program of the 1950s, women were recruited into manufacturing industries that paid lower salaries than those where men workers predominated.

Feminist research on women's economic and health problems in developing countries has been extensive, but even those who work for government organizations, United Nations agencies, or the World Bank have not had the power to make development or economic restructuring programs more women-friendly. Pooling resources through grass-roots organizing, women of different communities have joined together to fight against exploitation and for social services. They do so as mothers, for their children, and so have often been able to accomplish what more obvious political protest cannot, given the entrenchment of wealthy owners of land and factories.

The following excerpt is from a paper originally presented at an international conference, Women and Development: Focus on Latin America and Africa, sponsored by the Institute for Research on Women and the Center for Latin America and the Caribbean, which was held at the State University of New York at Albany in 1989. In it, Edna Acosta-Belén, a Latin American specialist, and Christine Bose, a sociologist, lay out feminist theories dealing with the effects of colonialism, why poor women today are called "the last colony," and strategies of coping by these women.

Gender and Development

Edna Acosta-Belén and Christine E. Bose

. . . It is difficult to address gender issues in the developing countries of Latin America and the Caribbean without recognizing that they are inextricably linked to a global capitalist and patriarchal model of accumulation and hence to the history of imperialist expansion and colonialism (Saffioti 1978; Mies et al. 1988). Although it is not always self-evident, both women and colonies have served as the foundations of industrial development of the economically dominant Western nations.

Colonialism, born in the fifteenth century—the gateway to discovery, exploration, and conquest—was to become the mainspring of European industrial development. Since the "discovery" of their existence by European settlers, primarily from Spain, Portugal, Great Britain, France, and the Netherlands, territories in the New World have served as the major sources of precious metals, labor, raw materials, and food products to support the commerce, consumption, and economic development of what are today's industrialized nations. The basis for the ascendancy of capitalism in Europe was the colonial exploitation of its overseas empires. Although the nature of colonization varied from one region of the world to another, the system was based on extracting the wealth of the new lands by using the labor of both the subjugated indigenous populations and that of the displaced and enslaved African populations to support the lavish lives of European aristocracies and the consumption needs of a rising bourgeoisie (Saffioti 1978; Etienne and Leacock 1980). The wealth and natural resources of the colonies were the essence of European mercantilist capitalism and, at a later stage, of its industrial revolution. The manufactured goods produced in European factories with the colonies' raw materials and labor found their way back into colonial markets. With some variations, this cycle has essentially perpetuated itself through the centuries.

In the Americas the United States emerged as a new colonial power to substitute for the Spanish, consolidating itself in the nineteenth century through the pursuit of its Manifest Destiny policies of territorial expansion and the Monroe Doctrine (1823), aimed at reducing European presence and influence in the hemisphere. After its Civil War (1861–65) the United States was determined to become the major economic and geopolitical power in the Americas.

In the twentieth century capitalism entered its new monopoly and multinational stages of development, and the neocolonial relations developed then still link the colonizing and colonized countries into a global economic network. The unequal relationship that has kept Latin American and Caribbean nations dependent helps explain the continuing internal turmoil and clamor for change emanating from most of these nations today.

It is quite evident in the colonial literature that from the beginning of the European monarchies' imperial expansion, the adventurers, missionaries, and officials who came to the New World had little regard for any patterns of communal and egalitarian relationships among the native populations subjugated during the colonial enterprise. In many pre-colonial societies women's position and participation in productive activities was parallel to that of men, rather than subservient (Saffioti 1978; Etienne and Leacock 1980). The imposition of European patriarchal relationships that presupposed the universal subordination of women in many instances deprived indigenous women of property and personal autonomy and restricted the productive functions and any public roles they might have played before colonization (Saffioti 1978; Etienne and Leacock 1980; Nash 1980). These policies continued through the centuries as colonial territories were integrated into the capitalist system of production, and persisted even after those countries gained independence, in part because of the neocolonial relations the industrialized nations still maintain with developing countries. The conditions of *internal colonialism* (Blauner 1972) that later emerged within Western metropolitan centers, wherein immigrant groups and racial minorities are relegated to a structurally marginal position, replicate the patterns of colonial relationships.

Before the work of Ester Boserup (1970), most of the classical development literature tended to ignore women's economic role and contributions. Assuming women were passive dependents, the literature relegated them to reproductive rather than productive roles, confining them to an undervalued domestic sphere isolated from the rest of the social structure. Little attention was paid to differences in productivity between women and men in different developing nations or to women's labor activities in the informal economy. One of Boserup's major contributions was to establish empirically the vital role of women in agricultural economies and to recognize that economic development, with its tendency to encourage labor specialization, was actually depriving women of their original productive functions and on the whole deteriorating their status. . . .

Women as a Last Colony

The conceptualization of women as a last colony, advanced by the work of German feminist scholars Mies, Bennholdt-Thomsen, and Werlhof (1988), has provided a valuable new interpretative model for feminist research on Third World issues. This framework underscores the convergences of race, class, and gender and recognizes one complex but coherent system of oppression. It also allows us to see that the patterns of sexism are compounded by a layer of oppression, shared by Third World men and women, brought about by the colonizing experience.

Werlhof (1988, 25) argues that the relationship of Third World subsistence workers of both genders to First World multinationals in some ways resembles the relationship between men and women worldwide. Women and colonies are both low-wage and nonwage producers, share structural subordination and dependency, and are overwhelmingly poor. Werlhof contends that in response to its accumulation crisis, capitalism is now implicitly acknowledging that the unpaid labor of women in the household goes beyond the reproductive sphere into the production of commodities. Nevertheless, housewives are frequently and explicitly excluded from what is defined as the economy in order to maintain the illusion of the predominance of the male wage worker. The problems with this definition are increasingly obvious, as many Latin American and Caribbean households, using multiple income strategies, rely on women's informal economy activities or subsistence work. . . .

Mies et al. (1988, 7) indicate there are actually three tiers in the capitalist pyramid of exploitation: (1) the holders of capital, (2) wage workers (mostly white men or the traditional proletariat) and nonwage workers (mostly women), and (3) housewives and subsistence producers (men and women) in the colonial countries. Using this model, both Werlhof (1988) and Bennholdt-Thomsen (1988) argue that the new international trend in the division of labor is toward the "housewifization" (*Hausfrauisierung*) of labor, namely, labor that exhibits the major characteristics of housework, and away from the classical proletariat whose labor is now being replaced. Of course, the housewife role entails different things across nations, ranging from cooking, cleaning, washing, and taking care of children and the elderly, to grinding maize, carrying water, or plowing the family plot. The determining factor is always whether or not these tasks are performed for wages. Werlhof (1988, 173) establishes a key link between the undervalued work performed by women and that of Third World populations, which leads her to conclude that the classical proletariat is being replaced by the Third World worker and the housewife as the new "pillars of accumulation." This conclusion also points to the contradiction between any cultural or economic devaluation of women's work and the important role it actually plays.

Following this line of argument, the three authors note that, since the latter part of the nineteenth century, patriarchal capitalist practice and ideology have colonized women by the "housewifization" of their work: by attempting to isolate women in the domestic sphere and devaluing the work they perform there; by ideologically justifying it as a genetic predisposition based on their capacity for motherhood; by regarding any type of income they generate as supplementary or secondary, thus ascribing a lower status to their occupations; and ultimately, by controlling their sexuality. These power relations between men and women are thus comparable to the international division of labor between First and Third World countries. The present-day world economic crisis is not just another cycle of capitalism but rather a new phase of development relying on female forms of labor (i.e., doing any kind of work at any time, unpaid or poorly paid) wherein the industrialized powers try to force Third World nations to "restructure" or adapt their national economies to the needs of the world system for such flexible labor. . . .

Women Organizing for Change

. . . Women are not passive victims in the socioeconomic processes that maintain their lower status. Instead, they are developing creative ways in which to resist the new forms of subordination. Latin American activists expect that changes in sexist practice and ideology can be obtained during economic crises—an experience quite different from that of feminists in the core capitalist countries whose achievements were made in the context of improving material conditions. In Latin America and the Caribbean various types of resistance, solidarity, and collective action are used by women in diverse geographic regions and under different sociopolitical structures, a pattern that is beginning to be recognized in comparative studies of women's movements (Margolis 1993).

Although Latin American women's subsistence activities as peasant producers can be seen as similar to the unpaid housework of women in Europe and the United States, the resultant political strategies are different . . . perhaps because of the class differences between them. In First World countries women have responded to cutbacks in government services to families by entering the paid labor force, especially in the service industry, and by taking over the tasks of eldercare and childcare. In Latin America and the Caribbean nations, though some women do create microenterprises, . . . take jobs in export processing zones, or enter the service sector, the vast majority respond to the breakdown of their subsistence economy by organizing collective meals, health cooperatives, mothers' clubs, neighborhood water-rights groups, or their own textile and craft collectives, which produce goods both for street vending and for international markets. Thus, rather than *privatizing* their survival problems, these women *collectivize* them and form social-change groups based on social reproduction concerns. In these new terms, the political discourse and arena of struggle is not worker exploitation and control of the means of production but rather moral persuasion to place demands on the state for rights related to family survival.

Many Latin American women activists contend that their traditional roles as wives and mothers are the basis for these collective actions on behalf of their families. Although most of the groups are composed of poor women, they do not organize either explicitly on a class basis or at the workplace. Instead, they organize at a neighborhood level around a broad list of issues that they redefine as women's concerns, such as running water or transportation for squatter communities. Some feminist scholars argue that this approach constitutes a movement of women but not necessarily a feminist movement; others feel these tactics represent a form of working-class feminism that promotes consciousness of how gender shapes women's lives (Sternback et al. 1992). . . .

References

Bennholdt-Thomsen, Veronika. 1988. "'Investment of the Poor': An Analysis of World Bank Policy." In *Women: The Last Colony,* ed. Maria Mies, Veronika Bennholdt-Thomsen, and Claudia von Werlhof, pp. 51–63. London: Zed.

Blauner, Robert. 1972. *Racial Oppression in America.* New York: Harper and Row.

Boserup, Ester. 1970. *Women's Role in Economic Development.* New York: St. Martin's Press.

Etienne, Mona, and Eleanor Leacock (eds.). 1980. *Women and Colonization: Anthropological Perspectives.* New York: Praeger.

Margolis, Diane Rothbard. 1993. "Women's Movements Around the World: Cross-Cultural Comparisons." *Gender & Society* 7:379–99.

Mies, Maria, Veronika Bennholdt-Thomsen, and Claudia von Werlhof. 1988. *Women: The Last Colony.* London: Zed.

Nash, June. 1980. "Aztec Women: The Transition from Status to Class in Empire and Colony." In *Women and Colonization: Anthropological Perspectives,* pp. 134–48.

Saffioti, Heleieth I. B. 1978. *Women in Class Society.* New York: Monthly Review.

Sternback, Nancy Saporta, Marysa Navarro-Aranguren, Patricia Chuchryk, and Sonia E. Alvarez. 1992. "Feminisms in Latin America: From Bogotá to San Bernardo." *Signs* 17:393–434.

Werlhof, Claudia von. 1988. "Women's Work: The Blind Spot in the Critique of Political Economy." In *Women: The Last Colony,* ed. Maria Mies, Veronika Bennholdt-Thomsen, and Claudia von Werlhof, pp. 13–26. London: Zed.

Post-colonial feminism equates women's status with their contribution to their family's economy and their control of economic resources. To be equal with her husband, it is not enough for a married woman to earn money; she has to provide a needed portion of her family's income and also have control over the source of that income and over its distribution as well. In a rural community, that means owning a piece of land, being able to market the harvest from that land, and deciding how the profit from the sale will be spent. In an urban economy, it may mean owning a store or small business, retaining the profit, and deciding what to spend it on or whether to put it back into the business.

There are societies in Africa and elsewhere in the world where women control significant economic resources and so have a high status. In contrast, in societies with patriarchal family structures where anything women produce, including children, belongs to the husband, women and girls have a low value. Post-colonial feminism's theory is that in any society, if the food or income women produce is the main way the family is fed, and women also control the distribution of any surplus they produce, women have power and prestige. If men provide most of the food and distribute the surplus, women's status is low. Whether women or men produce most of the food or bring in most of the family income depends on the society's economy. When a woman is able to own the means of production (land, a store, a business) like a man, she has the chance to be economically independent. If her income is barely above subsistence level because her choices are low-waged work in a factory, piece work in a sweatshop, or sex work as a prostitute, then the fact that she has a job does not give her a very high social status, especially if much of the money she earns is sent back home to her family. Thus, the mode of production and the kinship rules that control the distribution of any surplus are the significant determinants of the relative status of women and men in any society.

In addition to gendered economic analyses, post-colonial feminism addresses the political issue of women's rights versus national and cultural traditions. At the United Nations Fourth World Conference on Women and the NGO (nongovernmental organizations) Forum held in Beijing in 1995, the popular slogan was "human rights are women's rights and women's rights are human rights." The Platform for Action document that came out of the U.N. Conference condemned particular cultural practices that are oppressive to women—infanticide, dowry, child marriage, and female genital mutilation. The 187 governments that signed onto the Platform agreed to abolish these practices. However, since they are integral parts of cultural and tribal traditions, giving them up could be seen as kowtowing to Western ideas. The post-colonial feminist perspective, so critical of colonial and cultural imperialism and yet so supportive of women's rights, has found this issue difficult to resolve.

The women's own solution to this dilemma is community organizing around their productive and reproductive roles as mothers—so that what benefits them economically and physically is in the service of their families, not themselves alone. However, this same community organizing and family service can support the continuance of cultural practices, such as female genital mutilation, that Western post-colonial feminists want to see eradicated. The decision not to interfere with traditional cultural practices that are physically harmful to girls and at the same time work for the girls' education and better health care is a dilemma for post-colonial feminists.

Some post-colonial feminists argue that pushing developing countries into Western ways is the wrong way to go. They are especially critical of free-market capitalism, with its emphasis on industrialization and globalization. One of the most influential, Maria Mies, a German sociologist, argues that we need a new "moral economy," one that is centered on women and children, based in local community enterprises, and respectful of the environment. Her perspective is ecofeminist, and her views link post-colonial and radical feminism. She laid out these alternative economic principles in a paper first presented at the Sixth International Interdisciplinary Congress on Women, held in Adelaide, Australia, in 1996.

Decolonizing the Iceberg Economy: New Feminist Concepts for a Sustainable Society

Maria Mies

... We began to understand that the dominant theories about the functioning of our economy, including Marxism, were only concerned with the tip of the iceberg, the 11% rising above the water, namely only capital and wage labour. The whole base of that iceberg, the 89% under the water, was invisible, namely women's unpaid housework, caring work, nurturing work, or, as we then called it: the production of life or the subsistence production. . . . Since my friends and I had lived in "Third World" countries for a long time, we also recognized another part of the invisible economy—the work of millions of subsistence farmers and artisans. These producers in subsistence economies, who are mainly women, supply goods to meet basic local needs and to sustain life. And finally we saw that nature herself was considered to be a free good, to be appropriated and exploited with no or little costs for the sake of accumulation. We called all three parts of the submerged "hidden economy" under the water in our iceberg metaphor: the "Colonies of White Man." White Man stands here for the western industrial system which colonizes nature, women and "foreign" people and territories (Mies 1986/1991; Mies, Bennholdt-Thomsen and von Werlhof 1988). It is our thesis that permanent economic growth or capital accumulation can only continue as long as these colonies can be exploited free of costs, or with very little costs. Although the hidden-under-water part of this economy is excluded where people think about the "economy," it is the necessary foundation and precondition for the existence and flourishing of the over-the-water-tip and hence is part of the whole economy. One does not understand capitalism unless one includes this in one's analysis. On the other hand, this hidden part must also necessarily be excluded theoretically and ideologically from people's perception of reality; otherwise all laws, particularly all labour laws, all claims to equality and freedom and the concept of the rule of right, would then have also to be applied to this part of the economy. If all work in this world had to be paid, this would lead to a collapse of the accumulation model and the tip of the iceberg. Like an iceberg which tilts and sometimes overturns because of differential melting, the current economic model is fundamentally unstable. . . .

Alternative Economic Principles

The iceberg paradigm of unsustainability, with its pyramid of colonization and its destructive consequences, leads to a few theses about sustainable development:

"Catch-up development" is not possible for all people.

"Catch-up development" is not even desirable for the comparative few or top of the iceberg economy.

To preserve the foundations of life on earth, equality, justice and solidarity new models of society are needed which can lead towards true sustainability.

This leads to the difficulty of visualizing a sustainable society as a working, positive and inspiring concept. Clearly the existing iceberg model, topped by capital and submerging most of the world's people and nature itself, cannot produce and regenerate life. In an alternative paradigm, presently colonized and marginalised actors, activities and values will be put into the core (centre), because they are central to ensuring that life can go on in its regeneration and fullness. If the preservation of life is made central (the life or subsistence perspective), all other dimensions, mechanisms, institutions, must serve this goal. This core of life is not unlimited: efforts to expand and exploit it must recognize that happiness, freedom, justice, equality for all must be realized within these limits.

People's livelihood in a sustainable society will depend both on income from wage-labour/employment and on other forms of work, including unpaid work. In this context, the loss of wage-labour (employment) need not be catastrophic. Moreover, valuable, unpaid, necessary social labour can have prestige in the society when it is *shared by men and women equally.* Thus, moving from paid to unpaid work will not be a disaster leading to social exclusion, depression, isolation and poverty. Nor will socially and environmentally destructive work be necessary to ensure employment, monetary income and thus livelihood for people. A sustainable society will depend on regaining control of communities. Restoring local and regional community control of assets and resources can enhance better decision-making on the contradictory concerns for a healthy environment and the preservation of people's work and livelihood. Work and nature will no longer be antagonists.

A sustainable society implies a regional economy instead of one based on globalization and the principles of "free trade." Only in a regional economy can people have control over their communal resources, preserve nature and have true food security. A regional economy makes sure that there is no wasteful production for an anonymous global market. Instead production and consumption will again be linked. Producers will produce what people need—not what enhances capital accumulation. Consumers will feel responsible for the producers and the relationships of production. Producer-consumers' cooperatives (e.g., the Seikatsu Club in Japan) and urban supported agriculture are first steps in this direction. . . .

A New Concept of Productive Work

Sometimes scholars, policy-makers and the general public still assume that work, employment, labour and productive labour are identical. Since the late seventies, however, feminists have shown that such "productive" labour, which produces money or capital, can only exist because of the so-called "non-productive" unpaid work of women in the household. Feminists have also shown there to be a clearcut sexual division of labour between unpaid subsistence work done by women and employment or wage labour, typically dominated by men. Even when women are also employed, the responsibility for the unpaid housework is still theirs. All this unpaid work is not only exploited freely, without any labour laws, but it is also excluded from the GDP and not considered when people talk of the labour market.

A new concept of *productive work* would challenge one of the myths of classical economic theory, also not disputed by Marx, that the concepts of productive labour and of productivity be reserved for the labour of the capitalist and of the wage workers. A new definition of productive work would not exclude the work of a woman who gives birth to a baby and spends years feeding, caring for and loving the child, even though such work does not produce money directly. A different meaning of productivity would cease to give the semblance of life to money as the creator of life as happens when productivity is considered to be only money-producing and money-augmenting labour. I shall reserve this concept of work for the life-producing and life-sustaining work that has been done by women, tribals, small peasants and all those who still know that life comes out of our interaction with nature and with one another and not out of money.

The existing assumption that work is synonymous with money-earning employment would change once unpaid work were fully included and valued in economic theory and practice and no longer treated as the invisible colonized underground of mainstream economics. In this alternative vision, work for money income would play a secondary role, and many of the things and services people need would be produced locally or regionally and exchanged directly or for little money. In this vision, work becomes a joy as well as a burden, and this can only happen when people see again what they produce, for whom they produce and that it makes sense that they produce at all (Mies, 1986/1991; King, 1993).

To integrate unpaid work, both in and outside the household, again into the overall economic-social-cultural activities requires above all a change in the sexual division of labour. This means men will have to do as much of this unpaid work as women. They will have to share the responsibility for the care of children, the household, the sick, the old and to share the necessary unpaid ecological and community work. Political work will be done by both women and men. Caring, nurturing, mothering, taking care of relationships will no longer be seen as "female" qualities but as human qualities, expected from everyone.

References

King, Ursula (1993), *Women and Spirituality: Voices of Protest and Promise.* University Park: Pennsylvania State University Press.

Mies, Maria, Veronika Bennholdt-Thomsen, and Claudia von Werlhof (1988), *Women, the Last Colony.* London: Zed Books.

Mies, Maria (1986/1991), *Patriarchy and Accumulation: Women in the International Division of Labour,* 1st and 4th editions. London: Zed Books.

Critique. Post-colonial feminism has taken marxist and socialist feminist theories and expanded their application to nonindustrial economies and to societies in the process of industrializing. They have found many of the same phenomena that occurred during the nineteenth-century European and American industrial revolution—young, single factory girls exploited as cheap labor, working-class men getting the better-paid factory jobs, and middle- and upper-class men owning the means of production. They also found that the family remains a source of both exploitation and protection for women. Their labor is frequently used as a source of family income, but mothers also form grassroots service and community protest groups.

Western ideas of individualism are double-edged in developing countries. On the one hand, these ideas support the rights of girls and women to an education that will allow them to be economically independent. They are also the source of a concept of universal human rights, which can be used to fight subordinating and sometimes physically hurtful tribal practices, such as female genital mutilation. On the other hand, Western ideas undercut communal enterprises and traditional sharing of food production and childcare.

Summary

The global economy reflects state and private economic interests, and that means high production with cheap labor for maximum profits. Families all over the world need several workers in order to survive, often including children. Women and girls are doubly vulnerable—as workers and as family members. They are a prime source of low-paid wage workers whose earnings belong first to their families. They also work in family businesses, often unpaid; they make things at home to sell to supplement their family's food supply; they become prostitutes at a young age, often sold as a source of family income. At the same time, women physically maintain households and have babies, and frequently bury them within a year of birth.

There is no doubt that in many parts of the world today, as post-colonial feminism has shown, women are living in dire conditions. To redress their situation, whole economic structures and family and kinship systems need to be overhauled. However, the twentieth-century economic and social revolutions in the Soviet Union and China did not give women equality. Women became full-time workers, but, as in capitalist economies, they earned less than men and did almost all the child care and housework.

Post-colonial feminism makes very evident the political dilemmas of gender reform feminisms. Throughout the world, men own most of the private property, monopolize the better jobs, and make the laws. The outcome of this inequality is men's double exploitation of women in the job market and in the home. Procreative differences are not the cause of women's exploitation, but its justification. Women are subordinate in all industrial societies not because they are child bearers or child minders but because economies depend on them as low-paid workers who can be hired and fired as needed. The rationale is that women are, after all, "really" wives and mothers. Each form of exploitation of women's work reinforces the other. Women's economic value as waged and low-waged workers and as unpaid workers for the family are the *main* reasons for their subordination in modern societies.

Gender reform feminist politics is correct in pinpointing women's position in the world of paid work as the target for change. The problem is that the entire global economy needs drastic change. If the global economy is not made more equal for everyone, women in general, and poor women in particular, suffer the most. But since the gendered social order as a whole is the source of gender inequality, economic changes alone will not necessarily put women on an equal footing with men.

Note

1. For more than two thousand years, in a broad belt across the middle of Africa, little girls and young women have been subject to crude surgery that cuts away the clitoris and the lips of the vagina. The vaginal opening is sewn closed, except for a tiny opening for urination and menstruation. The purpose is to ensure women's virginity until marriage and to inhibit wives' appetites for sexual relations after marriage. Ironically, these mutilating practices do neither but result in the infliction of pain and the practice of anal intercourse as part of normal sexuality. Childbirth is more dangerous because of tearing and hemorrhage, and the risks of abscesses, fistulas, and urinary tract infection throughout life are high.

Suggested Readings in Post-Colonial Feminism

Bennholdt-Thomsen, Veronika, and Maria Mies. 2000. *The Subsistence Perspective: Beyond the Globalized Economy.* London: Zed Books.

Boserup, Ester. 1970. [second edition, 1987]. *Women's Role in Economic Development.* New York: St. Martin's Press.

Brydon, Lynn, and Sylvia Chant. 1989. *Women in the Third World: Gender Issues in Rural and Urban Areas.* New Brunswick, NJ: Rutgers University Press.

El Dareer, Asma. 1982. *Woman, Why Do You Weep? Circumcision and Its Consequences.* London: Zed Books.

Fernández-Kelly, María Patricia. 1983. *For We Are Sold, I and My People: Women and Industry in Mexico's Frontier.* Albany: State University of New York Press.

Harcourt, Wendy (ed.). 1994. *Feminist Perspectives on Sustainable Development.* London: Zed Books.

Jaquette, Jane (ed.). 1989. *The Women's Movement in Latin America: Feminism and the Transition to Democracy.* Winchester, MA: Unwin Hyman.

Kim, Seung-Kyung. 1997. *Class Struggle or Family Struggle? The Lives of Women Factory Workers in South Korea.* Cambridge, UK: Cambridge University Press.

Leacock, Eleanor and Helen I. Safa (eds.). 1986. *Women's Work: Development and the Division of Labor by Gender.* South Hadley, MA: Bergin & Garvey.

Lightfoot-Klein, Hanny. 1989. *Prisoners of Ritual: An Odyssey into Female Circumcision in Africa.* New York: Harrington Park Press.

Mies, Maria. 1982. *The Lace Makers of Narsapur: Indian Housewives Produce for the World Market.* London: Zed Books.

——. 1986. *Patriarchy and Accumulation on a World Scale: Women in the International Division of Labor.* London: Zed Books.

Mies, Maria, Veronika Bennholdt-Thomsen, and Claudia von Werlhof. 1988. *Women: The Last Colony.* London: Zed Books.

Moghadam, Valentine M. (ed.). 1994. *Identity Politics and Women: Cultural Reassertions and Feminisms in International Perspective.* Boulder, CO: Westview Press.

——. (ed.). 1996. *Patriarchy and Development: Women's Positions at the End of the Twentieth Century.* Oxford, UK: Clarendon Press.

Morrissey, Marietta. 1989. *Slave Women in The New World: Gender Stratification in the Caribbean.* Lawrence: University of Kansas Press.

Narayan, Uma. 1997. *Dislocating Cultures: Identities, Traditions, and Third World Feminism.* New York and London: Routledge.

Nash, June, and María Patricia Fernández-Kelly (eds.). 1983. *Women, Men, and the International Division of Labor.* Albany: State University of New York Press.

Redclift, Nanneke, and M. Thea Stewart (eds.). 1991. *Working Women: International Perspectives on Women and Gender Ideology.* New York and London: Routledge.

Scheper-Hughes, Nancy. 1992. *Death Without Weeping: The Violence of Everyday Life in Brazil.* Berkeley: University of California Press.

Silliman, Jael and Ynestra King (eds.). 1999. *Dangerous Intersections: Feminist Perspectives on Population, Environment, and Development.* Boston: South End Press.

Sparr, Pam (ed.). 1994. *Mortgaging Women's Lives: Feminist Critiques of Structural Adjustment.* London: Zed Books.

Tinker, Irene (ed.). 1990. *Persistent Inequalities: Women and World Development.* New York: Oxford University Press.

Visvanathan, Nalini et al. (ed.). 1997. *The Women, Gender and Development Reader.* London: Zed Books.

Ward, Kathryn (ed.). 1990. *Women Workers and Global Restructuring.* Ithaca, NY: ILR Books.

Young, Kate, Carol Wolkowitz, and Roslyn McCullagh (eds.). 1981. *Of Marriage and the Market: Women's Subordination in International Perspective.* London: CSE Books. ✦

Part III

Gender Resistance Feminisms

In the 1970s, feminist ideas began to make inroads into the public consciousness, and women entered many formerly all-men workplaces and schools. Derogatory remarks about women were no longer acceptable officially, but women became more and more aware of constant put-downs from men they saw every day—bosses and colleagues at work, professors and students in the classroom, fellow organizers in political movements, and worst of all, from boyfriends and husbands at home. These "microinequities" of everyday life—being ignored and interrupted, not getting credit for competence or good performance, being passed over for jobs that involve taking charge—crystallize into a pattern that insidiously wears women down. Mary Rowe, a woman doctor using a pseudonym (because it was too dangerous even in the late 1970s to openly call attention to what men colleagues were doing to women), termed it the "Saturn's Rings Phenomenon" at a Conference on Women's Leadership and Authority in the Health Professions, held in California in 1977. The seemingly trivial sexist incidents, she said, are like the dust particles in the rings around the planet Saturn—separately they are tiny, but when they coalesce, they form a very visible pattern.

The younger women working in the civil rights, anti–Vietnam War, and student new-left movements in the late 1960s had even earlier realized that they were being used as handmaidens, bed partners, and coffee-makers by the men in their protest organizations. Despite the revolutionary rhetoric the young men were flinging in the face of Western civilization in many countries, when it came to women, they might as well have been living in the eighteenth century.

Out of this awareness that sisters had no place in any brotherhood came the American and European gender resistance feminisms. Their watchword is *patriarchy,* or men's subordination of women. Gender resistance feminisms argue that patriarchy can be found wherever women and men are in contact with each other, in public life as well as in the family. It is very hard to eradicate because a sense of their superiority to women is deeply embedded in the consciousness of most men and is built into the structures of Western society. This privilege has come to be known as the patriarchal dividend. It may best be resisted by forming nonhierarchical, supportive, woman-only organizations, where women can think and act and create freely.

Radical feminism is characterized by small, leaderless, women-only consciousness-raising groups, where the topics of intense discussion come out of the commonalities of women's lives—housework, emotional and sexual service to men, menstruation, childbirth, menopause, the constant sexual innuendoes and come-ons in workplaces and on college campuses, the lack of control over procreation, the fear of physical and sexual abuse. Politically, radical feminism took on the violence in women's oppression—rape and wife beating, the depiction of women as sex objects in the mass media and as pieces of meat in pornography, the global commerce in prostitution. This sexual exploitation of women is the worst effect of patriarchy, according to radical feminism, because its goal is social control of all women. Even if they are not directly attacked, the threat can be enough to keep women fearful and timid.

Lesbian feminism argues that sexual violence and exploitation are the common downside of romantic heterosexual love, which itself is oppressive to women. Lesbian feminists are active in women-only political activities, such as Take Back the Night marches, and in cultural events, such as women-only festivals, as well as in women-run businesses. The lesbian feminist perspective has been an important part of gay and lesbian studies and gay and lesbian political activism.

Psychoanalytic feminism provides a psychological theory of why men oppress women. Using Freudian concepts of personality development, psychoanalytic feminism argues that men's fear of castration by their mothers and repression of their primal attachment to her is sublimated in a *phallic* (sexually male) culture that symbolically subordinates and controls women. Politically, French feminism counters with cultural productions, particularly literature, that celebrate women's bodies, sexuality, and maternality.

Standpoint feminism brought all these feminist theories and politics together in a research agenda: Not only culture but science and social science have to formulate questions and gather data from a *woman's standpoint*. For standpoint feminists, it has been crucial for women to do research from their own point of view and thus to create new bodies of knowledge in biology, psychology, economics, and sociology. This knowledge starts from premises that put women, not men, at the center.

The important theoretical contribution of gender resistance feminisms has been in showing that women's devaluation and subordination are part of the ideology and values of Western culture, as represented in religion, the mass media, sports, and cultural productions, and are built into the everyday practices of major institutions, such as medicine, the law, science, and social science. They also show how sexual exploitation and violence, especially rape and pornography, are a means of control of women.

Some political remedies—women-only consciousness-raising groups, alternative organizations, and lesbian separatism—are resistant to the gendered social order, but they are not able to transform it, as they stand apart from mainstream social institutions. They are vital in allowing women the "breathing space" to formulate important theories of gender inequality, to develop women's studies programs in colleges and universities, to form communities, and to produce knowledge, culture, ethics, and religions from a woman's point of view. But they alienate heterosexual White working-class women and women of disadvantaged racial or ethnic groups, who feel that their men are just as oppressed as they are by the dominant society. These women would not desert their brothers for a sisterhood they feel does not welcome them anyway.

More effective have been the feminist campaigns against sexual harassment, rape, battering, incest, pornography, and prostitution. They have, however, led to head-on confrontations with some men's sense of sexual entitlement and have produced considerable anti-feminist backlash. ✦

Chapter Four

Radical Feminism

Sources of Gender Inequality

- A system of men's oppression of women (*patriarchy*) that goes beyond discrimination.
- Men's violence and control of women through rape, battering, and murder.
- Legitimation of women's oppression in law, medicine, religion, and other social institutions.
- Objectification of women's bodies in advertisements, mass media, and cultural productions.
- Sexual exploitation in pornography and prostitution.

Remedies

- More effective laws against rape and battering.
- Rape crisis centers and battered women's shelters.
- Take Back the Night marches.
- Identification of sexual harassment as a form of discrimination.
- Praise for all kinds of women's bodies, women's sexuality, and maternal qualities.

Contributions

- Theory of patriarchy as a system of oppression of women.

- Recognition of violence against women as a means of direct and indirect control.
- Getting stronger legislation against rape and battering.
- Establishment of accessible rape crisis centers and battered women's shelters.
- Sexual harassment guidelines for workplaces and schools.
- Making evident the dangers of date rape.
- Women's studies programs in colleges and universities throughout the world.

The 1970s saw the growth of what has become a major branch of feminism. Originally used as a term for feminists who wanted to do away with the traditional family and motherhood, radical feminism became a perspective that makes motherhood into a valuable way of thinking and behaving. However, it continues to criticize the traditional family as a prime source of patriarchal oppression of women, as does marxist feminism.

Radical feminism expands the concept of *patriarchy* by defining it as a worldwide system of subordination of women by men through violence and sexual exploitation. In the radical feminist view, because of Western society's encouragement of aggressiveness in men and sexual display in women, most men are capable of, if not prone to, violence against women, and most women are potential victims. The constant threat of rape, battering, and murder is a powerful means of keeping women "in their place." Movies, TV, and advertisements in all media sexualize women's bodies. The pervasive sexual objectification encourages men's using women for their own needs. Also, if women are depicted as "sex objects," their intellectual and leadership capabilities disappear from view. Women running for political office have to look attractive but dare not look too sexy.

Sexual harassment is the commonest manifestation of the sexual exploitation of women in Western societies: Unwanted sexual invitations, sexually loaded remarks and jokes, and inappropriate comments on dress or appearance make it difficult for women and girls to do their work (or even to walk down the street unmolested). When the response to a work-related request is "Wow, that sweater really brings out your good points," the not-so-subtle intent is to turn a woman colleague into a "bimbo" and take her out of the running as a serious competitor. More obvious sexual harassment occurs when a boss or teacher threatens the loss of a job or a low grade if a worker or student will not "give a kiss" or if she responds to a grope with a slap. In the military and other hierarchical organizations, women feel that reporting a rape or coerced sex, let alone a pattern of demeaning comments, is useless when the higher-ups have the same sexist attitudes. Women who complain get tainted with a "troublemaker" label, or are harassed by the person they complain to, but their harassers are let off with a mild talking-to. Sexual harassment seems to get attention only when the media report a drunken attack on many women in a public place, or the same situation is found in army base after army base, or a high government official is involved.

When sexual harassment adversely affects a worker's or student's concentration, or contaminates the environment in which they work or study, it becomes a form of discrimination. Radical feminism has made these patterns of sexual harassment and their discriminatory results visible. Its analysis is reflected in the sexual harassment guidelines of many schools and workplaces. In these guidelines, a sexual involvement of any kind between a subordinate and a person in a position of power is considered coercive and is explicitly forbidden. Also actionable is any situation where sexual remarks or uninvited attentions make employees or students so uncomfortable that they are unable to concentrate on work. These guidelines set up formal processes for reports and complaints and rules for actions to be taken in cases of proven sexual harassment.

Although radical feminism's political battlefield has been protection of rape victims and battered women and condemnation of pornography, prostitution, and sexual harassment, some writers have attached the unequal power in heterosexual relationships as being oppressive to women. They argue that since all men derive power from their dominant social status, any sexual relationship between women and men takes place in a socially unequal context. Consent by women to heterosexual intercourse is, by this definition, often forced by emotional appeals and threats to end the relationship. When a woman fears that a date or friend or lover or husband will use physical violence if she does not give in, it is *date rape* or *marital rape* and is as abusive as any other kind of rape.

The following excerpt is by Catharine MacKinnon, a feminist lawyer whose theoretical and legal arguments that sexuality and violence form a continuum of oppression have become the foundation for radical feminism. It was developed for the National Conference on Women and the Law, which met in Boston in 1981.

Sex and Violence

Catharine A. MacKinnon

I want to raise some questions about the concept of this panel's title, "Violence Against Women," as a concept that may coopt us as we attempt to formulate our own truths. I want to speak specifically about four issues: rape, sexual harassment, pornography, and battery. I think one of the reasons we say that each of these issues is an example of violence against women is to reunify them. To say that aggression against women has this unity is to criticize the divisions that have been imposed on that aggression by the legal system. What I see to be the danger of the analysis, what makes it potentially cooptive, is formulating it—and it *is* formulated this way—these are issues of violence, *not* sex: rape is a crime of violence, not sexuality; sexual harassment is an abuse of power, not sexuality; pornography is violence against women, it is not erotic. Although battering is not categorized so explicitly, it is usually treated as though there is nothing sexual about a man beating up a woman so long as it is with his fist. I'd like to raise some questions about that as well.

I hear in the formulation that these issues are violence against women, not sex, that we are in the shadow of Freud, intimidated at being called repressive Victorians. We're saying we're *oppressed* and they say we're *repressed*. That is, when we say we're against rape, the immediate response is, "Does that mean you're against sex?" "Are you attempting to impose neo-Victorian prudery on sexual expression?" This comes up with sexual harassment as well. When we say we're against sexual harassment, the first thing people want to know is, "What's the difference between that and ordinary male-to-female sexual initiation?" That's a good question. . . . The same is also true of criticizing pornography. "You can't be against erotica?" It's the latest version of the accusation that feminists are anti-male. To distinguish ourselves from this, and in reaction to it, we call these abuses violence. The attempt is to avoid the critique—we're not against sex—and at the same time retain our criticism of these practices. So we rename as violent those abuses that have been seen to be sexual, without saying that we have a very different perspective on violence and on sexuality and their relationship. I also think a reason we call these experiences violence is to avoid being called lesbians, which for some reason is equated with being against sex. In order to avoid that, yet retain our opposition to sexual violation, we put this neutral, objective, abstract word *violence* on it all.

To me this is an attempt to have our own perspective on these outrages without owning up to having one. To have our point of view but present it as *not* a particular point of view. Our problem has been to label something as rape, as sexual harassment, as pornography in the face of a suspicion that it might be intercourse, it might be ordinary sexual initiation, it might be erotic. To say that these purportedly sexual events violate us, to be against them, we call them not sexual. But the attempt to be objective and neutral avoids owning up to the fact that women do have a specific point of view on these events. It avoids saying that from women's point of view, intercourse, sex roles, and eroticism can be and at times are violent to us as women.

My approach would claim our perspective; we are not attempting to be objective about it, we're attempting to represent the point of view of women. The point of view of men up to this time, called objective, has been to distinguish sharply between rape on the one hand and intercourse on the other; sexual harassment on the one hand and normal, ordinary sexual initiation on the other; pornography or obscenity on the one hand and eroticism on the other. The male point of view defines them by distinction. What women experience does not so clearly distinguish the normal, everyday things from those abuses from which they have been defined by distinction. Not just "Now we're going to take what *you* say is rape and call it violence"; "Now we're going to take what *you* say is sexual harassment and call it violence"; "Now we're going to take what *you* say is pornography and call it violence." We have a deeper critique of what has been done to women's sexuality and who controls access to it. What we are saying is that sexuality in exactly these normal forms often *does* violate us. So long as we say that those things are abuses of violence, not sex, we fail to criticize what has been made of *sex,* what has been done to us *through* sex, because we leave the line between rape and intercourse, sexual harassment and sex roles, pornography and eroticism, right where it is.

I think it is useful to inquire how women and men (I don't use the term *persons*, I guess, because I haven't seen many lately) live through the meaning of their experience with these issues. When we ask whether rape, sexual harassment, and pornography are questions of violence or questions of sexuality, it helps to ask, to whom? What is the perspective of those who are involved, whose experience it is—to rape or to have been raped, to consume pornography or to be consumed through it? As to what these things *mean* socially, it is important whether they are about sexuality to women and men or whether they are instead about "violence"—or whether violence and sexuality can be distinguished in that way, as they are lived out.

The crime of rape—this is a legal and observed, not a subjective, individual, or feminist definition—is defined around penetration. That seems to me a very male point of view on what it means to be sexually violated. And it is exactly what heterosexuality as a social institution is fixated around, the penetration of the penis into the vagina. Rape is defined according to what men think violates women, and that is the same as what they think of as the *sine qua non* of sex. What women experience as degrading and defiling when we are raped includes as much that is distinctive to us as is our experience of sex. Someone once termed penetration a "peculiarly resented aspect" of rape—I don't know whether that meant it was peculiar that it was resented or that it was resented with heightened peculiarity. Women who have been raped often do resent having been penetrated. But that is not all there is to what was intrusive or expropriative of a woman's sexual wholeness.

I do think the crime of rape focuses more centrally on what men define as sexuality than on women's experience of our sexual being, hence its violation. A common experience of rape victims is to be unable to feel good about anything heterosexual thereafter—or anything sexual at all, or men at all. The minute they start to have sexual feelings or feel sexually touched by a man, or even a woman, they start to relive the rape. I had a client who came in with her husband. She was a rape victim, a woman we had represented as a witness. Her husband sat the whole time and sobbed. They couldn't have sex anymore because every time he started to touch her, she would flash to the rape scene and see his face change into the face of the man who had raped her. That, to me, is sexual. When a woman has been raped, and it is sex that she then cannot experience without connecting it to that, it was her sexuality that was violated.

Similarly, men who are in prison for rape think it's the dumbest thing that ever happened. . . . It isn't just a miscarriage of justice; they were put in jail for something very little different from what most men do most of the time and call it sex. The only difference is they got caught. That view is nonremorseful and not rehabilitative. It may also be true. It seems to me we have here a convergence between the rapist's view of what he has done and the victim's perspective on what was done to her. That is, for both, their ordinary experiences of heterosexual intercourse and the act of rape have something in common. Now this gets us into intense trouble, because that's exactly how judges and juries see it who refuse to convict men accused of rape. A rape victim has to prove that it was not intercourse. She has to show that there was force and she resisted, because if there was sex, consent is inferred. Finders of fact look for "more force than usual during the preliminaries." Rape is defined by distinction from intercourse—not nonviolence, intercourse. They ask, does this event look more like fucking or like rape? But what is their standard for sex, and is this question asked from the *woman's point of view?* The level of force is not adjudicated at her point of violation; it is adjudicated at the standard of the normal level of force. Who sets this standard?

In the criminal law, we can't put everybody in jail who does an ordinary act, right? Crime is supposed to be deviant, not normal. Women continue not to report rape, and a reason is that they believe, and they are right, that the legal system will not see it from their point of view. We get very low conviction rates for rape. We also get many women who believe they have never been raped, although a lot of force was involved. They mean that they were not raped in a way that is legally provable. In other words, in all these situations, there was not *enough* violence against them to take it beyond the category of "sex"; they were not coerced enough. Maybe they were forced-fucked for years and put up with it, maybe they tried to get it over with, maybe they were coerced by something other than battery, something like economics, maybe even something like love.

What I am saying is that unless you make the point that there is much violence in intercourse, as a usual matter, none of that is changed. Also we continue to stigmatize the women who claim rape as having experienced a deviant violation and allow the rest of us to go through life feeling violated but thinking we've never been raped, when there were a great many times when we, too, have had sex and didn't want it. What this critique does that is different from the "violence, not sex" critique is ask a series of questions about normal, heterosexual intercourse and attempt to move the line between heterosexuality on the one hand—intercourse—and rape on the other, rather than allow it to stay where it is.

Having done that so extensively with rape, I can consider sexual harassment more briefly. The way the analysis of sexual harassment is sometimes expressed now (and it bothers me) is that it is an abuse of power, not sexuality. That does not allow us to pursue whether sexuality, as socially constructed in our society through gender roles, is *itself* a power structure. If you look at sexual harassment as power, not sex, what is power supposed to be? Power is employer/employee, not because courts are marxist but because this is a recognized hierarchy. Among men. Power is teacher/student, because courts recognize a hierarchy there. Power is on one side and sexuality on the other. Sexuality is ordinary affection, everyday flirtation.

Only when ordinary, everyday affection and flirtation and "I was just trying to be friendly" come into the context of *another* hierarchy is it considered potentially an abuse of power. What is not considered to be a hierarchy is women and men—men on top and women on the bottom. That is not considered to be a question of power or social hierarchy, legally or politically. A feminist perspective suggests that it is.

When we have examples of coequal sexual harassment (within these other hierarchies), worker to worker on the same level, involving women and men, we have a lot of very interesting, difficult questions about sex discrimination, which is supposed to be about gender difference, but does not conceive of gender as a social hierarchy. I think that implicit in race discrimination cases for a brief moment of light was the notion that there is a social hierarchy between Blacks and Whites. So that presumptively it's an exercise of power for a White person to do something egregious to a Black person or for a White institution to do something egregious systematically to many Black people. Situations of coequal power—among coworkers or students or teachers—are difficult to see as examples of sexual harassment unless you have a notion of male power. I think we lie to women when we call it not power when a woman is come onto by a man who is not her employer, not her teacher. What do we labor under, what do we feel, when a man—any man—comes and hits on us? I think we require women to feel fine about turning down male-initiated sex so long as the man doesn't have some *other* form of power over us. Whenever—every and any time—a woman feels conflicted and wonders what's wrong with her that she can't decline although she has no inclination, and she feels open to male accusations, whether they come from women or men, of "why didn't you just tell him to buzz off?" we have sold her out, not named her experience. We are taught that we exist for men. We should be flattered or at least act as if we are—be careful about a man's ego because you never know what he can do to you. To flat out say to him, "You?" or "I don't want to" is not *in* most women's sex-role learning. To say it is, is bravado. And that's because he's a man, not just because you never know what he can do to you because he's your boss (that's two things—he's a man and he's the boss) or your teacher or in some other hierarchy. It seems to me that we haven't talked very much about gender *as* a hierarchy, as a division of power, in the way that's expressed and acted out, primarily I think sexually. And therefore we haven't expanded the definition according to women's experience of sexuality, including our own sexual intimidation, of what things are sexual in this world. So men have also defined what can be called sexual about us. They say, "I was just trying to be affectionate, flirtatious and friendly," and we were just all felt up. We criticize the idea that rape comes down to her word against his— but it really *is* her perspective against his perspective, and the law has been written from his perspective. If he didn't mean it to be sexual, it's not sexual. If he didn't see it as forced, it wasn't forced. Which is to say, only male sexual violations, that is, only male ideas of what sexually violates us as women, are illegal. We buy into this when we say our sexual violations are abuses of power, not sex.

Just as rape is supposed to have nothing against intercourse, just as sexual harassment is supposed to have nothing against normal sexual initiation (men initiate, women consent—that's mutual?), the idea that pornography is violence against women, not sex, seems to distinguish artistic creation on the one hand from what is degrading to women on the other. It is candid and true but not enough to say of pornography, as Justice Stewart said, "I know it when I see it." *He* knows what he thinks it is when he sees it—but is that what *I* know? Is that the same "it"? Is he going to know what I know when I see it? I think pretty much not, given what's on the newsstand, given what is not considered hard-core pornography. Sometimes I think what is obscene is what does *not* turn on the Supreme Court—or what revolts them more. Which is uncommon, since revulsion is eroticized.

We have to admit that pornography turns men on; it is therefore erotic. It is a lie to say that pornography is not erotic. When we say it is violence, not sex, we are saying, there is this degrading to women, over here, and this erotic, over there, without saying to whom. It is overwhelmingly disproportionately men to whom pornography is erotic. It is women, on the whole, to whom it is violent, among other things. And this is not just a matter of perspective, but a matter of reality.

Pornography turns primarily men on. Certainly they are getting something out of it. They pay incredible amounts of money for it; it's one of the largest industries in the country. If women got as much out of it as men do, we would buy it instead of cosmetics. It's a massive industry, cosmetics. We are poor but we have *some* money; we are some market. We spend our money to set ourselves up as the objects that emulate those images that are sold as erotic to men. What pornography says about us is that we enjoy degradation, that we are sexually turned on by being degraded. For me that obliterates the line, as a line at all, between pornography on one hand and erotica on the other, if what turns men on, what men find beautiful, is what degrades women. It is pervasively present in art, also, and advertising. But it is definitely present in eroticism, if that is what it is. It makes me think that women's sexuality as such is a stigma. We also sometimes have an experience of sexuality authentic somehow in all this. We are not allowed to have it; we are not allowed to talk about it; we are not allowed to speak of it or image it as from our own point of view. And, to the extent we try to assert that we are beings equal with men, we have to be either asexual or virgins.

To worry about cooptation is to realize that lies make bad politics. It is ironic that cooptation often results from an attempt to be "credible," to be strategically smart, to be "effective" on existing terms. Sometimes you become what you're fighting. Thinking about issues of sexual violation as issues of violence not sex could, if pursued legally, lead to opposing sexual harassment and pornography through morals legislation and obscenity laws. It is actually interesting that this theoretical stance has been widely embraced but these legal strategies have not been. Perhaps women realize that these legal approaches would not address the subordination of women to men, specifically and substantively. These approaches are legally as abstract as the "violence not sex" critique is politically abstract. They are both not enough and too much of the wrong thing. They deflect us from criticizing everyday behavior that is pervasive and normal and concrete and fuses sexuality with gender in violation and is not amenable to existing legal approaches. I think we need to think more radically in our legal work here.

Battering is called violence, rather than something sex-specific: this is done to women. I also think it is sexually done to women. Not only in where it is done—over half of the incidents are in the bedroom. Or the surrounding events—precipitating sexual jealousy. But when violence against women is eroticized as it is in this culture, it is very difficult to say that there is a major distinction in the level of sex involved between being assaulted by a penis and being assaulted by a fist, especially when the perpetrator is a man. If women as gender female are defined as sexual beings, and violence is eroticized, then men violating women has a sexual component. I think men rape women because they get off on it in a way that fuses dominance with sexuality. . . . I think that when men sexually harass women it expresses male control over sexual access to us. It doesn't mean they all want to fuck us, they just want to hurt us, dominate us, and control us, and that *is* fucking us. They want to be able to have that and to be able to say when they can have it, to *know* that. That is in itself erotic. The idea that opposing battering is about saving the family is, similarly, abstracted, gender-neutral. There are gender-neutral formulations of all these issues: law and order as opposed to derepression, Victorian morality as opposed to permissiveness, obscenity as opposed to art and freedom of expression. Gender-neutral, objective formulations like these avoid asking *whose* expression, from whose point of view? Whose law and whose order? It's not just a question of who is free to express ourselves; it's not just that there is almost no, if any, self-respecting women's eroticism. The fact is that what we do see, what we are allowed to experience, even in our own suffering, even in what we are allowed to complain about, is overwhelmingly constructed from the male point of view. Laws against sexual violation express what men see and do when they engage in sex with women; laws against obscenity center on the display of women's bodies in ways that men are turned on by viewing. To me, it not only makes us cooptable to define such abuses in gender-neutral terms like violence; when we fail to assert that we are fighting for the affirmative definition and control of our own sexuality, of our own lives as women, and that these experiences violate *that,* we have already been bought.

Radical feminism is not only critical of men's violence and sexuality, it turns male-dominated culture on its head. It takes all the characteristics that are valued by men in Western societies—objectivity, distance, control, coolness, aggressiveness, and competitiveness—and blames them for wars, poverty, rape, battering, child abuse, and incest. It praises what women do—feed and nurture, cooperate and reciprocate, and attend to bodies, minds, and psyches. The important values, radical feminism argues, are intimacy, persuasion, warmth, caring, and sharing—the characteristics that women develop in their hands-on, everyday experiences with their own and their children's bodies and with the work of daily living. Men could develop these characteristics, too, if they "mothered," but they are much more prevalent in women because women are usually the primary child-carers and nurturers in a family.

These arguments for the enormous value of mothering support the radical feminist perspective that teenage pregnancy and single parenting should not be automatically condemned. Pregnancy and childbirth are emotional as well as physical experiences. All mothers and children are equally valuable and need the support and services of governments and health care systems in addition to that of their families and communities.

The political implications of "maternal thinking" are laid out in the following excerpt by Sara Ruddick, who has written on motherhood, peace, and feminism.

Maternal Thinking

Sara Ruddick

. . . Maternal thinking is only one aspect of "womanly" thinking. In artic-ulating and respecting the maternal, I do not underwrite the still current, false, and pernicious identification of womanhood with biological or adoptive mothering of particular children in families. For me, "maternal" is a social category. Although maternal thinking arises out of actual child-caring practices, biological parenting is neither necessary nor sufficient. Many women and some men express maternal thinking in various kinds of working and caring with others. And some biological mothers, especially in misogynistic societies, take a fearful, defensive distance from their own mothering and the maternal lives of any women.

Maternal thought does, I believe, exist for all women in a radically dif-ferent way than for men. It is because we are *daughters,* nurtured and trained by women, that we early receive maternal love with special atten-tion to its implications for our bodies, our passions, and our ambitions. We are alert to the values and costs of maternal practices whether we are determined to engage in them or avoid them.

It is now argued that the most revolutionary change we can make in the institution of motherhood is to include men equally in every aspect of childcare. When men and women live together with children, it seems not only fair but deeply moral that they share in every aspect of childcare. To prevent or excuse men from maternal practice is to encourage them to separate public action from private affection, the privilege of parenthood from its cares. Moreover, even when men are absent from the nursery, their dominance in every other public and private room shapes a child's earliest conceptions of power. To familiarize children with "natural" domi-nation at their earliest age in a context of primitive love, assertion, and sexual passion is to prepare them to find equally "natural" and exhaustive the division between exploiter and exploited that pervades the larger world. Although daughter and son alike may internalize "natural" domi-nation, neither typically can live with it easily. Identifying with and imitat-ing exploiters, we are overcome with self-hate; aligning ourselves with the exploited, we are fearful and manipulative. Again and again, family power dramas are repeated in psychic, interpersonal, and professional dramas, while they are institutionalized in economic, political, and international life. Radically recasting the power-gender roles in those dramas just might revolutionize social conscience.

Assimilating men into childcare both inside and outside the home would also be conducive to serious social reform. Responsible, equal childcaring would require men to relinquish power and their own favorable position in the division between intellectual/professional and service labor as that division expresses itself domestically. Loss of preferred status at home might make socially privileged men more suspicious of unnecessary divisions of labor and damaging hierarchies in the public world. Moreover, if men were emotionally and practically committed to childcare, they would reform the work world in parents' interests. Once no one "else" was minding the child, good day-care centers with flexible hours would be established to which parents could trust their children from infancy on. These day-care centers, like the workweek itself, would be managed flexibly in response to human needs as well as to the demands of productivity, with an eye to growth rather than measurable profit. Such moral reforms of economic life would probably begin with professions and managers servicing themselves. Even in nonsocialist countries, however, their benefits could be unpredictably extensive.

I would not argue that the assimilation of men into childcare is the primary social goal for mothers. Rather, we must work to bring a *transformed* maternal thought in the public realm, to make the preservation and growth of *all* children a work of public conscience and legislation. This will not be easy. Mothers are no less corrupted than anyone else by concerns of status and class. Often our misguided efforts on behalf of the success and purity of our children frighten them and everyone else around them. As we increase and enjoy our public effectiveness, we will have less reason to live vicariously through our children. We may then begin to learn to sustain a creative tension between our inevitable and fierce desire to foster our own children and the less compulsive desire that all children grow and flourish.

Nonetheless, it would be foolish to believe that mothers, just because they are mothers, can transcend class interest and implement principles of justice. All feminists must join in articulating a theory of justice shaped by and incorporating maternal thinking. Moreover, the generalization of attentive love to *all* children requires politics. The most enlightened thought is not enough.

Closer to home again, we must refashion our domestic life in the hope that the personal will in fact betoken the political. We must begin by resisting the temptation to construe "home" simplemindedly, as a matter of justice between mothers and fathers. Single parents, lesbian mothers, and coparenting women remind us that many ways to provide children with examples of caring do not incorporate sexual inequalities of power and privilege. Those of us who live with the fathers of our children will eagerly welcome shared parenthood—for overwhelming practical as well as ideological reasons. But in our eagerness, we must not forget that as long as a mother is not effective publicly and self-respecting privately, male presence can be harmful as well as beneficial. It does a woman no good to have the power of the Symbolic Father brought right into the nursery, often despite the deep, affectionate egalitarianism of an individual man. It takes a strong mother and father to resist temptations to domination and subordination for which they have been trained and are socially rewarded. And whatever the hard-won equality and mutual respect an individual couple may achieve, as long as a mother—even if she is no more parent than father—is derogated and subordinate outside the home, children will feel angry, confused, and "wildly unmothered."

Despite these reservations, I look forward to the day when men are willing and able to share equally and actively in transformed maternal practices. When that day comes, will we still identify some thought as maternal rather than merely parental? Might we echo the cry of some feminists—there shall be no more "women"—with our own—there shall be no more "mothers," only people engaging in childcare? To keep matters clear I would put the point differently. On that day there will be no more "fathers," no more people of either sex who have power over their children's lives and moral authority in their children's world, though they do not do the work of attentive love. There will be mothers of both sexes who live out a transformed maternal thought in communities that share parental care—practically, emotionally, economically, and socially. Such communities will have learned from their mothers how to value children's lives.

Reprinted from: Sara Ruddick, "Maternal Thinking," in *Rethinking the Family: Some Feminist Questions*, edited by Barrie Thorne, with Marilyn Yalom, pp. 89–91. Copyright © 1982 by The Institute for Research on Women & Gender, Stanford University. Reprinted by permission.

Radical feminism's view is that the presence of significant numbers of women can alter values and behavior because their ideas, their outlook, and their experiences are different from those of most men, almost to the point of giving women a different culture. *Ecofeminism* is a movement that applies maternal thinking and radical feminist ideas about the exploitation of women's bodies to protecting the environment and protesting against killing animals for fur and meat. The radical feminist praise of the qualities of women that derive from their nurturance and care of others, especially among those who speak of a woman's culture, has also led to feminist religions and ethics, and to the women's health care movement.

In *religion,* radical feminism argues that while more women clergy and gender-neutral liturgical language are very important in reforming religious practices, they do not make a religion less patriarchal unless there is also a place for women's prayers and rituals. So, at Passover, Jewish feminists hold all-women seders with specially written Haggadahs that tell of the Jews' exodus from Egypt and wanderings in the desert from a woman's point of view. They celebrate Miriam as well as Moses.

Feminist religious scholars have reinterpreted Judeo-Christian history and texts showing the original influence of women spiritual leaders and their gradual exclusion as Judaism became more patriarchal and later, as Christianity became institutionalized. Islamic feminists have found, in their reading of the Qur'an, that Mohammed intended women and men to be equal. Buddhism's many goddesses have been given a more important place in the pantheon by feminists.

As an alternative to teachings of organized religions, Catholic and Protestant feminist ethicists have developed an ethics that puts women's experiences at the center of moral choices. They work through an umbrella organization, called Woman-Church, that is composed of feminist groups engaged in reconstructing ethics and sexual morality. One of these groups, the Women's Alliance for Theology, Ethics, and Ritual (WATER), argues for the importance of considering situational contexts in moral judgments. Another group, Catholics for a Free Choice, says that the circumstances of a woman's life and that of her family should determine whether or not an abortion is justified.

Other radical feminists have discarded a traditional religious affiliation altogether and have formed wiccas, or witch's covens. Some feminist spiritual circles have derived their symbols and rituals from the earth and fertility goddesses of pre-Judeo-Christian and pre-Islamic religions. They say that the Virgin Mary is a cultural descendant of a fertility goddess, the Queen of the May, and that three pre-Islamic fertility goddesses were transformed into the daughters of Allah. The Teotihuacán Feathered Serpent of many Mexican cultures originally represented a goddess, and the introduction of Christianity by the Spaniards uprooted the native culture's Corn Mothers. In reviving women-centered religions, radical spiritual feminism is reclaiming women's sexuality, pregnancy and childbirth, menstruation, and menopause from men who have made them into sins or illnesses.

In *medicine,* the women's health care movement resisted medical practices dominated by men; at first, they did so outside of mainstream institutions, but then many of their recommended changes were incorporated into the mainstream. Many women entered medical school in the 1960s and 1970s in the United States and other countries where most of the physicians had been men, but they found it very difficult to change curricula or training. At that time, men's bodies were the norm in textbooks; women's bodies were a deviation because they menstruated and gave birth. Standard medical practice has treated normal pregnancies as illnesses and has used monitors and machines routinely in normal childbirth, distancing women from their own bodies. The new reproductive technologies for infertile couples detach conception from sexual intimacy: for example, in a petri dish, sperm produced by masturbation are mixed with ova that are harvested surgically.

In the 1970s in the United States, the women's health movement tried to take the control of women's bodies out of the hands of the medical system because the care women patients were getting from men doctors took few of their overall needs into consideration and allowed them very little control over their treatment. The solution was women-run clinics for women patients. Nurses and other health care workers taught gynecological self-examination, took a whole-person approach to diagnosis and treatment, and dispensed alternative medicines. The women's health movement did not consider women physicians to be much better than men physicians, since they had been trained in the same medical schools and hospitals. The activists in the women's health movement thought that by educating women patients to be more assertive and knowledgeable health consumers, they would put pressure on the medical system to modify the way men and women physicians are taught to practice.

The women's health movement has encouraged the training and employment of midwives and the experience of family-oriented childbirth at home and in birthing centers separated from hospitals. It has been critical of the new reproductive technologies, breast implants, and cosmetic surgery as violations of women's bodily integrity. The consumer movement in medicine has taken over most of the women's health movement's demands that medicine become more holistic and patient-oriented. Adapting the radical feminist critique and working within mainstream medicine, women physicians in the United States have, in the last few years, promoted research and held conferences on women's medical needs and have published a medical journal devoted to research on women's health. They have pushed for women to be part of all clinical trials for new drugs and have collected statistics on the likelihood of women to contract "men's" illnesses, such as AIDS and heart disease. Female bodies are no longer seen as a deviation from a male norm; rather, the definition of "normal" has been altered.

Critique. Radical feminism is a direct and open confrontation with the gendered social order. Its condemnation of Western society's encouragement of men's violence and aggressive sexuality has led to a critique of the unequal power in heterosexual relationships. It defends the value of mothering over paid work. Thus, it produces a schism among feminists, offending many of those who are in heterosexual relationships, who do not want children, or who are ambitious for careers. The contrast of women's emotional and nurturing capabilities with men's intrusive sexuality and aggressiveness in radical feminism has been seen as *essentialist*—rooted in deep-seated and seemingly intractable differences between two global categories of people.

This concentration on pervasive gender characteristics and oppression has led to accusations that radical feminism neglects racial, ethnic, religious, and social class differences among men and among women, and that it downplays other sources of oppression. However, radical feminism has joined with marxist, socialist, and post-colonial feminisms in political activism to improve the lives of poor and working-class women of disadvantaged racial ethnic groups in industrial and nonindustrial countries.

Another divisive issue has been radical feminism's views on sexuality and pornography's harmfulness. Some feminists do not think pornography is that harmful to women, unlike radical feminists, who are in the forefront of the fights against sexual exploitation, harassment, rape, and battering. Radical feminism's stance against sadomasochism and other forms of "kinky" sex at the 1981 Barnard College conference, "The Scholar and the Feminist IX: Toward a Politics of Sexuality," opened a feminist "sex war" that has not died down to this day.

Yet it was radical feminism's extremism ("radical" means down to the roots) and fury at the throwaway use of women's bodies, sexuality, and emotions that made men and women realize how deeply misogynist our supposedly enlightened social world is. Radical feminism deserves much credit for bringing rape, sexual abuse of children, battering, and sexual harassment to public attention. Those who try to raise the value of women by praising motherhood have been criticized by feminists who feel this strategy invokes traditional rationales for keeping women out of the public arena. But it does what some radical feminists want—to put women on the social map as different from men but worth just as much, if not more.

Summary

It may seem as if some radical feminists' slogan could be, "Women are not just as good as men, they are *better.*" (Others strongly repudiate such views.) If men are so violent and sexually aggressive, and women are so nurturant and emotionally sensitive, what the world needs is for women, not men, to run things. As leaders, women would be less hierarchical and authoritarian, more cooperative and consensual. They would respect the environment. Ethically, they would look out for others' needs, and spiritually, they would form loving, caring communities that included men.

Despite this utopian vision, radical feminism's practical actions focus on setting up rape crisis centers and battered women's shelters, teaching women karate and other forms of self-defense, developing guidelines against sexual harassment, and educating people about date rape. Radical feminist politics mounts campaigns against prostitution, pornography, and other forms of sex work, as well as against high-tech reproductive technologies, breast implants, cosmetic surgery, and other types of demeaning objectification of women's bodies.

Radical feminism was the theoretical rationale for women's studies programs in colleges and universities. It is not enough to add women to the curriculum as another social group to be studied; women's ways of thinking have to be brought to the forefront. Women's bodies, sexuality, and emotional relationships are different from men's, and so is women's literature, art, music, and crafts. If most of what is taught in schools is "men's studies," then what is needed is a separate focus on women's history, knowledge, and culture.

The same argument—that it is not enough to "add women and stir" but that women's experiences produce a radical rethinking—occurs in feminist ethics, religions, and medicine. Women's ethics are based on responsibility to others, not individual rights; women's religious rituals focus on their life cycles, not men's; and women's health care tends to the social as well as physical problems of girls and women.

Organizationally, radical feminists form nonhierarchical, supportive, woman-only spaces where women can think and act and create free of constant sexist put-downs, sexual harassment, and the threat of rape and violence. The heady possibilities of creating woman-oriented health care facilities, safe residences for battered women, counseling and legal services for survivors of rape, a woman's culture, and a woman's religion and ethics forge the bonds of sisterhood. Politically, their primary mission is fighting for women and against men's social supremacy.

Radical feminism, by refusing to go along with conventional assumptions, directly confronts the deep-seated denigration and control of women in the gendered social order. It pushes feminism into direct conflict with those in power. The battle cry is no longer "Women deserve equal rights," but "Sisterhood is powerful."

Suggested Readings in Radical Feminism

Adams, Carol J., and Josephine Donovan (eds.). 1995. *Animals and Women: Feminist Theoretical Explorations*. Durham, NC: Duke University Press.

Barry, Kathleen. 1979. *Female Sexual Slavery*. Englewood Cliffs, NJ: Prentice-Hall.

———. 1995. *Prostitution of Sexuality: Global Exploitation of Women*. New York: New York University Press.

Bart, Pauline B., and Eileen Geil Moran (eds.). 1993. *Violence Against Women: The Bloody Footprints*. Newbury Park, CA: Sage.

Boston Women's Health Book Collective. 1973. *Our Bodies, Ourselves*. New York: Simon and Schuster.

Brownmiller, Susan. 1975. *Against Our Will: Men, Women and Rape*. New York: Simon and Schuster.

Buckley, Thomas and Alma Gottlieb (eds.). 1988. *Blood Magic: The Anthropology of Menstruation*. Berkeley: University of California Press.

Caputi, Jane. 1987. *The Age of Sex Crime*. Bowling Green, OH: Bowling Green University Popular Press.

Clarke, Adele and Virginia L. Oleson (eds.). 1999. *Revisioning Women, Health, and Healing: Feminist, Cultural, and Technoscience Perspectives*. New York and London: Routledge.

Daly, Mary. 1973. *Beyond God the Father*. Boston: Beacon Press.

——. 1978. *Gyn/Ecology: The Metaethics of Radical Feminism.* Boston: Beacon Press.

Delaney, Janice, Mary Jane Lupton, and Emily Toth. 1977. *The Curse: A Cultural History of Menstruation.* New York: New American Library.

Dobash, R. Emerson and Russell Dobash. 1979. *Violence Against Wives: A Case Against the Patriarchy.* New York: Free Press.

Dworkin, Andrea. 1974. *Woman Hating.* New York: NAL Penguin.

——. 1981. *Pornography: Men Possessing Women.* New York: Perigee (Putnam).

——. 1987. *Intercourse.* New York: Free Press.

Ehrenreich, Barbara and Deirdre English. 1973. *Complaints and Disorders: The Sexual Politics of Sickness.* Westbury, NY: Feminist Press.

——. 1978. *For Her Own Good: 150 Years of the Experts' Advice to Women.* Garden City, NY: Doubleday Anchor.

Gimbutas, Marija. 1989. *The Language of the Goddess.* San Francisco: Harper & Row.

——. 1999. *The Living Goddesses.* (Edited and supplemented by Miriam Robbins Dexter.) Berkeley: University of California Press.

Griffin, Susan. 1982. *Pornography and Silence: Culture's Revenge Against Nature.* San Francisco: Harper & Row.

Holmes, Helen Bequaert, and Laura M. Purdy (eds.). 1992. *Feminist Perspectives in Medical Ethics.* Bloomington: Indiana University Press.

Jayakar, Pupul. 1990. *The Earth Mother: Legends, Ritual Arts, and Goddesses of India.* San Francisco: Harper & Row.

Knight, Chris. 1991. *Blood Relations: Menstruation and the Origins of Culture.* New Haven, CT: Yale University Press.

Laws, Sophie. 1990. *Issues of Blood: The Politics of Menstruation.* London: Macmillan.

Laws, Sophie, Valerie Hey, and Andrea Egan. 1985. *Seeing Red: The Politics of Premenstrual Tension.* London: Hutchinson.

Lederer, Laura (ed.). 1980. *Take Back the Night: Women on Pornography.* New York: Morrow.

MacKinnon, Catharine A. 1979. *Sexual Harassment of Working Women.* New Haven, CT: Yale University Press.

——. 1987. *Feminism Unmodified.* Cambridge, MA: Harvard University Press.

——. 1989. *Toward a Feminist Theory of the State.* Cambridge, MA: Harvard University Press.

Martin, Emily. 1987. *The Woman in the Body: A Cultural Analysis of Reproduction.* Boston: Beacon.

Merchant, Carolyn. [1980] 1989. *The Death of Nature: Women, Ecology, and the Scientific Revolution.* New York: Harper & Row.

Mies, Maria and Vandana Shiva. 1993. *Ecofeminism: Reconnecting a Divided World.* London, Zed Books.

Morgan, Robin (ed.). 1970. *Sisterhood Is Powerful.* New York: Vintage.

———. 1984. *Sisterhood Is Global: The International Women's Movement Anthology.* New York: Doubleday. Reprint edition, 1996, New York: Feminist Press.

O'Brien, Mary. 1981. *The Politics of Reproduction.* New York: Routledge & Kegan Paul.

———. 1989. *Reproducing the World: Essays in Feminist Theory.* Boulder, CO: Westview Press.

Pateman, Carole. 1988. *The Sexual Contract.* Stanford, CA: Stanford University Press.

Plaskow, Judith. 1990. *Standing Again at Sinai: Judaism From a Feminist Perspective.* San Francisco: Harper & Row.

Ratcliff, Kathryn Strother, Myra Marx Ferree, Gail O. Mellow, Barbara Drygulski Wright, Glenda D. Price, Kim Yanoshik, and Margie S. Freston (eds.). 1989. *Healing Technology: Feminist Perspectives.* Ann Arbor, MI: University of Michigan Press.

Rich, Adrienne. 1977. *Of Woman Born: Motherhood as Experience and as Institution.* New York: Norton.

Rothman, Barbara Katz. 1989. *Recreating Motherhood: Ideology and Technology in a Patriarchal Society.* New York: Norton.

Ruether, Rosemary Radford. 1983. *Sexism and God-talk: Toward a Feminist Theology.* Boston: Beacon Press.

Ruether, Rosemary Radford, and Eleanor McLaughlin (eds.). 1979. *Women of Spirit: Female Leadership in the Jewish and Christian Traditions.* New York: Simon and Schuster.

Russell, Diana E. H. 1998. *Dangerous Relationships: Pornography, Misogyny, and Rape.* Thousand Oaks, CA: Sage.

Ruzek, Sheryl Burt. 1978. *The Women's Health Movement: Feminist Alternatives to Medical Control.* New York: Praeger.

Sabbah, Fatna A. 1984. *Woman in the Muslim Unconscious.* (Trans. by Mary Jo Lakeland.) New York: Pergamon.

Trebilcot, Joyce (ed.). 1983. *Mothering: Essays in Feminist Theory.* Totowa, NJ: Rowman and Allenheld.

Voda, Anne M., Myra Dinnerstein, and Sheryl R. O'Donnell (eds.). 1982. *Changing Perspectives on Menopause.* Austin: University of Texas Press.

Yllö, Kersti, and Michele Bograd (eds.). 1988. *Feminist Perspectives on Wife Abuse.* Thousand Oaks, CA: Sage. ✦

Chapter Five

Lesbian Feminism

Sources of Gender Inequality

- Oppressive heterosexuality.
- Men's domination of women's social spaces.

Remedies

- Empowering women-identified women.
- Women-only workplaces, cultural events, and political organizations.
- Lesbian sexual relationships.

Contributions

- Critical analysis of heterosexual romantic love and sexual relationships.
- Exploration of women's sexuality.
- Expansion of lesbianism to include community and culture.
- Dual battles for women's rights and for homosexual rights.

Lesbian feminism takes the radical feminist pessimistic view of men to its logical conclusion. If heterosexual relationships are intrinsically exploitative because of men's social, physical, and sexual power over women, why bother with men at all? Women are more loving, nurturant, sharing, and understanding. Men like having women friends to talk about their problems with, but women can only unburden to other women. "Why not go all the way?" asks lesbian feminism. Stop sleeping with the "enemy," and turn to other women for sexual love as well as for intellectual companionship and emotional support.

Lesbianism, like male homosexuality, had always been underground in the United States and other countries, but fired by the social protest movements of the 1960s, both became increasingly visible and acceptable as alternative ways to have intimate relationships. Up to the 1960s, many women professionals and activists, most of whom did not identify themselves as lesbians, were nonetheless able to break the mold of conventional women's roles because of their deeply emotional, supportive friendships with other women, which may or may not have been sexual.

Despite popular opinion, most feminists are not lesbians, and many lesbians are not feminists. There is a continuum of relationships, from life-long friendships among women who identify themselves as heterosexuals and whose sexual partners are men, to women-identified women who are politically active in causes benefiting women and whose sexuality is varied, to women who identify themselves as lesbians and whose sexual and emotional partners are exclusively women.

In the following excerpt, Lillian Faderman, who has written two histories of lesbianism, discusses the changing meaning of women's emotional involvement with other women.

Romantic Friendship and Lesbian Love

Lillian Faderman

Passionate romantic friendship between women was a widely recognized, tolerated social institution before . . . [the twentieth] century. Women were, in fact, expected to seek out kindred spirits and form strong bonds. It was socially acknowledged that while a woman could not trust men outside her family, she could look to another female for emotional sustenance and not fear betrayal. Had a woman of an earlier era *not* behaved with her intimate friend . . . [in an emotional manner], she would have been thought strangely cold. But her relationship to another female went beyond such affectionate exchanges. It was not unusual for a woman to seek in her romantic friendship the center of her life, quite apart from the demands of marriage and family if not in lieu of them. When women's role in society began to change, however—when what women did needed to be taken more seriously because they were achieving some of the powers that would make them adult persons—society's view of romantic friendship changed.

Love between women—relationships which were *emotionally* in no way different from the romantic friendships of earlier eras—became evil or morbid. It was not simply that men now saw the female sexual drive more realistically. Many of the relationships that they condemned had little to do with sexual expression. It was rather that love between women, coupled with their emerging freedom, might conceivably bring about the overthrow of heterosexuality—which has meant not only sex between men and women but patriarchal culture, male dominance, and female subservience. Learning their society's view of love between women, females were compelled to suppress natural emotion; they were taught to see women only as rivals and men as their only possible love objects, or they were compelled to view themselves as "lesbian," which meant "twisted" either morally or emotionally. What was lovely and nurturing in love between women, what women of other centuries clearly understood, became one of the best-guarded secrets of the patriarchy.

In the sophisticated twentieth century women who chose to love women could no longer see themselves as romantic friends, unless they enveloped themselves in a phenomenal amount of naiveté and were oblivious to modern psychology, literature, and dirty jokes. If they persisted in same-sex love past adolescence, they would at least have to take into account what society thought of lesbians, and they would have to decide to what extent they would internalize those social views. If they were unusually strong or had a strong support group, they might escape regarding themselves as sick sinners. For many of them, without models to show that love between women was not intrinsically wrong or unhealthy, the experts' pronouncements about lesbianism worked as a self-fulfilling prophecy. They became as confused and tormented as they were supposed to be. But it was only during this brief era in history that tragedy and sickness were so strongly attributed to (and probably for that reason so frequently found in) love between women.

This changed with the rise of the second wave of feminism. Having made a general challenge to patriarchal culture, many feminists in the last decade began to challenge its taboos on love between women too. They saw it as their job to divest themselves of all the prejudices that had been inculcated in them by their male-dominated society, to reexamine everything regarding women, and finally to reclaim the meaning of love between women. Having learned to question both the social order which made women the second sex and the meaning behind the taboos on love between women, they determined to live their lives through new definitions they would create. They called themselves women-identified-women, or they consciously attempted to lift the stigma from the term "lesbian" and called themselves lesbian-feminists, by which they meant that they would put women first in their lives because men had proven, if not on a personal then on a cultural scale, that they were not to be trusted. Lesbian-feminists see men and women as being at odds in their whole approach to the world: men, as a rule, are authoritarian, violent, and cold, and women are the opposite. Like romantic friends before them, lesbian-feminists choose women, kindred spirits, for their love objects. Unlike most romantic friends, however, they understand through feminist doctrine the sociopolitical meaning of their choice.

Lesbian-feminists differ from romantic friends in a number of ways. Most significantly, the earlier women generally had no hope of actually spending their lives together despite often reiterated fantasies that they might; but also romantic friends did not have an articulated doctrine which would help them explain why they could feel closer to women than to men. And the primary difference which affected their relationship to the world is that romantic friends, unlike lesbian-feminists, seldom had reason to believe that society saw them as outlaws—even when they eloped together. . . . Lesbian-feminists understand, even when they are comfortable within a large support group, that the world outside views them as criminal and reduces their love to a pejorative term. Whatever anger they began with as feminists is multiplied innumerable times as lesbian-feminists as soon as they experience, either in reality or by observation, society's hostility to what is both logical and beautiful to them. Even if they do not suffer personally—if they do not lose their children in court or if they are not fired from their jobs or turned out by their families because of their political-sexual commitments—lesbian-feminists are furious, knowing that such possibilities exist and that many women do suffer for choosing to love other women. Romantic friends never learned to be angry through their love.

There is a good deal on which lesbian-feminists disagree, such as issues concerning class, whether or not to form monogamous relationships, the virtues of communal living, whether separatism is necessary in order to live as a lesbian-feminist, the nature of social action that is efficacious, etc. But they all agree that men have waged constant battle against women, committed atrocities or at best injustices against them, reduced them to grown-up children, and that a feminist ought not to sleep in the enemy camp. They all agree that being a lesbian is, whether consciously or unconsciously perceived, a political act, a refusal to fulfill the male image of womanhood or to bow to male supremacy. Perhaps for romantic friends of other eras their relationship was also a political act, although much more covert: With each other they could escape from many of the externally imposed demands of femininity that were especially stringent throughout much of the eighteenth and nineteenth centuries. They could view themselves as human beings and prime rather than as the second sex. But they did not hope that through their relationship they might change the social structure. Lesbian-feminists do.

They see their lesbian-feminism not just as a personal choice regarding life-style, even though it is certainly a most personal choice. But it is also a political choice which challenges sexism and heterosexism. It is a choice which has been made often in the context of the feminist movement and with an awareness of the ideology behind it. It has seemed the only possible choice for many women who believe that the personal is political, that to reject male supremacy in the abstract but to enter into a heterosexual relationship in which the female is usually subservient makes no sense. Contemporary lesbianism, on the other hand, makes a great deal of sense. It is a combination of the natural love between women, so encouraged in the days of romantic friendships, with the twentieth-century women's freedom that feminism has made possible.

While romantic friends had considerable latitude in their show of physical affection toward each other, it is probable that, in an era when women were not supposed to be sexual, the sexual possibilities of their relationship were seldom entertained. Contemporary women can have no such innocence. But the sexual aspects of their lesbian-feminist relationships generally have less significance than the emotional sustenance and the freedom they have to define themselves. While many lesbian-feminist relationships can and do continue long after the sexual component has worn off, they cannot continue without emotional sustenance and freedom of self-definition. Romantic friends of other eras would probably have felt entirely comfortable in many lesbian-feminist relationships had the contemporary label and stigma been removed.

But many women today continue to be frightened by love between women because the pejorative connotation of the contemporary label and stigma are still very real for them. Such fear is bound to vanish in the future as people continue to reject strict orthodoxy in sexual relationships:

Women will be less and less scared off by the idea of same-sex love without examining what it entails beyond "sexual abnormality." The notion of lesbianism will be neutralized. As females are raised to be more independent, they will not assume that heterosexual marriage is necessary for survival and fulfillment; nor will they accept male definitions of womanhood or non-womanhood. They will have no need to repress natural feelings of affection toward other women. Love between women will become as common as romantic friendship was in other eras. The twentieth-century combination of romantic friendship and female independence will continue to yield lesbian-feminism.

In an ideal world lesbian-feminism, which militantly excludes relationships with men, would not exist. And, of course, the romantic friendships such as women were permitted to conduct in other centuries—in which they might be almost everything to each other but in which a male protector was generally needed in order for them to survive—would not exist either. Instead, in a utopia men would not claim supremacy either in social or personal relationships, and women would not feel that they must give up a part of themselves in order to relate to men. Women with ambition and strength and a sense of themselves would have no reason to see men as the enemy out to conquer and subdue them. Nor would there be any attempt to indoctrinate the female with the notion that to be normal she must transfer the early love she felt for her mother first to her father and then to a father substitute—a man who is more than she is in all ways: older, taller, better educated, smarter, stronger. Women as well as men would not select their love objects on the basis of sexual politics, in surrender or in reaction to an arbitrary heterosexual ideology. They would choose to love another only in reference to the individual needs of their own personalities, which ideally had been allowed to develop untrammeled and free of sex-role stereotyping. Potential or actual bisexuality, which is today looked on by lesbian-feminists as a political betrayal and by heterosexuals as an instability, would be normal, both emotionally and statistically. But until men stop giving women cause to see them as the enemy and until there ceases to be coercion to step into prescribed roles without reference to individual needs and desires, lesbian-feminists will continue to view their choice as the only logical one possible for a woman who desires to be her own adult person.

As theory and in politics, lesbian feminism transforms love between women into an identity, a community, and a culture. Lesbian feminism praises women's sexuality and bodies, mother-daughter love, and the culture of women, thus expanding sexual and emotional relationships between women into a wholly engaged life. Politically, lesbian feminists fight on two fronts—for all women's betterment and for the civil rights and social worth of homosexuals.

Whether lesbians identify and act politically mostly as homosexuals or mostly as women varies. In Germany today, there are three self-identified political categories—women, feminists, and lesbians. In the United States, lesbians first identified with homosexual men in their resistance to harassment and discrimination, but after experiencing the same gender discrimination as women in the civil rights and draft-resistance movements, they turned to feminist organizations. There, unhappily, they experienced hostility to their sexuality from heterosexual women. Subsequently, some lesbian feminists developed an oppositional, woman-identified, separatist movement. But many lesbian activist groups welcome heterosexual women in their work for women's issues. Other lesbians have joined with gay men in their battle with the AIDS epidemic, for civil rights, and for legal recognition of committed relationships.

Lesbians are not monolithic. In the 1950s, lesbians playing the "fem" role were extremely feminine in their dress, demeanor, and expressions of sexuality, while "butches" were cool, masculine-looking, and assertive. There were also butch-fem role exchangers ("roll overs" or "kikis") who played both parts. Some lesbian women have biological children and raise them with a lesbian partner. Others have been critical of sexual monogamy, with or without children, as imitative of the institution of heterosexual marriage. These lesbians prefer alternative household arrangements of several partners, which may include gay men.

Lesbian feminism's defining stance on sexuality is that heterosexuality is oppressive and therefore women are better off having sexual relationships with women. But there are debates within lesbian feminism over the origin of women's sexual attraction to women—is it inborn and lifelong or can it develop at any time, perhaps beginning with an intense work or political involvement? Another split in lesbian feminism is over sadomasochistic sexual relationships between women, which seem to violate the egalitarian and nonviolent ethos of both feminism and lesbianism.

Bisexuality challenges lesbian feminism behaviorally and politically. Women bisexuals who have sexual relations with both women and men, sometimes simultaneously and sometimes serially, disturb the clear gender and sexual divisions that are the basis for woman-identification and lesbian separatism. Bisexuality may not undercut the identification with women as an oppressed social group, but it undermines the lesbian separatist solution. Paula Rust's sociological study of bisexuality and lesbianism explores the dilemmas for lesbian feminism that are posed by the possibility of a bisexual feminist political movement.

Bisexual Politics

Paula C. Rust

Many of the arguments that bisexuals are using to politicize bisexuality are very similar to arguments that lesbians used in the 1970s to politicize lesbianism. But there are also some important differences between the two movements, because the political arena in which bisexuals are struggling for recognition is substantially different from the one lesbians faced two decades ago. To a large extent, therefore, the bisexual movement is another revolution on the same political wheel, but perhaps the bisexual movement is also a revolution, period. To understand both possibilities, we have to look at the similarities and the differences between the lesbian movement of the early 1970s and the bisexual movement of the early 1990s.

The bisexual movement's roots in the lesbian/gay movement are analogous to the lesbian movement's roots in the feminist and gay movements. Contemporary bisexual activists concentrate much of their energy on building a home within the lesbian/gay movement by arguing that "bi liberation is gay liberation" and demanding that lesbian/gay organizations and events nominally and actually include bisexuals. Similarly, early lesbian feminists initially struggled to find a home within the feminist and gay movements. Like early lesbian feminists who argued that lesbians had been in the feminist movement all along but remained hidden because of feminists' homophobia, bisexuals argue that bisexuals have been in the lesbian/gay movement all along but remained hidden because of biphobia.

Lesbian feminists eventually lost patience with the homophobia of feminists and the sexism of gay men, and established an independent lesbian feminist movement. Among bisexuals, the vision of an independent bisexual movement is a minority opinion; the separatist BiCentrist Alliance is considered outside the mainstream of bisexual political thought. But at the same time, despite most activists' insistence that bisexuals rightfully belong in the lesbian/gay movement, they are building the structure of a separate bisexual movement complete with a national bisexual network and international conferences. Moreover, ideology is beginning to follow suit; most of the bisexual women who participated in my study in 1986 saw their interests as flowing from their genders and their "gayness," not from their bisexuality, whereas the bisexual activists whose opinions appeared in bisexual publications of the late 1980s and early 1990s identified unique bisexual interests. Whether the LesBiGay model of political organizing will continue to dominate bisexual political strategy, or whether bisexual ideology will continue to develop in an independent direction to be followed eventually by a shift in political strategy as occurred in the lesbian movement, remains to be seen.

One strategy used by both lesbians and bisexuals to politicize themselves is to present their movements as challenges to established ways of thinking. Lesbian feminists argued that heterosexuality is a political institution that upholds patriarchy and that lesbianism, as an alternative to heterosexuality, is therefore political and feminist. Early lesbian feminists also argued that lesbianism is feminist because it challenges gender—specifically, the male definition of feminine gender that defines a "real woman" as a female who has sex with men. Contrary to the feeling of feminists at the time that lesbians were marginal constituents of the feminist movement and that the movement should focus on the needs of "women," not "lesbians," lesbians argued that they were the quintessential women and that the movement should not only address lesbians' needs but recognize lesbians as the true feminists. Thus, lesbianism was initially constructed as a challenge to gender. But once "woman" was reconstructed to include "lesbian," lesbians became part of the prevailing gender structure. In effect, lesbianism was co-opted into gender and ceased to be a challenge to it. Furthermore, the rise of cultural feminism reified rather than challenged gender, maximized rather than minimized the differences between women and men, and created a concept of lesbianism that was dependent on the preservation of gender.

Similarly, bisexual activists argue that categorical Western thinking is oppressive because it limits people's options, and that bisexuality is political because it challenges categorical thinking. Specifically, bisexuality is a challenge to dichotomous thinking about both gender and sexuality.

Because bisexuality challenges these dichotomies, it undermines oppression based on them, i.e., sexism and heterosexism. Therefore, if lesbianism is political and feminist, bisexuality is political, feminist, and queer. If lesbianism undermines the heteropatriarchy, bisexuality undermines not only the heteropatriarchy but the fundamental structure of Western thought.

Given lesbians' initial challenge to gender, one might expect bisexuals' efforts to break down gender to be well received among lesbians. But because of the change in the relationship of lesbianism to gender that occurred with the reconstruction of womanhood and the rise of cultural lesbian feminism, bisexuals' contemporary challenge to gender is also a threat to lesbianism. Lesbianism is now part of the gender establishment that bisexuals seek to break down. Bisexuals' challenge to gender is no less than a challenge to the very existence of lesbianism, because of the dependence of lesbianism on gender for definition. Instead of being allies in the struggle against gender, because of the course taken by lesbian feminism in the two decades before the inception of the bisexual movement, lesbians and bisexuals have emerged with contrary political goals in reference to gender.

Bisexuality's challenge to dichotomous sexuality poses a threat to lesbianism that is even more direct. Lesbians contributed to the construction of dichotomous sexuality, primarily through their efforts to construct lesbians as an ethnic group. To become an ethnic group, lesbians had to distinguish themselves from nonlesbians and create the appearance of clear and fixed boundaries between themselves as the oppressed and heterosexuals as the oppressor. Lesbians are now part of the society that is based on dichotomous ways of thinking. If bisexuals are a threat to sexual dichotomy, they are a threat to lesbians.

This threat is multiple. At the very least, bisexuals are a material threat to lesbians because as the new category "bisexual" becomes available as an alternative to the homosexual/heterosexual dichotomy, some women who would otherwise have placed themselves in the lesbian category will place themselves in the new bisexual category. Lesbians will therefore lose numbers. However, the real threat is not to the size of the lesbian population, but to the ethnicity of lesbianism. By challenging and ultimately destroying the sexual dichotomy, bisexuals threaten to undermine the clarity of the distinction between lesbians and heterosexuals. If some people are bisexual—particularly if that bisexuality is conceptualized in hybrid terms—then the distinction between homosexuality and heterosexuality is not clear at all. If some people are both homosexual and heterosexual, then lesbians cannot be clearly distinguished from heterosexuals. If lesbians cannot be clearly distinguished from heterosexuals, then how can they claim to be oppressed by heterosexuals, and how can they struggle to win their liberation from heterosexuals? If the sexual dichotomy is destroyed, lesbians are deprived of their ethnicity, and of the strategies for liberation that flow from ethnicity.

If bisexuals were to construct themselves as an ethnic group, then the threat to lesbianism would be alleviated. The sexual dichotomy would be replaced by a sexual trichotomy, and the clarity of the category "lesbian" could be restored. But bisexuals show little indication that they will take this path, at least not in the near future. One might argue that the bisexual movement is simply too young to have yet constructed itself as an ethnic movement, but the lack of attention bisexuals are giving to the question of defining bisexuality stands in sharp contrast to the lively debates that occurred among lesbians on this issue in the early 1970s. The prevailing message in the bisexual press is that bisexuals should avoid establishing a single definition of bisexuality based on identifiable common characteristics, and little effort is being made to create bisexual ancestors or a bisexual heritage. Bisexuals are not constructing themselves as an ethnic group, precisely because they wish to remain a challenge to dichotomous gender and dichotomous sexuality. In so doing, they are not only refusing to place themselves into the ethnic political tradition; they are threatening to remove all of sexual identity politics from the realm of ethnic political discourse, thereby destroying other sexual minorities' abilities to utilize the language of ethnic politics to make their political claims.

Another strategy lesbian feminists used to politicize lesbianism was the desexualization of lesbianism. Because they were struggling to find a political voice in a period when sexuality was not recognized as political, to present themselves as political they had to distance themselves from sexuality. The rise of cultural feminism facilitated this effort by recalling the ideal of asexual womanly purity. But lesbians' efforts to politicize lesbianism contributed to the development of a sexual politics, and lesbians' efforts to desexualize lesbianism was one impetus for the rise of sex positivism. When bisexual activists appeared in the arena, sexuality was already politicized and sex positivism was in full swing. Because sex positivism is consistent with the bisexual emphasis on diversity, it was easily incorporated into the developing bisexual ideology, and because sexuality was politicized, this move was not antithetical to the process of bisexual politicization. Because of the historical period in which the bisexual movement has emerged, bisexuals can present themselves as both sexual and political; they can and do celebrate sexuality while simultaneously demanding recognition of their political voice.

Although they have largely escaped the desexualizing influence of lesbian feminism, bisexuals, especially bisexual women, cannot ignore the relationship that lesbian feminism constructed between lesbianism and feminism. . . . Lesbian feminists first constructed lesbianism as consistent with feminism, and then argued that lesbians are the best feminists because they are independent of men and have the vision and resources to create women's space. According to this analysis, bisexual women collaborate with the enemy (men) and are, in some senses, even more detrimental to the feminist movement than heterosexual women are. Contemporary bisexual activists, having claimed that bisexuality is feminist, have to reconstruct the relationship between feminism and sexuality to support their claim. Among the specific problems they face are how to build a mixed-gender movement that is feminist, and whether to welcome transgenderists to women's space within that movement. Building a feminist mixed-gender movement means challenging the argument that feminism depends on women's space and refuting the charge that by associating with men bisexuals are collaborating with the enemy. Welcoming transgenderists requires that bisexual women reject the reification of gender that took place with the growth of cultural feminism. Neither task will be easy, but their importance to bisexual women is evident in the number of authors who have addressed the task of constructing a feminist bisexuality.

Another difference between the lesbian and bisexual movements that is attributable to the different contexts in which they developed lies in their willingness to universalize their identities and interests. Many early lesbian feminists declared that "all women are lesbians." This claim served to present the lesbian movement as a movement for all women, and was based either on a concept of universal bisexuality, on arguments about the artificiality of culturally imposed heterosexuality, or on the redefinition of lesbianism as a form of feminist resistance. The concept of a universal bisexuality seems ready-made for a bisexual movement that might also want to emphasize its broad applicability and large constituency, but surprisingly, this idea has not been picked up enthusiastically by activists writing in the bisexual press. It was expressed by many of the bisexual women who took part in my study in 1986, but the fact that it does not appear consistently in the bisexual press suggests that the bisexual women in my study encountered the idea within lesbian feminism and found it personally gratifying. As such, it was evidence of the influence lesbian ideology had on them, not evidence of the beginnings of a bisexual ideology. Instead of proclaiming "everyone is bisexual," activists warn each other to respect the self-identities of those who choose not to identify as bisexual. The fact that bisexuals advocate respect for others' self-identities reflects the fact that the bisexual movement is developing in a context in which sexuality has already been politicized and lesbians and gay men have already constituted themselves as interest groups and invested heavily in their identities. . . .

This does not imply that lesbian feminists did not also consider self-identity important. They did, but for very different reasons than bisexuals. At the height of lesbian feminism, identity was considered a political statement, or a means toward an end. Women should, therefore, identify themselves as lesbians for political reasons regardless of what they thought they "really" were sexually. In contrast, bisexuals consider self-identity important because self-determination is important; bisexual identity is not an identity to be adopted for political reasons, but because that is how one wishes to define oneself for whatever reason, and others should respect that self-definition. This might be partially due to the early stage of the bisexual movement; after all, early lesbian feminists also advocated the right of women to sexual self-determination. As bisexual ideology develops and bisexuality acquires specific political meanings, it is quite possible that individuals will begin to adopt bisexual identity for political reasons. . . .

Finally, the role of race and ethnicity within the lesbian and bisexual movements differs, largely because of the different historical time periods in which the two movements developed. Lesbian feminism began, and remained, primarily a white movement. Lesbians who felt that the movement should pay attention to racial and ethnic issues shouldered the burden of calling other lesbians' attention to the problem and constructing elaborate arguments about the relationships among oppressions in order to convince them of the importance of the issue. Considerable debate occurred over the exact relationship among different oppressions; for example, do all oppressions arise from the same root, or is one oppression fundamental? If one is fundamental, is it classism, racism, or sexism? Contemporary bisexual activists not only inherit these arguments, but have come forth in a historical period in which the celebration of racial/ethnic diversity and efforts to eliminate racial/ethnic oppression need no justification. Therefore, they do not spend a great deal of energy asserting that the bisexual movement should be multicultural. From its inception, bisexuals declared the movement to be multicultural; the work that remains is the work of making sure that it is in fact multicultural.

In summary, bisexuals, like lesbians, are faced with the task of politicizing a sexual identity, but bisexuals live in a very different political world than early lesbian feminists did. Not only have politics in general changed in the intervening two decades, but the lesbian/gay movement itself has created an entirely new political tradition. As a result of the lesbian/gay movement, sexuality has been politicized, and lesbians and gays are established political interest groups. To establish their own political voice, bisexuals must insert themselves into an ongoing discourse of sexual identity politics. In a very real sense, the lesbian/gay movement created bisexuals as an oppressed group by creating a discourse in which lesbians/gays and heterosexuals, but not bisexuals, were defined into political existence. Thus, the lesbian/gay movement not only altered the political arena by creating a new political tradition; it also created the need for a bisexual movement . . . .

Critique. Lesbian feminism began by claiming that all women can be considered lesbian in their emotional identification with women, even though they may be heterosexual in their sexual relationships. This gender identification was soon submerged by an insistence that lesbian sexual relationships are more feminist than heterosexual relationships, because intimacy with a man undercuts a woman's independence. But feminists who take up with women for political reasons in turn annoy lesbians who feel that sexual orientation is not something you can turn off and on.

A second unresolved argument is over the structure of lesbian relationships. The ideal type of lesbian relationship has been conventionalized as a sexually monogamous, emotionally satisfying bond between two loving women, weakening the critical edge of the lesbian boycott of the conventional family. Even if the structure of lesbian relationships resembles that of heterosexual pairs, lesbians argue that the quality of their relationships is entirely different. Free of male dominance, partners can be fully egalitarian and reciprocal in their behavior toward each other. Many lesbians, like many gay men, would like to have the legal benefits of marriage. They do not see why they, and not heterosexual feminists, have to give up the goal of legally recognized couple relationships to fight against the subordination of women in the traditional family.

Summary

As an offshoot of radical feminism, lesbian feminism pushes the critique of heterosexuality and conventional family life to its logical extreme. Theoretically, lesbian feminism argues that all heterosexual relationships, especially those that are romantic and sexual, are intrinsically coercive of women. Given men's dominant social position and tendency to oppress women in everyday interaction, it is better to have as little to do with them as possible. Women have to work with men and deal with them in many public arenas, but in their private lives and especially in sexual relationships, a woman is a far better partner.

Lesbian feminist separatists go further, and create cultural communities, social lives, and political organizations that are for women only. Caring, nurturance, intimacy, and woman-to-woman love of all kinds are the ideals of these women's worlds. In recent years, however, the boundaries between lesbians and heterosexual feminists and between lesbians and gay men are giving way. Lesbians invite heterosexual women into their feminist political activities, and they work with gay men politically. With the advent of men's feminism, lesbian feminism is less wary of even heterosexual men. In many political organizations today, neither gender nor sexual orientation is a significant marker of who sides with whom.

Suggested Readings in Lesbian Feminism

Abelove, Henry, Michèle Aina Barale, and David M. Halperin (eds.). 1993. *The Lesbian and Gay Studies Reader*. New York and London: Routledge.

Allen, Jeffner (ed.). 1990. *Lesbian Philosophies and Cultures*. Albany: State University of New York Press.

Bristow, Joseph, and Angelia R. Wilson (eds.). 1993. *Activating Theory: Lesbian, Gay, and Bisexual Politics*. London: Lawrence & Wishart.

Faderman, Lillian. 1981. *Surpassing the Love of Men: Romantic Friendship and Love Between Women from the Renaissance to the Present*. New York: William Morrow.

——. 1991. *Odd Girls and Twilight Lovers: A History of Lesbian Life in Twentieth-Century America*. New York: Columbia University Press.

Feinberg, Leslie. 1993. *Stone Butch Blues*. Ithaca, NY: Firebrand Press.

Frye, Marilyn. 1983. *The Politics of Reality: Essays in Feminist Theory*. Trumansburg, NY: The Crossing Press.

Hoagland, Sarah, and Julia Penelope (eds.). 1991. *For Lesbians Only: A Separatist Anthology*. London: Radical Feminist Lesbian Publishers.

Johnston, Jill. 1973. *Lesbian Nation: The Feminist Solution*. New York: Simon and Schuster.

Leong, Russell (ed.). 1996. *Asian American Sexualities: Dimensions of the Gay and Lesbian Experience*. New York and London: Routledge.

Lorde, Audre. 1984. *Sister Outsider*. Trumansburg, NY: The Crossing Press.

Phelan, Shane. 1989. *Identity Politics: Lesbian Feminism and the Limits of Community*. Philadelphia: Temple University Press.

Ratti, Rakesh (ed.). 1993. *A Lotus of Another Color: An Unfolding of the South Asian Gay and Lesbian Experience*. Boston: Alyson Publications.

Rich, Adrienne. 1980. "Compulsory Heterosexuality and Lesbian Existence." *Signs* 5:631–60.

Rust, Paula C. 1995. *Bisexuality and the Challenge to Lesbian Politics: Sex, Loyalty, and Revolution*. New York: New York University Press.

Snitow, Ann, Christine Stansell, and Sharon Thompson (eds.). 1983. *Powers of Desire: The Politics of Sexuality*. New York: Monthly Review Press.

Stein, Arlene (ed.). 1993. *Sisters, Sexperts, Queers: Beyond the Lesbian Nation*. New York: Plume.

——. 1997. *Sex and Sensibility: Stories of a Lesbian Generation*. Berkeley: University of California Press.

Storr, Merl (ed.). 1999. *Bisexuality: A Critical Reader*. London and New York: Routledge.

Taylor, Verta, and Leila Rupp. 1993. "Women's Culture and Lesbian Feminist Activism: A Reconsideration of Cultural Feminism." *Signs* 19:32–61.

Valverde, Mariana. 1985. *Sex, Power and Pleasure*. Toronto: Women's Press.

Vance, Carole S. (ed.). 1984. *Pleasure and Danger: Exploring Female Sexuality*. Boston: Routledge & Kegan Paul.

Weston, Kathleen M. 1991. *Families We Choose: Lesbians, Gays, Kinship*. New York: Columbia University Press.

Wittig, Monique. 1992. *The Straight Mind and Other Essays*. Boston: Beacon Press.

Zimmerman, Bonnie, and Toni A. H. McNaron. 1996. *The New Lesbian Studies: Into the Twenty-First Century*. New York: Feminist Press. ✦

Chapter Six

Psychoanalytic Feminism

Sources of Gender Inequality

- Gendered personality structures—ego-bound men and ego-permeable women.
- Men's sublimated fear of women.
- Cultural domination of men's phallic-oriented ideas and repressed emotions.

Remedies

- Shared parenting, so men as well as women parent intensively.
- Cultural productions that feature women's emotions, sexuality, and connectedness with the body.

Contributions

- Analysis of the unconscious sources of masculinity and femininity.
- Making evident the dominance of the *phallus* (symbol of masculine power) in Western culture.
- Counteracting with literature written out of women's experiences with their bodies, sexuality, and emotions.

In the 1970s, British, American, and French feminists began to reread and reinterpret Freud. Instead of Freud's primary focus on the personality development of boys, psychoanalytic feminism gives equal attention to the personality development of girls. It locates the origins of Freud's theories in the European patriarchal family structure of the early twentieth century and criticizes the extensive cultural and social effects of men's fear of castration, men's emotional repression, and their ambivalence toward women.

Psychoanalytic feminism claims that the source of men's domination of women is men's unconscious ambivalent need for women's emotionality and their simultaneous rejection of women as potential castrators. Women submit to men because of women's unconscious desires for emotional connectedness. These gendered personalities are the outcome of the *Oedipus complex*—the psychological separation from the mother as the child develops a sense of individual identity.

Because the woman is the primary parent, infants bond with her. According to Freudian theory, boys have to separate from their mothers and identify with their fathers in order to establish their masculinity. This identification causes them to develop strong ego boundaries and a capacity for the independent action, objectivity, and rational thinking so valued in Western culture. Women are a threat to their independence and masculine sexuality because they remind men of their dependence on their mothers. However, men need women for the emotional sustenance and intimacy they rarely give each other. Their ambivalence towards women comes out in heterosexual love-hate relationships.

Girls continue to identify with their mothers, and so they grow up with fluid ego boundaries that make them sensitive, empathic, and emotional. It is these qualities that make them potentially good mothers and keep them open to men's emotional needs. But because the men in their lives have developed personalities that are emotionally guarded, women want to have children to bond with. Thus, psychological gendering of children is continually reproduced. To develop nurturing capabilities in men, and to break the cycle of the reproduction of gendered personality structures, psychoanalytic feminism recommends shared parenting— after men are taught how to parent with emotional intimacy.

In an article published in 1976 in a special issue of *Social Problems*, "Feminist Perspectives: The Sociological Challenge," sociologist and psychoanalyst Nancy Chodorow laid out the processes and consequences of the Oedipus complex for women and men. It is a brief summary of the psychoanalytic theories presented in her influential book, *The Reproduction of Mothering*.

Oedipal Asymmetries and Heterosexual Knots

Nancy J. Chodorow

As a result of being parented by a woman, both sexes are looking for a return to this emotional and physical union. A man achieves this directly through the heterosexual bond which replicates for him emotionally the early mother-infant exclusivity which he seeks to recreate. He is supported in this endeavor by women, who, through their own development, have remained open to relational needs, have retained an ongoing inner affective life, and have learned to deny the limitations of masculine lovers for both psychological and practical reasons.

Men, generally, though, both look for and fear exclusivity. Throughout their development, they have tended to repress their affective relational needs and sense of connection, and to develop and be more comfortable with ties based more on categorical and abstract role expectations, particularly in relation to other males. Even when they participate in an intimate heterosexual relationship, it is likely to be with the ambivalence created by an intense relationship which one both wants and fears, demanding from women, then, what they are at the same time afraid of receiving. The relationship to the mother thus builds itself directly into contradictions in masculine heterosexual commitment.

As a result of being parented by a woman and growing up heterosexual, women have different and a more complex set of relational needs, in which exclusive relationship to a man is not enough. This is because women experience themselves as part of a relational triangle in which their father and men are emotionally secondary, or at most equal, in importance to their mother and women. Women, therefore, need primary relationships to women as well as to men. In addition, the relation to the man itself has difficulties. Idealization, growing out of a girl's relation to her father, involves denial of real feelings and to a certain extent an unreal relationship to men.

The contradictions in women's heterosexual relationships, though, do not inhere only in the outcome of early childhood relationships. As I have suggested, men themselves, because of their own development and socialization, grow up rejecting their own and others' needs for love, and, therefore, find it difficult and threatening to meet women's emotional needs. Thus, given the masculine personality which women's mothering produces, the emotional secondariness of men to women, and the social organization of gender and gender roles, a woman's relationship to a man is unlikely to provide satisfaction for the particular relational needs which women's mothering and the concomitant social organization of gender have produced in women.

The two structural principles of the family, then, are in contradiction with each other. The family reproduces itself in form: for the most part people marry, and marry heterosexually; for the most part, people form couples heterosexually. At the same time, it undercuts itself in content: as a result of men and women growing up in families where women mother, these heterosexual relations, married or not, are liable to be strained in the regularized ways I have described.

In an earlier period, father absence was less absolute, production centered in the home, and economic interdependence of the sexes meant that family life and marriage was not and did not have to be a uniquely or fundamentally emotional project. The heterosexual asymmetry which I have been discussing was only one aspect of the total marital enterprise, and, therefore, did not overwhelm it. Women in this earlier period could seek relationships to other women in their daily work and community. With the development of industrial capitalism, however—and the increasingly physically isolated, mobile, and neolocal nuclear family it has produced—other primary relationships are not easy to come by on a routine, daily, ongoing basis. At the same time, the public world of work, consumption, and leisure leaves people increasingly starved for affection, support, and a sense of unique self. The heterosexual relationship itself gains in emotional importance at the very moment when the heterosexual strains which mothering produces are themselves sharpened. In response to these emerging contradictions, divorce rates soar, people flock to multitudes of new therapies, politicians decry and sociologists document the end of the family. And there develops a new feminism.

In France, feminists took on the Freudian-oriented cultural critics Jacques Lacan and Jacques Derrida, who say that women cannot create culture because they lack a sense of difference (from the mother) and a phallus (identification with the powerful father). French psychoanalytic feminism focuses on the ways that cultural productions (novels, drama, art, opera, music, movies) reflect and represent the masculine unconscious, especially fear of castration. In French feminist psychoanalytic theory, a major part of patriarchal culture reflects the sublimation of men's suppressed infantile desire for the mother and fear of the loss of the phallus, the symbol of masculine difference from powerless women. Women's wish for a phallus and repressed sexual desire for their fathers is sublimated into wanting to give birth to a son; men's repressed sexual desire for their mothers and fear of the father's castration of them are sublimated into cultural creations.

Phallic cultural productions, according to psychoanalytic feminism, are full of men's aggression, competition between men, men's flight from women or domination of them. The underlying subtext is fear of castration—of becoming women. What women represent in phallic culture is the sexual desire and emotionality men must repress in order to become like their fathers—men who are self-controlled and controlling of others. No matter what role women play in cultural productions, the *male gaze* sees them as potentially engulfing mothers or as potentially castrating objects of desire. Carmen must be killed over and over again.

To resist and to counter this phallic centrality with woman-centeredness, French feminism calls for women to write from their biographical experiences and their bodies—about menstruation, pregnancy, childbirth, intimacy with their mothers and their friends, their sexual desires for women as well as for men. Women's cultural productions will be very different from men's. Carmen can love—and live to love again.

In America, feminists applied psychoanalytic concepts to relationships in everyday life. Using the concept of *sadomasochism,* sociologist Lynne Chancer analyzes the psychological "chains of command" underlying work organizations' hierarchies. Since in so many workplaces, the higher positions are held by men, she argues that many women workers experience a sense of psychological masochism and dependency towards their bosses, who in turn are likely to be conscious or unconscious sadists in their enactments of power. Note, however, that as Chancer points out, the superior in any hierarchical relationship, whether a woman or a man, is likely to feel and act the same towards inferiors of either gender. The psychological aspects come from the situation, not the person, because the same person can be sadistic towards inferiors and masochistic towards superiors.

Sadomasochism and the Workplace

Lynn S. Chancer

While working for several years as a legal secretary in one of the largest corporate law firms in New York City, I perceived a high degree of dependency between secretaries and attorneys. To date, most secretaries at the firm are women, the lawyers predominantly men (statistically speaking, however, women lawyers are more common than male secretaries). Although in general one secretary worked for two attorneys, a sign of status for the higher-ranked partner was to have *his* (or, as in four or five cases, *her*) own secretary. Language itself, then, provided a clue to the texture of this employed/employer relationship, for what did it imply to the secretary to hear the attorney refer to his or her secretary as if a possession one controls, to hear the attorney boast, "I'll have my secretary bring this to you or get on the phone"? Being asked to serve coffee to the boss's clients or to perform personal tasks for him or her were not simply job functions but also demonstrations of the attorney's status; the boss/secretary relationship reflected considerations of power as much as efficiency. If one of the secretary's unspoken job functions was to endow the boss/attorney with greater predominance and status, she would certainly feel less powerful and less important by comparison. In the firm where I worked, a quasi-caste system had quietly but rigidly carved a chasm between lawyers and the secretarial staff. While it might be acceptable for lawyers to have affairs with secretaries, for instance, such actions as living with them, marrying them, or introducing them socially to other attorneys were in general frowned upon. Little wonder, then, if the secretary came to be dependent on the attorney not only for the specifying of tasks to be done but for the provision of a vicarious sense of self-importance undermined by the relative powerlessness implicit in her or his own situation.

However powerless and dependent a secretary might come to feel in relation to an attorney, the structure of this corporately organized firm did bestow relative status and power upon the secretary in contrast with people further down the chain of command such as Xerox operators, mail room workers, and messengers. The partner's secretary felt superior to the secretary of a mere associate. Here, a potential for subordinate sadism may exist (though not, of course, necessarily be enacted) for persons like the secretary cast in positions that structurally might tend to produce dominant masochism. Nor were these simultaneous dual roles confined to secretaries, being built in just as solidly to the attorneys' own daily lives.

Attorneys were divided along the axes of relative power and power-lessness according to whether they were associates or partners. As in most large law firms, the majority of attorneys were younger associates whose goal was partnership, a reward attainable only after seven years and only for one in every six or seven candidates. Thus, the associates also found themselves in positions of extreme dependency, sharing more with secretaries than they might care to admit, yet compensated for this sobering similarity by their relatively higher status. The secretary looked to her or his boss for approval and legitimation, since the boss had the power to continue or discontinue her or his livelihood as well as to reject her or his work. This behavior was not particularly different from that of the associate trying to please the partner. The corporate rung might vary, but anxieties were invoked everywhere along the ladder: a secretary worries about whether she or he has done a good enough typing job or presented a sufficiently pleasant front to the world on the attorney's behalf: an associate frets as to whether the partner will like the brief he or she has written. Will the partner think I'm sharp and hardworking enough, the associate wonders, or that I am a good enough team player (terminology borrowed typically from the world of sports)?

At a most fundamental level, then, the associate, like the secretary, is structurally dependent on his or her relative superiors: like the secretary, the associate seeks approval, legitimation, the sense of fitting in, and is surrounded by the uncomfortable reality that the partner's opinions and judgments count far more than his or her own. It is the partner who controls and has extraordinary significance in determining the associate's future fate: the partner's gestures and tone of voice may be nervously scanned for shades of approval or disapproval, just as the associate's own voice may be laden with extreme significance for the secretary dependent upon him or her. Within this framework, is the associate a dominant sadist or dominant masochist? Relative to the secretary, he or she may be a dominant sadist (with a potential for subordinate masochism in relation to the partner); relative to the partner, he or she may be a dominant masochist (with a potential for subordinate sadism, now in relation to the secretary). Based on this analysis, all the characters on stage—from the partner to the associate to the partner's secretary to the associate's secretary all the way through to Xerox operator and messenger boy—are enmeshed within the same psychosocial structure.

I am suggesting that the structure of modern bureaucracies, which Max Weber described as featuring fixed chains of command and rationalized rules and regulations, may itself contribute to producing a sadomasochistic orientation. Should this thesis have any validity, then cultures steeped in bureaucracy are potentially implicated—if, that is, they are organized in such a way that questioning or challenging those rules and regulations results in extreme reprisal. Again, in and of itself, the existence of hierarchy within bureaucratic structures need not suggest the presence of sadomasochistic dynamics. But when bureaucracy is combined with capitalist social structure in such a way that hierarchies are unquestionable, I would argue that then the potential for sadomasochism arises. (This allows for communist societies based on bureaucratic collectivism to also be analyzed through this framework.). . .

In *The Managed Heart*, sociologist Arlie Hochschild implies that excessive dependency for certain service workers may characterize not only the *relationship* between employee and employed at a particular job, but *the character of the work itself*. She notes that in 1983, less than 8 percent of workers were employed on assembly lines whereas the number of people engaged in "emotional labor" had grown to approximately one third of the workplace and one half of all working women. By Hochschild's definition, emotional labor involves the suppression of one's own feelings in order to produce a particular state of mind in an other. Using airline flight attendants as an example, Hochschild writes that they are trained to place the satisfaction of passengers above their own emotional gratification at all times. Passengers, they are taught, wish the attendant to smile, to reflect pleasantness and contentment. If a passenger should happen to anger the attendant by obnoxious behavior, she or he . . . is advised to "think about the *other* person and why they're so upset, [then] you've taken attention off of yourself and your own frustration. And you won't feel so angry."[1] One should not respond as one actually feels. The labor itself demands that the feelings and needs of the other be prioritized over one's own, a demand similarly placed by the sadist of the sadomasochistic dynamic upon the masochist. It is as though jobs based on emotional labor are not content to control body and mind but insist on reaching out to grab the soul as well. Though studying flight attendants in particular, Hochschild contends that her analysis holds true for a broad range of occupations: it would certainly apply to the secretary's predicament as I and others experienced it. One passage is worth quoting at length, as Hochschild describes

> the secretary who creates a cheerful office that announces her company as "friendly and dependable" and her boss as "up-and-coming," the waitress or waiter who creates an "atmosphere of pleasant dining," the

tour guide or hotel receptionist who makes us feel welcome, the social worker whose look of solicitous concern makes the client feel cared for, the salesman who creates a sense of protective outreach but even-handed warmth—all of them must confront in some way or another the requirements of emotional labor:[2]

Another important example of emotional labor is cited by sociologist Judith Rollins in her excellent book *Between Women: Domestics and Their Employers.* In this case, labor does not take place within a public capitalistic workplace but is far more privatized. Not only is a class relationship involved between employer and employee, but also a gendered interaction between two women of different races. According to Rollins's description, this relation is frequently sadomasochistically tinged, by this book's definition, involving forms of "emotional labor" that give the employee little choice but excessive dependency. Here, the usually white female employer may herself be cast in a role of subordinate masochism toward her white male husband (in relation to whom she is relatively powerless) at the same time that she acts out predominant sadism in relation to the usually black female employee. As an employer, she often demands that rituals of deference be followed. As Rollins writes about a change in her own behavior while working as a domestic,

> She [the employer] did not question the change; my behavior now expressed my belief in my inferiority in relation to her and thus my acceptance of her superiority in relation to me. Her desire for that confirmation from me was apparently strong enough to erase from her memory the contradiction of my previous behavior.[3]

But Rollins also notes that the supposedly "inferior" domestic, allegedly cast in the dependent position, is nonetheless astutely aware of the rules of the dynamic in which she has been asked to engage. The domestic makes her own quite independent judgments about her employer, often rebelling inside and exerting much more control over the situation than the employer ever recognizes. Hochschild's analysis of "emotional labor" might be relevant even to people working in positions supposedly more prestigious, whose jobs require and are desired for their ability to yield large salaries, bonuses, or commissions. In this respect, the law firm example is apt insofar as the young associate eager to please the boss knows only too well that it is not just his or her mind and attention the superior judges; subtler cultural indicators (how cool the associate is under pressure, how well he or she is able to make jokes and exchange social niceties) are also being constantly assessed out of a corner of the partner's eye. . . .

Whether referring to factory, service, or domestic workers, or to modern young urban professionals, then, a symbiotic situation can arise that is again analogous at the social level to the individual psychic symbiosis with which sadomasochism has already been associated. For the employed persons we have looked at—whether factory workers, secretaries, flight attendants, domestic employees, law associates, or investment bank trainees—questioning the rules and regulations of the workplace is often difficult or impossible, for challenging the boss's authority may be tantamount to committing job suicide.

Notes

1. Arlie Russell Hochschild, *The Managed Heart: Commercialization of Human Feelings* (Berkeley and Los Angeles, Calif.: University of California Press, 1983), p. 25, in which Hochschild describes a training seminar at Delta Airlines.

2. Ibid., p. 11.

3. Judith Rollins, *Between Women: Domestics and Their Employers* (Philadelphia: Temple University Press, 1985), p. 162.

Critique. Psychoanalytic theories of gender and sexuality are based on the bourgeois Western nuclear family, in which the woman is the prime parent and the man is emotionally distant from his children. Feminist psychoanalytic theories are just as narrowly based in a family consisting of two heterosexual parents. There are few tests of Freudian theories of each gender's personality development in single-parent and other types of households. The involvement of fathers in parenting varies enormously in societies throughout the world. Furthermore, it is not only heterosexual women who want the emotional attachment of mothering. Many lesbians who have deep and intense relationships with women also want children. Situational analyses of feelings and behavior in workplaces and in single-parent and lesbian and gay families have shown that psychological attributes may not be so deeply embedded or so clearly gendered. Women and men in similar situations may be more alike than women and men in different situations are to those of the same gender.

Psychoanalytic feminism's theory of culture is also too generalized— it assumes that all men in Western culture are misogynist and emotionally repressed, and all women are at ease with emotional intimacy. By encouraging women to produce woman-centered art and literature, psychoanalytic feminism has opened our eyes to the strengths of female bodies and sexualities. But it can lock women artists, musicians, and writers into a categorically female sensibility and emphasize their difference from men and the dominant culture even more. Women's emotional and erotic power is unleashed and made visible in women's cultural productions, but they are separated from men's culture, which is still dominant.

Summary

A culture's symbol system communicates both obvious and subliminal meanings. Ordinary language reflects gender hierarchies in conscious and deliberate devaluation (as in referring to adult women as "girls") and in careless language that renders women invisible (referring to men and women peers as "the guys"). Symbolic language, however, does not just name in ways that praise and denigrate; symbolic language reflects and creates the culture's "unconscious." Psychoanalytic feminism shows how Western culture represents men's fear of women and dread of emotional involvement in plays, operas, art, movies, and rap music and on MTV.

In Freudian theory, gendered personality development comes out of the resolution of the Oedipus complex, in which the young boy represses his emotional attachment to his mother and identifies with his more powerful father because he is afraid that otherwise, like her, he will lose his penis. Western culture is the product of men's fear of losing the phallus, the symbol of masculine power. Since women do not have a penis to lose, they do not participate in the creation of culture.

A little girl continues to be emotionally attached to her mother in the development of her feminine identity. When she grows up, she finds that men cannot fill her emotional needs because they are too detached, and the taboo against homosexuality turns her away from sexual relationships with women. The normal woman, in Freudian theory, will want to mother a child. Her attachment to her child, girl or boy, reproduces the cycle of gendered personality development all over again.

Psychoanalytic feminism's solution to these patterns of gendered personalities and phallic cultural productions is twofold. First, men have to be taught how to be emotionally attached parents to their sons and daughters. With a man as an intimate parent to bond with, a boy will not have to detach emotionally to develop a masculine identity. Second, women have to create art, music, and literature out of their emotional and sexual experiences and their sense of their female bodies. The dominance of the phallus (symbolic masculinity) in Western culture will thus be undermined by the changes in men's unconscious as well as by women's creativity.

Suggested Readings in Psychoanalytic Feminism

Baruch, Elaine Hoffman. 1991. *Women, Love, and Power: Literary and Psychoanalytic Perspectives*. New York: New York University Press.

Benjamin, Jessica. 1988. *The Bonds Of Love: Psychoanalysis, Feminism, and the Problem of Domination*. New York: Pantheon.

Buhle, Mary Jo. 1998. *Feminism and Its Discontents: A Century of Struggle with Psychoanalysis*. Cambridge, MA: Harvard University Press.

Chancer, Lynn S. 1992. *Sadomasochism in Everyday Life: The Dynamics of Power and Powerlessness*. New Brunswick, NJ: Rutgers University Press.

Chodorow, Nancy. 1978. *The Reproduction of Mothering*. Berkeley: University of California Press.

——. 1989. *Feminism and Psychoanalytic Theory*. New Haven, CT: Yale University Press.

——. 1994. *Femininities, Masculinities, Sexualities: Freud and Beyond*. Lexington: University Press of Kentucky.

——. 1999. *The Power of Feelings: Personal Meanings in Psychoanalysis, Gender, and Culture*. New Haven, CT: Yale University Press.

Cixous, Hélène, and Catherine Clément. [1975] 1986. *The Newly Born Woman*. (Trans. by Betsy Wing.) Minneapolis: University of Minnesota Press.

Gallop, Jane. 1982. *The Daughter's Seduction: Feminism and Psychoanalysis*. Ithaca, NY: Cornell University Press.

Hochschild, Arlie Russell. 1983. *The Managed Heart: Commercialization of Human Feeling*. Berkeley: University of California Press.

Irigaray, Luce. [1974] 1985. *Speculum of the Other Woman*. (Trans. by Gillian C. Gill.) Ithaca, NY: Cornell University Press.

———. [1977] 1985. *This Sex Which Is Not One*. (Trans. by Catherine Porter with Carolyn Burke.) Ithaca, NY: Cornell University Press.

McClary, Susan. 1991. *Feminine Endings: Music, Gender, and Sexuality*. Minneapolis: University of Minnesota Press.

Mitchell, Juliet. 1975. *Psychoanalysis and Feminism*. New York: Vintage.

Mitchell, Juliet, and Jacqueline Rose (eds.). 1985. *Feminine Sexuality: Jacques Lacan and the École Freudienne*. New York: Norton.

Mulvey, Laura. 1989. *Visual and Other Pleasures*. Bloomington: Indiana University Press. ✦

Chapter Seven

Standpoint Feminism

Sources of Gender Inequality

- The neglect of women's perspective and experiences in the production of knowledge.
- Women's exclusion from the sciences.
- Invisibility of women's perspective in the social sciences.

Remedies

- Making women central to research in the physical and social sciences, as researchers and as subjects.
- Asking research questions from a woman's point of view.

Contributions

- Reframing research questions and priorities.
- Challenging the universality of scientific "facts."
- Creating a feminist paradigm for the production of knowledge.

Radical, lesbian, and psychoanalytic feminist theories of women's oppression converge in standpoint feminism, which argues that knowledge must be produced from a woman's as well as a man's point of view. The main idea among the gender resistance feminisms is that women's experiences and perspectives should be central, not invisible or marginal, in the production of knowledge and culture. This idea is the basis for standpoint feminism. Simply put, standpoint feminism says that women's "voices" are different from men's, and they must be heard.

Standpoint feminism is a critique of mainstream science and social science, a methodology for feminist research, and an analysis of the power that lies in producing knowledge. The sciences and social sciences are supposed to be universal in their application, but they present the world as it is seen through men's eyes. Men have dominated the production of knowledge in laboratories and in social science research. Standpoint feminism argues that this knowledge is not universal because it is shaped by *men's* views of the world. Women see the world from a different angle, and they are still excluded from much of science. In the social sciences, it is only in the last 25 years that questions have been asked from a woman's point of view. In anthropology, for example, men writing on evolution represented our early primate ancestors as chest-beating, aggressive male gorillas; women in the same field argued that humans were more like the gentler, cooperative male and female chimpanzees.

In the twentieth century, philosophers, psychologists, and physicists have argued that the social location, experiences, and point of view of the investigator or "looker," as well as those of the subjects or the "looked at," interact in producing what we know. A complete picture of a school, for instance, has to include the perspectives of the researcher, the teachers, students, their families, the school administrators, the bureaucrats of the department of education, and the politicians who set the school's budget.

The impact of the everyday world in its experiential reality and the structures that limit, shape, organize, and penetrate it are different for people in different social locations—but especially different for women and men because Western society is so gender-divided. Consider the school again—won't viewpoints be different if the teachers and involved parents are mostly women and the school and departmental administrators and politicians mostly men? Is a man or a woman researcher more likely to see the gendered concentration of power and its impact on curriculum and sports programs? Similarly, in a racially or ethnically divided community, it makes a lot of difference in the way research is done when the researcher is a member of the disadvantaged rather than the advantaged community.

Although men could certainly do research on and about women, and women on men, standpoint feminism argues that women are more sensitive to how other women see problems and set priorities and therefore would be better able to design and conduct research from their point of view. It is not enough, however, to just add more women to research teams or even to have them head a team—these women have to have a feminist viewpoint. They have to be critical of mainstream concepts that justify established lines of power, and they should recognize that "facts" can reflect stereotypical values and beliefs about women and men.

In addition to *phenomenology* (the philosophy that says that what we know comes out of our social location and experience), the grounding for standpoint feminism comes from marxist and socialist feminist theory, which applies Marx's concept of class consciousness to women and men, and from psychoanalytic feminist theory, which describes the gendering of the unconscious. Standpoint feminism argues that as physical and social producers of children—out of bodies, emotions, thought, and sheer physical labor—women are grounded in material reality in ways that men are not. Women are responsible for most of the everyday work, even if they are highly educated, while highly educated men concentrate on the abstract and the intellectual. Because they are closely connected to their bodies and their emotions, women's unconscious as well as conscious view of the world is unitary and concrete. If women produced knowledge, it would be much more in touch with the everyday, material world and with the connectedness among people, because that is what women experience.

In the following excerpt, Nancy Hartsock, one of the first standpoint feminists, defines "standpoint" and describes why a woman's labor makes her way of thinking different from a man's.

The Nature of a Standpoint

Nancy C. M. Hartsock

A standpoint is not simply an interested position (interpreted as bias) but is interested in the sense of being engaged. It is true that a desire to conceal real social relations can contribute to an obscurantist account, and it is also true that the ruling gender and class have material interests in deception. A standpoint, however, carries with it the contention that there are some perspectives on society from which, however well intentioned one may be, the real relations of humans with each other and with the natural world are not visible. This contention should be sorted into a number of distinct epistemological and political claims: (1) Material life (class position in Marxist theory) not only structures but sets limits on the understanding of social relations. (2) If material life is structured in fundamentally opposing ways for two different groups, one can expect that the vision of each will represent an inversion of the other, and in systems of domination the vision available to the rulers will be both partial and perverse. (3) The vision of the ruling class (or gender) structures the material relations in which all parties are forced to participate, and therefore cannot be dismissed as simply false. (4) In consequence, the vision available to the oppressed group must be struggled for and represents an achievement which requires both science to see beneath the surface of the social relations in which all are forced to participate, and the education which can only grow from struggle to change those relations. (5) As an engaged vision, the understanding of the oppressed, the adoption of a standpoint exposes the real relations among human beings as inhuman, points beyond the present, and carries a historically liberatory role. . . .

The feminist standpoint which emerges through an examination of women's activities is related to the proletarian standpoint, but deeper going. Women and workers inhabit a world in which the emphasis is on change rather than stasis, a world characterized by interaction with natural substances rather than separation from nature, a world in which quality is more important than quantity, a world in which the unification of mind and body is inherent in the activities performed. Yet, there are some important differences, differences marked by the fact that the proletarian (if male) is immersed in this world only during the time his labor power is being used by the capitalist. If, to paraphrase Marx, we follow the worker home from the factory, we can once again perceive a change in the *dramatis personae*. He who before followed behind as the worker, timid and holding back, with nothing to expect but a hiding, now strides in front while a third person, not specifically present in Marx's account of the transaction between capitalist and worker (both of whom are male) follows timidly behind, carrying groceries, baby, and diapers. . . .

Women's activity as institutionalized has a double aspect—their contribution to subsistence, and their contribution to childrearing. Whether or not all of us do both, women as a sex are institutionally responsible for producing both goods and human beings and all women are forced to become the kinds of people who can do both . . . .

Let us trace both the outlines and the consequences of woman's dual contribution to subsistence in capitalism. Women's labor, like that of the male worker, is contact with material necessity. Their contribution to subsistence, like that of the male worker, involves them in a world in which the relation to nature and to concrete human requirements is central, both in the form of interaction with natural substances whose quality, rather than quantity, is important to the production of meals, clothing, etc., and in the form of close attention to the natural changes in these substances. Women's labor both for wages and even more in household production involves a unification of mind and body for the purpose of transforming natural substances into socially defined goods. This too is true of the labor of the male worker.

There are, however, important differences. First, women as a group work more than men.[1] We are all familiar with the phenomenon of the "double day," and with indications that women work many more hours per week than men. Second, a larger proportion of women's labor time is devoted to the production of use values than men's. Only some of the goods women produce are commodities (however much they live in a society structured by commodity production and exchange). Third, women's production is structured by repetition in a different way than men's. While repetition for both the woman and the male worker may take the form of production of the same object, over and over—whether apple pies or brake linings—women's work in housekeeping involves a repetitious cleaning.[2]

Thus, the male worker in the process of production is involved in contact with necessity, and interchange with nature as well as with other human beings, but the process of production or work does not consume his whole life. The activity of a woman in the home as well as the work she does for wages keeps her continually in contact with a world of qualities and change. Her immersion in the world of use—in concrete, many-qualitied, changing material processes—is more complete than his. And if life itself consists of sensuous activity, the vantage point available to women on the basis of their contribution to subsistence represents an intensification and deepening of the materialist world view and consciousness available to the producers of commodities in capitalism, an intensification of class consciousness. The availability of this outlook to even nonworking-class women has been strikingly formulated by Marilyn French in *The Women's Room:*

> Washing the toilet used by three males, and the floor and walls around it, is, Mira thought, coming face to face with necessity. And that is why women were saner than men, did not come up with the mad, absurd schemes men developed; they were in touch with necessity, they had to wash the toilet bowl and floor.[3]

The focus on women's subsistence activity rather than men's leads to a model in which the capitalist (male) lives a life structured completely by commodity exchange and not at all by production, and at the furthest distance from contact with concrete material life. The male worker marks a way station on the path to the other extreme of the constant contact with material necessity in women's contribution to subsistence. There are, of course important differences along the lines of race and class. For example, working class men seem to do more domestic labor than men higher up in the class structure—car repairs, carpentry, etc. And until very recently, the wage work done by most women of color replicated the housework required by their own households. Still, there are commonalities present in the institutionalized sexual division of labor which make women responsible for both housework and wage work.

The female contribution to subsistence, however, represents only a part of women's labor. Women also produce/reproduce men (and other women) on both a daily and a long-term basis. This aspect of women's "production" exposes the deep inadequacies of the concept of production as a description of women's activity. One does not (cannot) produce another human being in anything like the way one produces an object such as a chair. Much more is involved, activity which cannot easily be dichotomized into play or work. Helping another to develop, the gradual relinquishing of control, the experience of the human limits of one's action—all these are important features of women's activity as mothers. Women as mothers, even more than as workers, are institutionally involved in processes of change and growth and, more than workers, must understand the importance of avoiding excessive control in order to help others grow.[4] The activity involved is far more complex than the instrumental working with others to transform objects. (Interestingly, much of women's wage work—nursing, social work, and some secretarial jobs in particular—requires and depends on the relational and interpersonal skills women learned by being mothered by someone of the same sex.)

This aspect of women's activity too is not without consequences. Indeed, it is in the production of men by women and the appropriation of this labor and women themselves by men that the opposition between feminist and masculinist experience and outlook is rooted, and it is here that features of the proletarian vision are enhanced and modified for the woman and diluted for the man. The female experience in reproduction represents a unity with nature which goes beyond the proletarian experience of interchange with nature . . . .

1. For a discussion of women's work, see Elise Boulding, "Familial Constraints on Women's Work Roles," in Martha Blaxall and B. Reagan, eds., *Women and the Workplace* (Chicago: University of Chicago Press, 1976), esp. the charts on pp. 111, 113 . . . .

2. Simone de Beauvoir holds that repetition has a deeper significance and that women's biological destiny itself is repetition. (See *The Second Sex*, tr. H. M. Parshley [New York: Knopf, 1953,] p. 59.) But see also her discussion of housework in Ibid., pp. 434ff. There her treatment of housework is strikingly negative. For de Beauvoir, transcendence is provided in the historical struggle of self with other and with the natural world. The oppositions she sees are not really stasis vs. change, but rather transcendence, escape from the muddy concreteness of daily life, from the static, biological, concrete repetition of "placid femininity."

3. Marilyn French, *The Women's Room* (New York: Jove, 1978), p. 214.

4. Sara Ruddick, "Maternal Thinking," presents an interesting discussion of these and other aspects of the thought which emerges from the activity of mothering. Although I find it difficult to speak the language of interests and demands she uses, she brings out several valuable points. Her distinction between maternal and scientific thought is very intriguing and potentially useful. (*Feminist Studies* 6: (1980), 350–53.)

Reprinted from: Nancy C. M. Hartsock, "The Feminist Standpoint: Developing the Ground for a Specific Feminist Historical Materialism," in *Feminism and Methodology*, edited by Sandra Harding, pp. 159–60, 164–66. Copyright © 1987 by Indiana University Press. Reprinted by permission.

Standpoint feminism is arguing for more than equal representation of all viewpoints. There is a power issue here as well. Whoever sets the agendas for scientific research shapes the content of education, chooses the symbols that permeate cultural productions, and decides political priorities has *hegemonic power*. *Hegemony* is the value base that legitimates a society's unquestioned assumptions. In Western society, the justifications for many of our ideas about women and men come from science. We believe in scientific "facts" and rarely question their objectivity. That is why standpoint feminism puts so much emphasis on demonstrating that scientific knowledge produced mostly by men is not universal and general but partial and particular.

But is all men's and women's experience the same? Is not all knowledge partial? Racial categories, ethnicity, religion, social class, age, and sexual orientation are also social locations. They intersect with gender to produce varied life experiences and outlooks. There may be a common core to women's experiences, perhaps because they share similar bodies, but standpoint feminism cannot ignore the input from social characteristics that are as important as gender. All men may be dominant over the women of their group, but some are certainly subordinate to other men.

As Patricia Hill Collins, one of the major theorists of Black feminism, points out in a recent critique of standpoint theory, these experiences are not individual but common to the members of a *group*; thus, they are a vital source of both a worldview and a sense of identity. When a group's experiences frame the production of knowledge and culture and set political agendas, that group has power. Most racial and ethnic groups in a heterogeneous society do not have such power; their experiential life-world views do not become part of the mainstream.

Where's the Power?

Patricia Hill Collins

. . . First, the notion of a standpoint refers to historically shared, *group*-based experiences. Groups have a degree of permanence over time such that group realities transcend individual experiences. For example, African Americans as a stigmatized racial group existed long before I was born and will probably continue long after I die. While my individual experiences with institutionalized racism will be unique, the types of opportunities and constraints that I encounter on a daily basis will resemble those confronting African Americans as a group. Arguing that Blacks as a group come into being or disappear on the basis of my participation seems narcissistic, egocentric, and archetypally postmodern. In contrast, standpoint theory places less emphasis on individual experiences within socially constructed groups than on the social conditions that construct such groups.

I stress this difference between the individual and the group as units of analysis because using these two constructs as if they were interchangeable clouds understanding of a host of topics, in this case, the very notion of a group-based standpoint. Individualism continues as a taproot in Western theorizing, including feminist versions. Whether bourgeois liberalism positing notions of individual rights or postmodern social theory's celebration of human differences, market-based choice models grounded in individualism argue that freedom exists via the absence of constraints of all sorts, including those of mandatory group membership. Freedom occurs when individuals have rights of mobility in and out of groups, much as we join clubs and other voluntary associations.

But the individual as proxy for the group becomes particularly problematic because standpoint theory's treatment of the group is not synonymous with a "family resemblance" of individual choice expanded to the level of voluntary group association. The notion of standpoint refers to groups having shared histories based on their shared location in relations of power—standpoints arise neither from crowds of individuals nor from groups analytically created by scholars or bureaucrats. Take, for example, the commonality of experiences that emerges from long-standing patterns of racial segregation in the United States. The degree of racial segregation between Blacks and Whites as *groups* is routinely underestimated. Blacks and Whites live in racially segregated neighborhoods, and this basic feature generates distinctive experiences in schools, recreational facilities, shopping areas, health-care systems, and occupational opportunities. Moreover, middle-class Blacks have not been exempt from the effects of diminished opportunities that accompany racial segregation and group discrimination. It is common location within hierarchical power relations that creates groups, not the results of collective decision making of the individuals within the groups. Race, gender, social class, ethnicity, age, and sexuality are not descriptive categories of identity applied to individuals. Instead, these elements of social structure emerge as fundamental devices that foster inequality resulting in groups. . . .

What we now have is increasing sophistication about how to discuss group location, not in the singular social class framework proposed by Marx, nor in the early feminist frameworks arguing the primacy of gender, but within constructs of multiplicity residing in social structures themselves and not in individual women. Fluidity does not mean that groups themselves disappear, to be replaced by an accumulation of decontexualized, unique women whose complexity erases politics. Instead, the fluidity of boundaries operates as a new lens that potentially deepens understanding of how the actual mechanisms of institutional power can change dramatically while continuing to reproduce long-standing inequalities of race, gender, and class that result in group stability. In this sense, group history and location can be seen as points of convergence within hierarchical, multiple, and changing structural power relations.

A second feature of standpoint theory concerns the commonality of experiences and perspectives that emerge for groups differentially arrayed within hierarchical power relations. Keep in mind that if the group has been theorized away, there can be no common experiences or perspectives. Standpoint theory argues that groups who share common place-ment in hierarchical power relations also share common experiences in such power relations. Such shared angles of vision lead those in similar social locations to be predisposed to interpret these experiences in a com-parable fashion. The existence of the group as the unit of analysis means neither that all individuals within the group have the same experiences nor that they interpret them in the same way. Using the group as the focal point provides space for individual agency. While these themes remain meritorious, they simply do not lie at the center of standpoint theory as a theory of group power and the knowledges that group location and power generate.

Unfortunately, the much-deserved attention to issues of individual agency and diversity often overshadow investigating the continued sali-ence of group-based experiences. But group-based experience, especially that of race and/or social class, continues to matter. For example, African American male rates of incarceration in American jails and prisons remain the highest in the world, exceeding even those of South Africa. Tran-scending social class, region of residence, command of English, ethnic background, or other markers of difference, all Black men must in some way grapple with the actual or potential treatment by the criminal justice system. Moreover, as mothers, daughters, wives, and lovers of Black men, Black women also participate in this common experience. Similarly, chil-dren from poor communities and homeless families are unlikely to attend college, not because they lack talent, but because they lack opportunity. Whatever their racial/ethnic classification, poor people as a group con-front similar barriers for issues of basic survival. In this sense, standpoint theory seems especially suited to explaining relations of race and/or social class because these systems of power share similar institutional structures. Given the high degree of residential and occupational segregation sepa-rating Black and/or working-class groups from White middle-class reali-ties, it becomes plausible to generate arguments about working-class and/or Black culture that emerge from long-standing shared experiences. For both class and race, a much clearer case of a group standpoint can be constructed. Whether individuals from or associated with these groups accept or reject these histories, they recognize the saliency of the notion of group standpoint.

But gender raises different issues, for women are distributed across these other groups. In contrast to standpoints that must learn to accom-modate differences within, feminist standpoints must be constructed across differences such as these. Thus, gender represents a distinctly different intellectual and political project within standpoint theory. How effectively can a standpoint theory that was originally developed to explicate the wage exploitation and subsequent impoverishment of European, working-class populations be applied to the extremely heterogeneous population of women in the contemporary United States, let alone globally? For example, Black women and White women do not live in racially integrated women's communities, separated from men and children by processes such as gender steering into such communities, experience bank redlining that results in refusal to lend money to women's communities, attend inferior schools as a result of men moving to all-male suburban areas, and the like. Instead, Black and White women live in racially segregated communities, and the experiences they garner in such communities reflect the racial politics operating overall. Moreover, proximity in physical space is not necessarily the same as occupying a common location in the space of hierarchical power relations. For example, Black women and women of color routinely share academic office space with middle-class and/or White women academics. It is quite common for women of color to clean the office of the feminist academic writing the latest treatise on standpoint theory. While these women occupy the same physical space—this is why proximity should not be confused with group solidarity—they occupy fundamentally different locations in hierarchical power relations. These women did not just enter this space in a random fashion. An entire arsenal of social institutions collectively created paths in which the individuals assigned to one group received better housing, health care, education, and recreational facilities, while those relegated to the other group did with worse or did without. The accumulation of these different experiences led the two groups of women to that same academic space. The actual individuals matter less than the accumulation of social structures that lead to these outcomes. In this sense, developing a political theory for women involves confronting a different and more complex set of issues than that facing race theories or class-based theories because women's inequality is structured differently. . . .

Critique. A woman-centered perspective is a needed corrective to a gender-blind neutralism that erases women's experience. But the exclusive focus on "woman" is troublesome. Are women so much alike that they can be expected to always have similar experiences and a unitary perspective? Does standpoint feminism create a universal Woman who is actually middle-class, Western, heterosexual, and White? Does this universal Woman suppress other women's voices? How can they be heard? For that matter, don't men also differ by racial category, ethnicity, religion, social class, and sexual orientation?

Standpoint feminism's answer to the diversity-sameness issue is that what binds all women together is their bodies and their connectedness to people through their work for their families and their nurturing. A strong critique of this view focuses on these claims of essential differences between men and women and the promotion of a separate and distinctive woman's culture rooted in female bodies and nurturing abilities. Many feminists feel that these views are a throwback to biological justifications of women's inferiority.

However, if women's standpoint is not located in the female body but in their caretaking work, and in their place in a gendered social order that allows them to be constantly threatened by violence, rape, and sexual harassment, then we can speak of a shared woman's standpoint without reverting to a direct biological cause. Standpoint feminism can legitimately argue that women's bodies are the source of their sexual oppression because of the ways they are used and abused by men, and that their consciousness is shaped by their family role as the primary parent. Women's bodies are not erased but are mediated by social processes.

Similarly, it is not male biology that makes men dominant but their social power, which they get because they have a visible mark of identity that sets them off from women—a penis. Men in diverse social circumstances have something in common—the privileges of dominant status. (Its *symbol* is the *phallus*.) Social locations and experiences, such as growing up a girl or a boy in a poor Black community, create particular women's and men's identities and standpoints. These shared particular identities are like concentric circles within the larger circle of womanhood and manhood. Both the common and the diverse ways of thinking are needed for fully representative knowledge.

Summary

Standpoint feminism claims that what people think is universal, objective knowledge is biased because it does not include the life experiences of those who are not members of the dominant group. It challenges the claim that what is represented as "fact" is applicable to everyone. Phenomenologists and perception psychologists have argued that knowledge is produced out of experience. If that is so, then knowledge produced without women's experiences is not applicable to the universe but only to half of it. In order to balance out the dominance of men's experiences in most knowledge production, standpoint feminism elevates *women's experience*.

Using marxist, socialist, and psychoanalytic feminisms' analyses of how women's lives and work shape their conscious and unconscious thinking, standpoint feminism says that women's distinctive perspectives must be used in producing knowledge.

We think that science is detached from the particulars of everyday life. That is not even true of astronomy and physics, which have a social impact in space travel and nuclear power, but it is especially false when it comes to research on people. When we want to know what makes people think and act the way they do, we are using the data of everyday life. The lives of women and of men of diverse racial categories, ethnicities, religions, social classes, and sexual orientations must be part of these data.

Standpoint feminism challenges the sciences and social sciences to take a more critical view of their basic assumptions, especially about women and men. It criticizes the research on sex/gender differences because women's social and experiential reality are ignored. Modern Western societies today believe in science as an explanation for the way things are; past generations believed life circumstances were God-given. Standpoint feminism claims that when it comes to sex and gender, there is as much faith as fact in men's science.

Suggested Readings in Standpoint Feminism

Alcoff, Linda, and Elizabeth Potter (eds.). 1993. *Feminist Epistemologies*. New York and London: Routledge.

Belenkey, Mary Field, Jill Mattuck Tarule, Nancy Rule Goldberger (eds.). 1986. *Women's Ways of Knowing: The Development of Self, Voice, and Mind*. New York: Basic Books.

DeVault, Marjorie. 1999. *Liberating Method: Feminism and Social Research*. Philadelphia: Temple University Press.

Embree, Lester, and Linda Fisher (eds.). 1997. *Feminism and Phenomenology.* Dordrecht and Boston: Kluwer.

Gilligan, Carol. 1982. *In a Different Voice.* Cambridge, MA: Harvard University Press.

Goldberger, Nancy Rule and Jill Mattuck Tarule (eds.). 1996. *Knowledge, Difference, and Power: Essays Inspired by Women's Ways of Knowing.* New York: Basic Books.

Haraway, Donna. 1989. *Primate Visions.* New York and London: Routledge.

——. 1991. *Simians, Cyborgs, and Women: The Reinvention of Nature.* New York and London: Routledge.

——. 1997. *Modest_Witness@Second_Millennium. FemaleMan(c)_Meets_Oncomouse™: Feminisms and Technoscience.* New York and London: Routledge.

Harding, Sandra. 1986. *The Science Question in Feminism.* Ithaca, NY: Cornell University Press.

——. 1991. *Whose Science? Whose Knowledge? Thinking from Women's Lives.* Ithaca, NY: Cornell University Press.

——. 1998. *Is Science Multicultural? Postcolonialisms, Feminisms, and Epistemologies.* Bloomington: Indiana University Press.

Keller, Evelyn Fox. 1985. *Reflections on Gender and Science.* New Haven, CT: Yale University Press.

Laslett, Barbara, Sally Gregory Kohlstedt, Helen Longino, and Evelyn Hammonds (eds.). 1996. *Gender and Scientific Authority.* Chicago: University of Chicago Press.

Levesque-Lopman, Louise. 1988. *Claiming Reality: Phenomenology and Women's Experience.* Totowa, NJ: Rowman & Littlefield.

Reinharz, Shulamit. 1992. *Feminist Methods in Social Research.* New York: Oxford University Press.

Scheibinger, Londa L. 1989. *The Mind Has No Sex?: Women in the Origins of Modern Science.* Cambridge, MA: Harvard University Press.

——. 1999. *Has Feminism Changed Science?* Cambridge, MA: Harvard University Press.

Smith, Dorothy E. 1987. *The Everyday World as Problematic.* Toronto: University of Toronto Press.

——. 1990. *The Conceptual Practices of Power: A Feminist Sociology of Knowledge.* Toronto: University of Toronto Press.

——. 1990. *Texts, Facts, and Femininity: Exploring the Relations of Ruling.* New York and London: Routledge.

——. 1999. *Writing the Social: Critique, Theory, Investigations.* Toronto: University of Toronto Press. ✦

Part IV

Gender Rebellion Feminisms

G ender rebellion feminisms have long roots in historical, political, social psychological, and cultural studies. Since the late 1980s, they have become major perspectives, amounting to what some have called *third-wave feminisms*. They address the limits of gender resistance feminisms, especially the problems of the unity of women, the privileged perspective of women's standpoint, and the source of identity in identity politics. They are also part of the postmodern questioning of assumptions underlying what we think and believe.

Multicultural feminism whose roots are in the history and politics of disadvantaged groups, argues that the major social statuses of a society produce a complex hierarchical stratification system. By teasing out multiple strands of oppression and exploitation, multicultural feminism shows that gender, racial categories, and ethnicity are intertwined social structures: How people are gendered differs according to whether they are members of dominant or subordinate racial and ethnic groups. Social class is also an especially crucial dimension, given the wide differences between the poor and the rich throughout the world.

Multicultural feminism (which can equally well be called multiracial or multiethnic feminism) creates theories and politics of gender inequality that interweave gender with the continuum of dominance and subordination of other social statuses. It argues that feminist political activism can no longer be based only on gender but must consider racial identifications, ethnicity, and social class as well. Thus, African American

143

women have developed a "womanist" rather than a feminist approach. The battle for rights and dignity includes men, but women's perspectives and cultural contributions are made visible as well.

Men's feminism, drawing on marxist analyses of social class, has focused on the interlocking structures of power that make one group of men dominant and rank everyone else in a complex hierarchy of privilege and disadvantage. It documents the gender practices that both exclude women from competition with men and determine which men are able to attain positions of great power. The culture of violence in many Western societies and its enactment in sports has come under criticism by men's feminism. Like multicultural feminism, men's feminism uses racial categories, ethnicity, religion, social class, and sexual orientation in its analyses of men's social statuses.

In many ways, men's feminism and multicultural feminism are producing parallel data about the ways gender inequality plays itself out within and between different social groups of women and men. One focuses on men and the other on women, but in their overall perspective, they are talking about gender as part of the structure of power and privilege that affects the lives of women and men of all different groups.

Social construction feminism comes out of symbolic interaction in social psychology, which shows how people construct multiple meanings and identities in their daily encounters. Social construction feminism analyzes the general processes that create what we perceive to be the differences between women and men. These processes also construct racial and ethnic stereotypes and beliefs about homosexuality as contrasted with heterosexuality. They impose categorical divisions on physiological and behavioral continuums and use visible markers, such as skin color or genitals, as signs of supposedly inborn and essential behavioral characteristics. Because these physiological markers are usually hidden (people do not walk on the streets naked) and varied (some African Americans have pale skin), other identifiers of social status are needed: Clothing, jewelry, and hair styles are the most common. In face-to-face encounters, visible cues of gender, class, ethnicity, and so on pattern subsequent behavior. (They act like team colors.) Evident differences within categories of people and similarities between groups are repressed or ignored.

Social construction feminism argues that multiple categories would better reflect the variety in people, but the gendered social order is built on a binary division of labor that needs clearly differentiated categories of women and men who can be assigned to gender-typed roles in the family, jobs in the workforce, and positions in government, the professions, and the arts.

Postmodern feminism and *queer theory,* located for the most part in cultural studies, challenge conventional binary oppositions even more. They claim that gender and sexuality are performances, and that individuals modify their displays of masculinity and femininity to suit their own purposes. Males can easily masquerade as women, and females can pass for men. Like clothing, sexuality and gender can be put on. Indeed, the exaggerations and parodies of gender by performers such as Michael Jackson and Madonna show how much manliness and womanliness are "put-ons."

Gender rebellion feminisms' theories destabilize what many people think is normal and natural and moral, but they have only begun to develop new practices for work, family life, and intimate relationships. They need to translate multiple categories into everyday living, which could be revolutionary enough. But to fulfill their political potential, these feminisms need to spell out what precisely has to be done in all the institutions and organizations of a society—family, workplace, government, the arts, religion, and so on—to ensure equal participation and opportunity for every person in every group. ✦

Chapter Eight

Multicultural Feminism

Sources of Gender Inequality

- The intersection of racial, ethnic, class, and gender discrimination.
- Continued patterns of disadvantage built into the social structure.
- Cultural devaluation of women and men of subordinated racial and ethnic groups.

Remedies

- Equal access to education, good jobs, and political power.
- Science and other knowledge production that reflects the subordinate group's perspectives.
- Cultural productions by women and men of varied racial and ethnic heritages.

Contributions

- Analysis of multiple, intertwined systems of oppression.
- Development of a complex politics of identity.
- *Womanist* and *subaltern* fiction, poetry, art, music, crafts—cultural productions from the perspective of the "other."

Coming in a long line of critical theory and activist politics, multicultural feminism (sometimes called multiethnic or multiracial feminism) focuses on the *intersectionality* of gender, racial categories, ethnicity, and social class. It argues that you cannot look at one of these social statuses alone, nor can you add them one after another. Their interaction is synergistic: together they construct a social location. Some locations are more oppressive than others because they are the result of *multiple systems of domination.*

Gender, racial categories, ethnicity, and social class comprise a complex hierarchical stratification system in the United States, in which upper-class white men and women oppress lower-class women and men of disadvantaged racial groups, ethnicities, and religions. In teasing out the multiple strands of oppression and exploitation, multicultural feminism has shown that gender is intertwined with and cannot be separated from other social statuses that confer advantage and disadvantage. The social location of a man and woman of the same racial, ethnic, or social class status differs. Men of the subordinate group may be as oppressed as the women but often in different ways. For example, Black men in the United States are rewarded for success in boxing and football, but are punished for violent behavior outside the sports arena; Black women are hired to take care of White children but are stigmatized for having many children of their own.

A woman member of a disadvantaged group may not be more disadvantaged than the man; in some economies, she may be able to get a job and a man may be out of work. White college students in the United States are pretty evenly divided by gender, but there is a gender gap for Blacks. According to a recent report by the National Urban League, from 1977 to 1997, the number of bachelor's degrees awarded to Black men rose by 30 percent, to Black women by 77 percent. For master's degrees, the figures were an 8 percent increase for Black men and a 39 percent increase for Black women. As of 1997, twice as many Black women as Black men in the United States had master's degrees.

There is a different social map for the men and the women of the same racial or ethnic group, just as there is a different social map for Whites and "others." There is also a different social map for the very wealthy, the rich, the middle income, the "just bill-payers", and those who scrape together a variety of survival sources. But if you made one map that included everyone, you would find clusters and patterns: the wealthy are mostly White men and the survivors mostly women of color; disadvantaged racial and ethnic groups and women are more numerous at the bottom of the hierarchy.

Not only life chances, but values, identity, and consciousness of self are rooted in all the major social categories; they are the walls and windows of our lives—combined, they structure what we experience, do, feel, see, and ultimately believe about ourselves and others. Multicultural feminism therefore talks of the outlooks and behavior of Black working-class women and Black working-class men, wealthy White women and wealthy White men, middle-class Latinas and middle-class Latinos, poor Chinese women and poor Chinese men, and so on.

The most advantaged group's values and ideas about the way people should behave usually dominate policies and social agendas. Multicultural feminism's politics focuses on this issue, especially with regard to the family. If the White, middle-class, two-parent family is taken as the norm, then the Black extended family of grandmothers, mothers, aunts, and "othermothers"—all responsible for the children of the household and pooling resources—is a deviant or problem family that needs changing. Health care is another area where the dominant group's perspective translates into allocation of resources. If psychological stress is defined as resulting from pressure in a high-powered job, then the pressures of living in a ghetto are ignored.

Eating disorders are a case in point. Among young White women, anorexia and bulimia are usually attributed to a desire for a thin, sexually attractive body because there is a culture of thinness in Western societies. For some African American and Hispanic women, however, binge eating and purging are ways of coping with the traumas of their lives—sexual abuse, poverty, racism, and injustice. In all these cases, the underlying cause of the eating disorder is social pressure, but the pressures differ enormously.

The following excerpt by Maxine Baca Zinn and Bonnie Thornton Dill, sociologists who have done extensive research on how gender intertwines with racial ethnic statuses, lays out the structural premises of what they call multiracial feminism.

What Is Multiracial Feminism?

Maxine Baca Zinn and Bonnie Thornton Dill

A new set of feminist theories have emerged from the challenges put forth by women of color. Multiracial feminism is an evolving body of theory and practice informed by wide-ranging intellectual traditions. This framework does not offer a singular or unified feminism but a body of knowledge situating women and men in multiple systems of domination. U.S. multiracial feminism encompasses several emergent perspectives developed primarily by women of color: African Americans, Latinas, Asian Americans, and Native Americans, women whose analyses are shaped by their unique perspectives as "outsiders within"—marginal intellectuals whose social locations provide them with a particular perspective on self and society. Although U.S. women of color represent many races and ethnic backgrounds—with different histories and cultures—our feminisms cohere in their treatment of race as a basic social division, a structure of power, a focus of political struggle, and hence a fundamental force in shaping women's and men's lives. . . .

We use "multiracial" rather than "multicultural" as a way of underscoring race as a power system that interacts with other structured inequalities to shape genders. Within the U.S. context, race, and the system of meanings and ideologies which accompany it, is a fundamental organizing principle of social relationships. Race affects all women and men, although in different ways. Even cultural and group differences among women are produced through interaction within a racially stratified social order. Therefore, although we do not discount the importance of culture, we caution that cultural analytic frameworks that ignore race tend to view women's differences as the product of group-specific values and practices that often result in the marginalization of cultural groups which are then perceived as exotic expressions of a normative center. Our focus on race stresses the social construction of differently situated social groups and their varying degrees of advantage and power. Additionally, this emphasis on race takes on increasing political importance in an era where discourse about race is governed by color-evasive language and a preference for individual rather than group remedies for social inequalities. Our analyses insist upon the primary and pervasive nature of race in contemporary U.S. society while at the same time acknowledging how race both shapes and is shaped by a variety of other social relations.

In the social sciences, multiracial feminism grew out of socialist feminist thinking. Theories about how political economic forces shape women's lives were influential as we began to uncover the social causes of racial ethnic women's subordination. But socialist feminism's concept of capitalist patriarchy, with its focus on women's unpaid (reproductive) labor in the home, failed to address racial differences in the organization of reproductive labor. As feminists of color have argued, "reproductive labor has divided along racial as well as gender lines, and the specific characteristics have varied regionally and changed over time as capitalism has re-organized" (Glenn 1992). Despite the limitations of socialist feminism, this body of literature has been especially useful in pursuing questions about the interconnections among systems of domination.

Race and ethnic studies was the other major social scientific source of multiracial feminism. It provided a basis for comparative analyses of groups that are socially and legally subordinated and remain culturally distinct within U.S. society. This includes the systematic discrimination of socially constructed racial groups and their distinctive cultural arrangements. Historically, the categories of African American, Latino, Asian American, and Native American were constructed as both racially and culturally distinct. Each group has a distinctive culture, shares a common heritage, and has developed a common identity within a larger society that subordinates them.

We recognize, of course, certain problems inherent in an uncritical use of the multiracial label. First, the perspective can be hampered by a biracial model in which only African Americans and whites are seen as racial categories and all other groups are viewed through the prism of cultural differences. Latinos and Asians have always occupied distinctive places within the racial hierarchy, and current shifts in the composition of the U.S. population are racializing these groups anew.

A second problem lies in treating multiracial feminism as a single analytical framework, and its principle architects, women of color, as an undifferentiated category. The concepts "multiracial feminism," "racial ethnic women," and "women of color" "homogenize quite different experiences and can falsely universalize experiences across race, ethnicity, sexual orientation, and age" (Andersen and Collins 1992, xvi). The feminisms created by women of color exhibit a plurality of intellectual and political positions. We speak in many voices, with inconsistencies that are born of our different social locations. Multiracial feminism embodies this plurality and richness. Our intent is not to falsely universalize women of color. Nor do we wish to promote a new racial essentialism in place of the old gender essentialism. Instead, we use these concepts to examine the structures and experiences produced by intersecting forms of race and gender.

It is also essential to acknowledge that race is a shifting and contested category whose meanings construct definitions of all aspects of social life. In the United States it helped define citizenship by excluding everyone who was not a white, male property owner. It defined labor as slave or free, coolie or contract, and family as available only to those men whose marriages were recognized or whose wives could immigrate with them.

Additionally, racial meanings are contested both within groups and between them.

Although definitions of race are at once historically and geographically specific, they are also transnational, encompassing diasporic groups and crossing traditional geographic boundaries. Thus, while U.S. multiracial feminism calls attention to the fundamental importance of race, it must also locate the meaning of race within specific national traditions.

The Distinguishing Features of Multiracial Feminism

By attending to these problems, multiracial feminism offers a set of analytic premises for thinking about and theorizing gender. The following themes distinguish this branch of feminist inquiry.

First, multiracial feminism asserts that gender is constructed by a range of interlocking inequalities, what Patricia Hill Collins calls a "matrix of domination" (1990). The idea of a matrix is that several fundamental systems work with and through each other. People experience race, class, gender, and sexuality differently depending upon their social location in the structures of race, class, gender, and sexuality. For example, people of the same race will experience race differently depending upon their location in the class structure as working class, professional managerial class, or unemployed; in the gender structure as female or male; and in structures of sexuality as heterosexual, homosexual, or bisexual.

Multiracial feminism also examines the simultaneity of systems in shaping women's experience and identity. Race, class, gender, and sexuality are not reducible to individual attributes to be measured and assessed for their separate contribution in explaining given social outcomes, an approach that Elizabeth Spelman calls "popbead metaphysics," where a woman's identity consists of the sum of parts neatly divisible from one another (1988, 136). The matrix of domination seeks to account for the multiple ways that women experience themselves as gendered, raced, classed, and sexualized.

Second, multiracial feminism emphasizes the intersectional nature of hierarchies at all levels of social life. Class, race, gender, and sexuality are components of both social structure and social interaction. Women and men are differently embedded in locations created by these cross-cutting hierarchies. As a result, women and men throughout the social order experience different forms of privilege and subordination, depending on their race, class, gender, and sexuality. In other words, intersecting forms of domination produce *both* oppression *and* opportunity. At the same time that structures of race, class, and gender create disadvantages for women of color, they provide unacknowledged benefits for those who are at the top of these hierarchies—whites, members of the upper classes, and males. Therefore, multiracial feminism applies not only to racial ethnic women but also to women and men of all races, classes, and genders.

Third, multiracial feminism highlights the relational nature of dominance and subordination. Power is the cornerstone of women's differences. This means that women's differences are *connected* in systematic ways. Race is a vital element in the pattern of relations among minority and white women. . . .

Fourth, multiracial feminism explores the interplay of social structure and women's agency. Within the constraints of race, class, and gender oppression, women create viable lives for themselves, their families, and their communities. Women of color have resisted and often undermined the forces of power that control them. From acts of quiet dignity and steadfast determination to involvement in revolt and rebellion, women struggle to shape their own lives. Racial oppression has been a common focus of the "dynamic of oppositional agency" of women of color (Mohanty et al. 1991, 13). . . .

Fifth, multiracial feminism encompasses wide-ranging methodological approaches, and like other branches of feminist thought, relies on varied theoretical tools as well. . . . In the last decade, the opening up of academic feminism has focused attention on social location in the production of knowledge. Most basically, research by and about marginalized women has destabilized what used to be considered as universal categories of gender. Marginalized locations are well suited for grasping social relations that remained obscure from more privileged vantage points. Lived experience, in other words, creates alternative ways of understanding the social world and the experience of different groups of women within it. Racially informed standpoint epistemologies have provided new topics, fresh questions, and new understandings of women and men. . . .

Sixth, multiracial feminism brings together understandings drawn from the lived experiences of diverse and continuously changing groups of women. Among Asian Americans, Native Americans, Latinas, and Blacks are many different national cultural and ethnic groups. Each one is engaged in the process of testing, refining, and reshaping these broader categories in its own image. Such internal differences heighten awareness of and sensitivity to both commonalities and differences, serving as a constant reminder of the importance of comparative study and maintaining a creative tension between diversity and universalization. . . .

References

Andersen, Margaret L., and Patricia Hill Collins (eds.). 1992. *Race, Class and Gender: An Anthology.* Belmont, CA: Wadsworth.

Collins, Patricia Hill. 1990. See Suggested Readings.

Glenn, Evelyn Nakano. 1992. "From Servitude to Service Work: Historical Continuities in the Racial Division of Paid Reproductive Labor." *Signs* 18:1–43.

Mohanty, Chandra Talpade, Ann Russo, and Lourdes Torres (eds.). 1991. *Third World Women and the Politics of Feminism.* Bloomington: Indiana University Press.

Spelman, Elizabeth. 1988. See Suggested Readings.

For both women and men, the dominant group sets the standards for what behavior is valued, what faces and bodies are considered beautiful, what cultural productions represent "everybody." The subordinate group is always less influential unless it can turn the dominant values upside down, as standpoint feminism does when it says women's values and experiences have to be given as much credit as men's.

Multicultural feminism takes the standpoint perspective a step further. It is not enough to dissect a social institution or area of social thought from a woman's point of view; the viewpoint has to include the experiences of women of different racial and ethnic groups and must also take into consideration social class and local economic conditions.

Multicultural feminism has made a political statement out of women's culture within these cultures. What women produce in everyday life, it claims as art: quilts, folk songs, celebratory dances, festive food, decorated dishes, embroidered tablecloths. These manifestations of a vibrant women's culture reflect women's history and current social status. Like everyday language, they are rooted in the material world, yet they are emotionally expressive as well. They are the equivalent of multicultural men's subversive cultural productions, such as jazz and rap, and equally distinctive from the dominant group's way of talking and thinking.

In the following excerpt, Nhlanhla Jordan, who teaches rural and gender sociology at the University of the Transkei in South Africa, shows how she used women's songs in her research. Her questions about their meaning became an entré into the rural community, and they also told her about how the women of the community saw themselves and their relationships with their men. Finally, she was able to interpret the protests conveyed symbolically in the songs, using the women's point of view as she had learned it.

Toward an Indigenous Method

Nhlanhla Jordan

The studies that were done in Transkei among rural women were conducted from the women's perspectives from an indigenous Afrocentric standpoint. The need for this methodology or analysis comes from the limitations placed on the non-positivistic methods by positivistic ones and other traditional research methodologies based on a Eurocentric approach. The researchers have continuously debated the question of "what methods should be used in feminist analysis of society?" Are other methods, other than the traditional research methods, appropriate for a feminist analysis of rural women? Such questions have been raised and debated by feminists critics of the social sciences (Mowrey 1995; hooks 1994). . . .

This view is meant as an attempt at transforming the research process, in particular that of the indigenous cultures. What stands out from the experiences gained in this type of research is the fact that rural women's experiences of oppression afford them a better insight into their problems that they can articulate . . . in a manner that will convey their lived experiences, unconsciously, through for example, song and dance. The following song describes some aspects of rural women's experiences:

He wethu, awuyazi oyifunayo (repeated in soprano)
He wethu, awuyazi oyifunayo (repeated in alto and bass)
Ndikunike'isandla, ndikunika nengalo, ndikunik'amabele
Awuyaz'oyifunayo

The English translation would read like:

Hey friend, you don't know what you want (repeat)
Hey friend, you don't know what you want (repeat)
I give you my hand, I give you my arm, I give you my breast
You don't really know what you want.

This is a song of protest, commonly sung by women with a rhythm. The dance that accompanies the song is very graphic and informing. From merely watching the dance and the actions that go along with the song one gets an informed view of the situation under which women live. The interpretation again can be confusing and misleading if taken literally. The song has a power dimension to it, the power that women have, that has not been acknowledged. It spells out the women's protest against men's controlling and sexual behaviours. It's a warning against those who want to own, possess, and exploit women's friendships. From the song one gets to understand the problems that women experience in their relationship with men.

Thus song and dance give us that ability to comprehend expressions of people's innermost feelings. They show us how those concerned are shaped into a community and are urged into action. Be it at a funeral, a wedding, a circumcision ceremony, a graduation or at work, a complex set of codes is being communicated and enforced. Singing in African culture is found in all walks of life, it occupies a centre stage. It is a form of innate art and has an aesthetic value, as part of the aesthetic knowledge of the African people. It needs no practice. When African people celebrate anything they sing, their celebration is expressed through songs. When they perform their daily tasks working at the mines, in prison, at church, at political rallies, in war, in the fields. Singing is the corner stone of their existence. It is about who they are and what they do. Why should we not therefore use such opportunities as methods to capture what the women are about? The songs reveal a certain approach to life which is descriptive, analytical, systematic and reveals the innermost feelings. This power to convey how one feels and how one has internalized, and is able to project, one's experiences in a manner that is rather disturbing to the positivistic methodologists has led to the debate on: "Are there different ways of knowing?"

It is a method that approaches the informant in a comfortable, non-threatening manner, starting from where the informant is. I have often wondered what went wrong with our African civilization system. The problem, I would want to believe, is partly found in our failure in marginalising those members of our society (viz. the rural, old, less formally educated people) who can meaningfully contribute to the epistemological foundations of our cultural development. These people have been marginalised by western epistemological ways of knowing. It is lamentable that even the African gate-keepers of knowledge seem not to desire to centre the rural and old people and to include them as sources and creators of knowledges.

. . . Allowing people to use the traditional way to share what they know, allows us the opportunity to enter their world views. When the women sing and dance, they in a way re-live their lives. They get into their world and express their innermost emotions. Getting into their worlds at such moments can be a productive experience for any researcher, provided the correct approach is used.

For me doing research among rural women in Transkei has called for a methodology that approaches the study from the informants' position, "going native" in a manner that will not cloud or confuse one's ultimate goal. Listening to their songs and watching their movements as they have allowed me to enter their space and attempt to learn of their experiences and also to understand them better has given me a better understanding of their lives and experiences. Listening and analyzing the songs that women sing as they go about their daily tasks, be it in agricultural work— working in the fields— or performing daily tasks like fetching water from the rivers, doing washing at the river site, collecting wood from the forests, has allowed me to get a better perspective of their lives and enter their world views. In fact it has also helped me in the process of gaining entry into their world because I began my interviews by asking what the songs were about. Often this has been met by laughter and more singing and at times I got explanations of what the songs were about . . . But often the interpretation of the songs was left to me. And the interpretation of the songs can be problematic if not properly handled. For instance, the song which follows depicts exactly what I'm talking about when I make reference to misinterpretations that are often made by outsiders when interpreting songs.

"*Wathinta umfazi, wathinta imbokodo.*" This is a very popular song which has even become a slogan for African women. The Eurocentric translation that has been imported is: "You strike a woman, you strike a rock." This is obviously, seriously flawed, and gives a wrong contextual meaning for the African women. In the first place, the literal translation does not convey what the song/slogan is about. Second, the linguistic equivalence of *thinta* is not *strike* as it is made to be or to mean. Again, *imbokodo* is not a *rock* in this context. Properly interpreted the song should mean: *Touching a woman is like touching a crushing stone— imbokodo*. The *imbokodo* is a smooth, roundish, stone that is used for crushing mealies on a grinding stone. The grinding stone has a hollow shape in the middle to allow for the grinding of the mealies. What is used to crush the mealies is the roundish crushing stone called *imbokodo*. The grinding of mealies is an art that not every woman has. The song conveys the power that the women have. The fact that when the women take over, then we must know that they will perform the task with precision and the end results will be good.

Historically, African songs of rural people, especially women, have been dismissed on the basis of their verbal texts, and yet it has been shown that the texts are in fact complex and require careful decoding and a critical analysis in order that they portray symbolic meanings (Stewart 1995). It is worth noting that in the textual analysis of the songs one can gain a lot of things. Women use songs to air their grievances and begin to negotiate for better resolutions of conflict. It provides a type of healing for the singers. I would like to agree with Stewart (1995), who suggests that women display a profound insight into their subordinate position in a patriarchal society and have found creative ways of resisting domination by using song as a voice. Referring to rural Zulu women, Stewart (1995, 10) attests that:

> songs recorded while the singers were cutting cane or hoeing fields demonstrate that the rural Zulu women have adopted and adapted the tradition of corn threshing or corn pounding songs as a means of finding an individual and collective voice of a social protest against male domination and their state of powerlessness.

There are a number of benefits in using this type of analysis: First, there is the ability to know what the women are experiencing and how, without them consciously making an effort at doing so. Second, from the informants, the easiness with which they relate to the researchers is further proof of the importance of the method. Third, the importance of this methodology is seen in the production of work (around the home as they plaster [*ukutyabeka*] their huts and in the fields as well). One can think of how production occurs at many levels. There is also the production of knowledge as we get to know their world better, understand their frustrations and concerns through the songs they sing. For the social scientist the method is descriptive, however for the ordinary person this is subject to many interpretations and misinterpretations as well. . . .

What the paper advocates is the existence of a type of methodology that I refer to as African feminist or, better still, indigenous African women research, which is known in other circles as "reality research" (American Indian Research and Policy Institute [AIRPI] 1996). "Reality research" uses methods which respect and incorporate basic tenets of a culture which makes the research more meaningful. It reflects the realities of an indigenous people and tells their stories as never before, from their own point of view and from an indigenous oral-history standpoint. Doing indigenous research not only affords knowledge to the African women, but to the wider community as well. Indigenous research is a method that is inclusive and reflective of African women's world views. It reflects the reality of African women and allows them to tell their stories in a different manner, from an African women's standpoint.

This method is important for research in rural areas amongst African women because African songs portray a kind of oral history. Using a method of research which respects and incorporates such basic tenets of a people's culture makes our research more meaningful to African communities. Here, sound research is translated into terms understood by Africans and the results are good and benefit our communities (AIRPI 1996).

References

American Indian Research and Policy Institute (AIRPI) (1996). "Reality Research," USA.

hooks, bell. (1994). See Suggested Readings.

Mowrey, M. (1995). "Feminist Ethics and the Postmodernist Debates." *The Annual of the Society of Christian Ethics*, pp. 275–284.

Stewart, D. (1995). In the *Centre for Science Development (CSD) Bulletin*. July/August Vol.2:6, Pretoria, HSRC.

Critique. Some multicultural feminist protests are universal, understood by disadvantaged women everywhere, and some are specific to women's different racial and ethnic groups. African American women, Latinas, and Asian American women may all encounter racial prejudice in social encounters, but they have markedly different experiences in the job market. A question that is difficult to answer is whether the discrimination these women experience is specific to them as women or whether they share racial and ethnic oppression with their men. If racial, ethnic, and gender identity are as intertwined as multicultural feminism claims, then political unity with men of the same racial or ethnic group could severely undermine a consciousness of oppression as women.

Among African Americans, there has been a controversy over whether Black women's independence and assertiveness threaten their men's ego and sense of masculinity. When this view is adopted by White politicians, it becomes an agenda for family policies that make it extremely difficult for battered women to leave abusive men. Where, then, do a woman's loyalty, identification, and politics lie? It may not be with the men of her own racial or ethnic group, who may oppress their own women because of a traditional patriarchal culture or because they themselves are oppressed by men at the top of the pyramid. Men's and women's standpoints within the same group may differ considerably, even though they may share a sense of injustice from their mutual racial or ethnic status.

Politically, however, women of oppressed groups may feel they have to stand by their men. In one Portuguese working-class community in which a woman was repeatedly raped in a pool hall, the women of the town first rallied around her. When the national media came in and began to vilify the men racially, the women turned on the rape victim, accusing her of sexual looseness and child neglect, and they supported the men at the trial.

A politics based on identity is a complex of interlocking coalitions and oppositional groups. Consciousness of subordination and the forms of struggle may have to be different for women and men. The man who is Other may need to find the voice suppressed by the dominant men; the woman who is Other may need to find the voice suppressed by both dominant *and* subordinate men.

Summary

Throughout the twentieth century, social critics have argued about which aspect of inequality is the most damaging. Feminists have focused on women's oppression, and civil rights activists on raising the status of the members of a particular disadvantaged racial or ethnic group. Marxist and socialist men and women have been in the forefront of working-class political struggles. Multicultural feminism argues that all these aspects of subordination have to be fought at the same time.

The important point made by multicultural feminism is that a member of a subordinate group is not disadvantaged just by gender or racial category, or ethnicity or social class, but by a *multiple system of domination*. Multicultural feminism is therefore critical of feminist theories that contrast two global groups—"women" and "men." It argues that in racist societies, no one is just a woman or man; they are, in the United States, for example, a White woman or a Black woman, a White man or a Black man.

The combination of social statuses makes for a particular group standpoint and culture—values, sense of appropriate behavior, and outlook on life (which may be completely distinctive or may overlap with that of other groups). The dominant group's standpoint is the one that prevails in the definition of social problems, in the attribution of their causes, and in allocation of resources to research and to political solutions. Dominant cultures tend to swamp native cultures, as witnessed by the spread of MacDonald's, Starbucks, and MTV. Members of disadvantaged racial, ethnic, and economic groups have fought to have their points of view heard, as have women. In the political arena, however, sometimes women band with other women and sometimes with men of their own social group. The politics of identity, as multicultural feminism is so aware, is a complex of shifting sides.

Multicultural feminism brings to feminism the tools of racial, ethnic, and class analysis. It gives us a powerful theory of the intersectionality of the multiple social statuses that shape individual lives and organize local communities and nations. Politically, however, multicultural feminism is often caught between the politics of race and ethnicity and that of gender, just as marxist feminists were divided over whether class position is more important than being a woman.

Suggested Readings in Multicultural Feminism

Amott, Teresa, and Julie Matthaei. 1991. *Race, Gender, and Work: A Multicultural Economic History of Women in the United States*. Boston: South End Press.

Anzuldúa, Gloria E. [1987] 1999. *Borderlands/La Frontera: The New Mestiza*. San Francisco, CA: Spinsters/Aunt Lute.

Collins, Patricia Hill. 1990. *Black Feminist Thought: Knowledge, Consciousness, and the Politics of Empowerment*. Boston: Unwin Hyman.

———. 1998. *Fighting Words: Black Women and the Search for Justice*. Minneapolis: University of Minnesota Press.

Davis, Angela Y. 1983. *Women, Race and Class*. New York: Vintage.

DuBois, Ellen Carol, and Vicki L. Ruiz (eds.). 1990. *Unequal Sisters: A Multicultural Reader in U.S. Women's History*. New York and London: Routledge.

Espiritu, Yen Le. 1997. *Asian American Women and Men*. Thousand Oaks, CA: Sage.

Glenn, Evelyn Nakano. 1986. *Issei, Nissei, War Bride*. Philadelphia: Temple University Press.

hooks, bell. [1984] 2000. *Feminist Theory: From Margin to Center.* Boston: South End Press.

——. 1989. *Talking Back: Thinking Feminist, Talking Black.* Boston: South End Press.

——. 1990. *Yearning: Race, Gender, and Cultural Politics.* Boston: South End Press.

——. 1994. *Outlaw Culture: Resisting Representations.* New York and London: Routledge.

Jones, Jacqueline. 1986. *Labor of Love, Labor of Sorrow: Black Women, Work, and the Family from Slavery to the Present.* New York: Vintage.

Joseph, Gloria I., and Jill Lewis. 1981. *Common Differences: Conflicts in Black and White Feminist Perspectives.* Garden City, NY: Doubleday Anchor.

Ladner, Joyce A. 1971. *Tomorrow's Tomorrow: The Black Woman.* Garden City, NY: Doubleday.

Melhuus, Marit, and Kristi Anne Stolen (eds.). 1997. *Machos, Mistresses, Madonnas: Contesting the Power of Latin American Gender Imagery.* New York and London: Verso.

Moraga, Cherríe, and Gloria Anzaldúa (eds.). 1981. *This Bridge Called My Back: Writings by Radical Women of Color.* Watertown, MA: Persephone Press.

Naples, Nancy A. 1998. *Grassroots Warriors: Activist Mothering, Community Work, and the War on Poverty.* New York and London: Routledge.

Newell, Stephanie (ed.). 1997. *Writing African Women: Gender, Popular Culture and Literature in West Africa.* London: Zed Books.

Nfah-Abbenyi, Juliana Makuchi. 1997. *Gender in African Women's Writing: Identity, Sexuality, and Difference.* Bloomington: Indiana University Press.

Smith, Barbara (ed.). [1983] 2000. *Home Girls: A Black Feminist Anthology.* New Brunswick, NJ: Rutgers University Press.

Spelman, Elizabeth. 1988. *Inessential Woman: Problems of Exclusion in Feminist Thought.* Boston: Beacon Press.

Spivak, Gayatri Chakravorty. 1988. *In Other Worlds: Essays in Cultural Politics.* New York and London: Routledge.

Stack, Carol B. 1975. *All Our Kin: Strategies for Survival in a Black Community.* San Francisco: Harper & Row.

Trinh, T. Minh-ha. 1989. *Woman, Native, Other: Writing Postcoloniality and Feminism.* Bloomington: Indiana University Press.

Walker, Alice. 1984. *In Search of Our Mothers' Gardens: Womanist Prose.* New York: Harcourt Brace.

Wallace, Michele. [1978] 1990. *Black Macho and the Myth of the Superwoman.* London: Verso.

Williams, Patricia J. 1991. *The Alchemy of Race and Rights.* Cambridge, MA: Harvard University Press. ✦

Chapter Nine

Men's Feminism

Sources of Gender Inequality

- Dominance of economic and educational resources and political power by one group of men.
- Institutionalized privileges that benefit all men.
- Social values that encourage men's violence and sexual exploitation of women.

Remedies

- Share resources and power.
- Enhance women's status and also that of disadvantaged men, including homosexuals.
- Make men responsible for controlling their own violent behavior.

Contributions

- Analysis of men's gender as part of a set of institutionalized relationships of dominance and subordination.
- Recognition of men's dominance of other men as well as of women.
- Critique of the culture of violence in sports.

Men's feminism applies feminist theories to the study of men and masculinity. Men's feminism took on the task called for by feminists studying women in relationship to men—to treat men as well as women as a gender and to scrutinize masculinity as carefully as femininity.

Genders—men's and women's—are relational and embedded in the structure of the social order. The object of analysis in men's feminism is thus not masculinity alone but its oppositional relationship to femininity. Much of masculinity is nonfemininity (and vice versa). Thus, neither men nor women can be studied separately.

The *patriarchal dividend* gives all men an advantageous status compared to women. Men's feminism argues that although a pattern of social dominance over women is prevalent, there are many subordinate men—as earlier studies of working-class men, Black men, and men under colonial domination made very clear.

The main theory developed in men's feminism, which has been used to dissect the differences between and within groups of upper-, middle-, and working-class men of different ethnic groups and sexual orientations in Western society, is that of *hegemonic masculinity*. Men who have the most valued characteristics—in Western society, those who are economically successful, from racially and ethnically privileged groups, and visibly heterosexual—are at the top of the social ladder. In the United States, many are of poor or working-class origins, but most have been educated at good colleges and universities and have professional or managerial careers. Their dominant status is legitimated by these valued or hegemonic attributes. They are both born to these characteristics (e.g., Whiteness) and achieve them (education). But what they can achieve depends partly on what they are born to.

Dominant men within a society monopolize privileges, resources, and power. Because newly independent countries are still suffering from the effects of colonization, hegemonically masculine men in Western societies, which have been economically and socially dominant for the past 500 years, have a double advantage. One might say that they have a double measure of patriarchal privilege. In the following excerpt, Bob Connell, an Australian social scientist who is one of the main theorists of men's feminism, describes this phenomenon. His paper is based on an address he gave in 1997 at the University of Natal-Durban at a colloquium on "Masculinities in Southern Africa."

Masculinities and Globalization

R. W. Connell

Masculinities do not first exist and then come into contact with femininities; they are produced together, in the process that constitutes a gender order. Accordingly, to understand the masculinities on a world scale, we must first have a concept of the globalization of gender.

This is one of the most difficult points in current gender analysis because the very conception is counterintuitive. We are so accustomed to thinking of gender as the attribute of an individual, even as an unusually intimate attribute, that it requires a considerable wrench to think of gender on the vast scale of global society. Most relevant discussions, such as the literature on women and development, fudge the issue. They treat the entities that extend internationally (markets, corporations, intergovernmental programs, etc.) as ungendered in principle—but affecting unequally gendered recipients of aid in practice, because of bad policies. Such conceptions reproduce the familiar liberal-feminist view of the state as in principle gender-neutral, though empirically dominated by men.

But if we recognize that very large scale institutions such as the state are themselves gendered, in quite precise and specifiable ways (Connell 1990), and if we recognize that international relations, international trade, and global markets are inherently an arena of gender formation and gender politics (Enloe 1990), then we can recognize the existence of a world gender order. The term can be defined as the structure of relationships that interconnect the gender regimes of institutions, and the gender orders of local society, on a world scale. That is, however, only a definition. The substantive questions remain: what is the shape of that structure, how tightly are its elements linked, how has it arisen historically, what is its trajectory into the future? Current business and media talk about globalization pictures a homogenizing process sweeping across the world, driven by new technologies, producing vast unfettered global markets in which all participate on equal terms. This is a misleading image. As Hirst and Thompson (1996) show, the global economy is highly unequal and the current degree of homogenization is often overestimated. Multinational corporations based in the three major economic powers (the United States, European Union, and Japan) are the major economic actors worldwide.

The structure bears the marks of its history. Modern global society was historically produced, as Wallerstein (1974) argued, by the economic and political expansion of European states from the fifteenth century on and by the creation of colonial empires. It is in this process that we find the roots of the modern world gender order. Imperialism was, from the start, a gendered process. Its first phase, colonial conquest and settlement, was carried out by gender-segregated forces, and it resulted in massive disruption of indigenous gender orders. In its second phase, the stabilization of colonial societies, new gender divisions of labor were produced in plantation economies and colonial cities, while gender ideologies were linked with racial hierarchies and the cultural defense of empire. The third phase, marked by political decolonization, economic neocolonialism, and the current growth of world markets and structures of financial control, has seen gender divisions of labor remade on a massive scale in the "global factory" (Fuentes and Ehrenreich 1983), as well as the spread of gendered violence alongside Western military technology. . . .

More important, I would argue, is a process that began long before electronic media existed, the export of institutions. Gendered institutions not only circulate definitions of masculinity (and femininity), as sex role theory notes. The functioning of gendered institutions, creating specific conditions for social practice, calls into existence specific patterns of practice. Thus, certain patterns of collective violence are embedded in the organization and culture of a Western-style army, which are different from the patterns of precolonial violence. Certain patterns of calculative egocentrism are embedded in the working of a stock market; certain patterns of rule-following and domination are embedded in a bureaucracy.

Now, the colonial and postcolonial world saw the installation in the periphery, on a very large scale, of a range of institutions on the North Atlantic model: armies, states, bureaucracies, corporations, capital markets, labor markets, schools, law courts, transport systems. These are gendered institutions and their functioning has directly reconstituted masculinities in the periphery. This has not necessarily meant photocopies of European masculinities. Rather, pressures for change are set up that are inherent in the institutional form. To the extent that particular institutions become dominant in world society, the patterns of masculinity embedded in them may become global standards. Masculine dress is an interesting indicator: almost every political leader in the world now wears the uniform of the Western business executive. The more common pattern, however, is not the complete displacement of local patterns but the articulation of the local gender order with the gender regime of global-model institutions. Case studies such as Hollway's (1994) account of bureaucracy in Tanzania illustrate the point; there, domestic patriarchy articulated with masculine authority in the state in ways that subverted the government's formal commitment to equal opportunity for women.

We should not expect the overall structure of gender relations on a world scale simply to mirror patterns known on the smaller scale. In the most vital of respects, there is continuity. The world gender order is unquestionably patriarchal, in the sense that it privileges men over women. There is a patriarchal dividend for men arising from unequal wages, unequal labor force participation, and a highly unequal structure of ownership, as well as cultural and sexual privileging. This has been extensively documented by feminist work on women's situation globally (e.g., Taylor 1985), though its implications for masculinity have mostly been ignored. The conditions thus exist for the production of a hegemonic masculinity on a world scale, that is to say, a dominant form of masculinity that embodies, organizes, and legitimates men's domination in the gender order as a whole.

The conditions of globalization, which involve the interaction of many local gender orders, certainly multiply the forms of masculinity in the global gender order. At the same time, the specific shape of globalization, concentrating economic and cultural power on an unprecedented scale, provides new resources for dominance by particular groups of men. The dominance may become institutionalized in a pattern of masculinity that becomes, to some degree, standardized across localities. I will call such patterns globalizing masculinities, and it is among them, rather than narrowly within the metropole, that we are likely to find candidates for hegemony in the world gender order. . . .

Masculinity Politics on a World Scale

Recognizing global society as an arena of masculinity formation allows us to pose new questions about masculinity politics. What social dynamics in the global arena give rise to masculinity politics, and what shape does global masculinity politics take?

The gradual creation of a world gender order has meant many local instabilities of gender. Gender instability is a familiar theme of poststructuralist theory, but this school of thought takes as a universal condition a situation that is historically specific. Instabilities range from the disruption of men's local cultural dominance as women move into the public realm and higher education, through the disruption of sexual identities that produced "queer" politics in the metropole, to the shifts in the urban intelligentsia that produced "the new sensitive man" and other images of gender change.

One response to such instabilities, on the part of groups whose power is challenged but still dominant, is to reaffirm local gender orthodoxies and hierarchies. A masculine fundamentalism is, accordingly, a common response in gender politics at present. A soft version, searching for an essential masculinity among myths and symbols, is offered by the mytho-poetic men's movement in the United States and by the religious revivalists of the Promise Keepers (Messner 1997). A much harder version is found, in that country, in the right-wing militia movement brought to world attention by the Oklahoma City bombing (Gibson 1994), and in contemporary Afghanistan, if we can trust Western media reports, in the militant misogyny of the Taliban. It is no coincidence that in the two latter cases, hardline masculine fundamentalism goes together with a marked anti-internationalism. The world system—rightly enough—is seen as the source of pollution and disruption. Not that the emerging global order is a hotbed of gender progressivism. Indeed, the neoliberal agenda for the reform of national and international economies involves closing down historic possibilities for gender reform. I have noted how it subverts the gender compromise represented by the metropolitan welfare state. It has also undermined the progressive-liberal agendas of sex-role reform represented by affirmative action programs, antidiscrimination provisions, child care services, and the like. Right-wing parties and governments have been persistently cutting such programs, in the name of either individual liberties or global competitiveness. Through these means, the patriarchal dividend to men is defended or restored, without an explicit masculinity politics in the form of a mobilization of men.

Within the arenas of international relations, the international state, multinational corporations, and global markets, there is nevertheless a deployment of masculinities and a reasonably clear hegemony. The transnational business masculinity described above has had only one major competitor for hegemony in recent decades, the rigid, control-oriented masculinity of the military, and the military-style bureaucratic dictatorships of Stalinism. With the collapse of Stalinism and the end of the cold war, Big Brother (Orwell's famous parody of this form of masculinity) is a fading threat, and the more flexible, calculative, egocentric masculinity of the fast capitalist entrepreneur holds the world stage.

We must, however, recall two important conclusions of the ethnographic moment in masculinity research: that different forms of masculinity exist together and that hegemony is constantly subject to challenge. These are possibilities in the global arena too. Transnational business masculinity is not completely homogeneous; variations of it are embedded in different parts of the world system, which may not be completely compatible. We may distinguish a Confucian variant, based in East Asia, with a stronger commitment . . . to hierarchy and social consensus, from a secularized Christian variant, based in North America, with more hedonism and individualism and greater tolerance for social conflict. In certain arenas, there is already conflict between the business and political leaderships embodying these forms of masculinity: initially over human rights versus Asian values, and more recently over the extent of trade and investment liberalization.

If these are contenders for hegemony, there is also the possibility of opposition to hegemony. The global circulation of "gay" identity (Altman 1996) is an important indication that nonhegemonic masculinities may operate in global arenas, and may even find a certain political articulation, in this case around human rights and AIDS prevention. . . . I have argued that the global gender order contains, necessarily, greater plurality of gender forms than any local gender order. This must reinforce the consciousness that masculinity is not one fixed form. The plurality of masculinities at least symbolically prefigures the unconstrained creativity of a democratic gender order.

References

Altman, Dennis. 1996. "Rupture or Continuity? The Internationalisation of Gay Identities." *Social Text* 48(3): 77–94.

Connell, R. W. 1990. "The State, Gender and Sexual Politics." *Theory and Society* 19:507–44.

Enloe, Cynthia. 1990. *Bananas, Beaches, and Bases: Making Feminist Sense of International Politics.* Berkeley: University of California Press.

Gibson, J. William. 1994. *Warrior Dreams: Paramilitary Culture in Post-Vietman America.* New York: Hill and Wang.

Hirst, Paul, and Grahame Thompson. 1996. *Globalization in Question: The International Economy and the Possibilities of Goverance.* Cambridge, MA: Polity.

Hollway, Wendy. 1994. "Separation, Integration and Difference: Contradictions in a Gender Regime." In *Power/Gender: Social Relations in Theory and Practice,* edited by H. Lorraine Radtke and Henderikus Stam, 247–69. London: Sage.

Messner, Michael A. 1997. See Suggested Readings.

Taylor, Debbie. 1985. "Women: An Analysis." In *Women: A World Report,* 1–98. London: Methuen.

Wallerstein, Immanuel. 1974. *The Modern World-System: Capitalist Agriculture and the Origins of the European World-Economy in the Sixteenth Century.* New York: Academic Press.

Reprinted from: "Masculinities and Globalization," in *Men and Masculinities* 1(1):7–8, 11–12, 16–19. Copyright © 1998 Sage Publications, Inc. Reprinted by permission.

In many countries, young working-class urban men's impoverished environment and "taste for risk" have made them an endangered species. They put their bodies on the line in confronting seeming slurs on their manhood, and they incur physical traumas in their work, in recreation, and especially when they become professional athletes. Men and boys in any social strata engage in gang rape as a way of showing off their sexual prowess to their friends. Men's feminism blames sports, the military, fraternities, and other arenas of male bonding for encouraging physical and sexual violence and misogyny. It deplores the social pressure on men to identify with but not be emotionally close to their fathers and to be "cool" and unfeeling toward the women in their lives and distant from their own children.

Although men's feminism uses psychoanalytic theories of the need to detach from the mother to explain men's emotional repression, it is critical of men's movements that foster a search for the inner primitive, or "wild man." It also regards religiously oriented men's organizations, such as Promise Keepers, as dangerous to women's autonomy because they link responsibility to family with patriarchal concepts of manhood. Men's feminism argues that these movements seek to change individual attitudes and do not address the structural conditions of gender inequality or the power differences between men and women and among men.

The gender politics that men's feminism concentrates on is embedded in the stratification systems of Western societies—racial and economic—as well as in the masculine dread of homosexuals. Prominent men of all racial and ethnic groups in politics, sports, and the mass media must appear heterosexual, which sometimes leads to constant womanizing. Men's feminism also criticizes the jockeying for leading positions in whatever arena men find themselves. It is not an accident that so much of the language of competition is the language of sports, because organized sports not only are an immediate site for demonstrations of masculinity but also are a source for vicarious competitiveness and for the creation of icons of masculine strength and beauty. Unfortunately, some athletes who have attained icon status feel free to use physical and sexual violence against women.

Men's feminism says that office-bound men's identification with the bruisers on the football field allows them to feel masculine and yet above such gross displays of physicality. White middle-class men who participate vicariously in the violent professional sports played by mostly Black and Hispanic men from economically disadvantaged backgrounds (but now very rich) admire their masculine physical prowess, extravagant wealth, and flaunted sexuality, but they also maintain their own racial and class superiority. White middle-class men who are themselves involved in professional sports are most of the owners, lawyers, agents, financial managers, journalists, and advertisers who make the athletes' careers. As a significant source of the social construction of masculinities in Western society, sport stratifies men, as can be seen from the following excerpt by Michael A. Messner, who was president of the North American Society for the Sociology of Sport.

Watching Men's Sport, Constructing Masculinities

Michael A. Messner

What does televised sport mean to male viewers? The mythology and symbolism of today's most popular spectator sports are probably meaningful to viewers on a number of levels: patriotism, militarism, violence, and meritocracy are all dominant themes. But it is reasonable to speculate that gender is a salient organizing theme in the construction of meanings, especially with respect to the more aggressive and violent aspects of sport. For example, when I was interviewing a thirty-two-year-old white professional-class male, and I asked him how he felt about the fact that recently a woman had been promoted to a position of authority in his workplace, he replied, "A woman can do the same job as I can do—maybe even be my boss. But I'll be *damned* if she can go out on the [football] field and take a hit from Ronnie Lott."

At the most obvious level, we can read this man's statement as an indication that he is identifying with Ronnie Lott as a man, and the basis of the identification is the violent male body. Football, based as it is on the fullest potential of the male body (muscular bulk, explosive power), is clearly a world apart from women, who are relegated to the roles of sex objects on the sidelines, rooting their men on. In contrast to the bare and vulnerable bodies of the cheerleaders, the armored male bodies of the football players are elevated to mythical status and thus give testimony to the undeniable "fact" that here is at least one place where men are clearly superior to women. Yet it is also significant that this man was quite aware that he (and perhaps 99 percent of the rest of the male population of the United States) was probably equally incapable of taking a "hit" from the likes of Ronnie Lott and living to tell of it. I would speculate that by recognizing the simultaneous construction of identification and difference among men, we may begin to understand the major role that televised sport plays in the current gender order.

Identification. With the twentieth-century decline of the practical relevance of physical strength in work and in warfare, representations of the male body as strong, virile, and powerful have taken on increasingly important ideological and symbolic significance in gender relations. Indeed, the body plays such a central role in the contemporary gender order because it is so closely associated with the "natural." Yet, as we have seen, though the body is popularly equated with nature, it is nevertheless an object of social practice: The development of men's bodies for athletic competition takes a tremendous amount of time, exercise, weight training, and even use of illegal and dangerous drugs such as steroids. But the sport media tend to obscure the reality of this social construction, weaving a cloak of symbol and interpretation around these gendered bodies that naturalizes them.

Some recent theorists have suggested that the true significance of sport as mediated spectacle lies in male spectators having the opportunity to identify narcissistically with the muscular male body. . . . Rather than concluding that televised sport violence has no meaning, it is reasonable to speculate that if men are using sport spectatorship to identify with the male body as a thing of beauty and power, perhaps the violence is an important aspect of the denial of the homoerotic element of that identification.

Difference. It is also possible that the media's framing of sport violence plays another important role: the construction of difference among men. As we have seen, it is disproportionately males from lower socioeconomic and ethnic minority backgrounds who commit themselves to athletic careers, and who end up participating at the higher levels of aggressive, violent sports. Privileged men might, as Woody Guthrie once suggested, commit violence against others "with fountain pens," but with the exception of domestic violence against women and children, physical violence is rarely a part of the everyday lives of these men. Yet violence among men may still have important ideological and psychological meaning for men from privileged backgrounds. There is a curious preoccupation among middle-class males with movie characters who are "working-class tough guys," with athletes who are fearsome "hitters" and who heroically "play hurt." These violent "tough guys" of the culture industry—the Rambos, the Ronnie Lotts—are at once the heroes who "prove" that "we men" are superior to women and the "other" against whom privileged men define themselves as "modern.". . .

Men's feminism overlaps with gay studies in analyzing the social dimensions of male homosexuality. Examining homosexuality from a gender perspective shows that homosexual men are *men*, not a third gender, and partake of the privileges (or lack of them) and life style of men of the same ethnic group and social class. Nonetheless, because homosexual men do not have sexual relationships with women—an important marker of manhood in Western society—they are considered not-quite-men. Thus, like other men who do not have the marks of dominant status (being White, economically successful, heterosexual), homosexual men are lower on the scale of privilege and power in Western society. Homosexual men, however, do not subvert the gender order, because they retain some of the "patriarchal dividend" of men's status.

Critique. Men's feminism provides a needed corrective in bringing men into gender research as a specific subject of study, but it does not offer a new theoretical perspective. Rather, men's feminism is an amalgam of psychoanalytic, multicultural, social construction, and gay studies. Women feminists have also written about masculinity, men's roles at work and in the family, and how men are changing—but slowly. The question, then, is whether men's feminism brings a different view on men's status because men themselves are writing about it critically.

Feminist men's politics include trying to educate young men about date rape and fraternity gang rape. Others who were athletes have written and lectured about the violent values in sport. Black and Hispanic men feminists have analyzed the dangers of risk taking and machismo. Gay men have analyzed and documented the history of the social construction of homosexuality, and its recent path from the headiness of the

Greenwich Village Stonewall riot to the tragedies of AIDS. There is a comprehensive body of knowledge in men's feminism, but politically, the men's movement has been taken over by the Iron Johns and the Promise Keepers, who offer versions of masculinity that are not much different from the conventional beliefs in men's intrinsic "wildness" or need to be the "head of the house."

Another strand in the nonfeminist politics of masculinity is the argument that says that men's power is a myth because so many men's roles are dangerous. They, and not women, are exploited—fighting wars, fires, criminals, and terrorists. Women feminists, not men, have countered this argument with studies of women in the military, the police, and other occupations where formerly only men showed they had the "right stuff." (Women could not enter such occupations until fairly recently.) A woman feminist has documented men's rapid rise up the "glass escalator" to the top positions in *women's* occupations. Both types of data—that women can do the dangerous work men do and that men doing women's work have the advantage of their dominant gender status—are analyses that came from women's, not men's, feminism.

If men's feminism is to add the dimension of the insider's view, men have to turn the gender lens on themselves in all the arenas where they still dominate—fundamentalist religions, science, politics, the higher echelons of finance, and the capitalist markets of the global economy.

Summary

Men's feminism has brought attention to the fact that men as well as women have a gender status. Men's gender status is dominant in most societies, although there is a hierarchy of dominant and subordinate men. Even though disadvantaged men may be lower on the status scale than dominant men, they are usually dominant over the women of their own group. The analysis of the structure of privilege, as well as the sexist practices and violent behavior that maintain men's dominance, has been dissected and deplored by men's feminism.

In particular, men's feminism has shown that the racial and economic stratification in sports and its culture of violence take a high toll on the players and on aspiring teenagers. A few professional athletes have careers that are rewarding financially and in popularity, but for the most part, the money in sport is made by White, middle-class men. In the health field, the high death rate of young men from poor urban centers and the short life expectancy of older men have been attributed to gendered, racial, ethnic, and economic pressures.

Men's feminism should be distinguished from the men's movements that focus on individual change. From the point of view of men's feminism, bonding with symbolic brothers and fathers and dancing to drums in the woods may make men more emotionally expressive, but it does nothing about the structural sources of gender inequality. Men's feminism also criticizes movements that offer men a rightful place as heads of their families in exchange for the promise of taking responsibility for the welfare of their wives and children. Men's feminism would rather see men and women sharing family work and economic support as equal partners. Men's feminism has also undertaken an active program of anti-rape and anti-battering education.

Men's feminism uses many of the ideas of women's feminism. It focuses on men and masculinity, but with overlaps in research on the body, sexuality, violence, personality development, health, and family relationships. These overlaps make men's feminism an increasingly valuable part of feminist studies.

Suggested Readings in Men's Feminism

Brod, Harry, and Michael Kaufman (eds.). 1994. *Theorizing Masculinities*. Newbury Park, CA: Sage.

Cockburn, Cynthia. 1983. *Brothers: Male Dominance and Technological Change*. London: Pluto Press.

Connell, R. W. 1995. *Masculinities*. Berkeley: University of California Press.

Cornwall, Andrea and Nancy Lindisfarne (eds.). 1994. *Dislocating Masculinity: Comparative Ethnographies*. New York and London: Routledge.

Digby, Tom (ed.). 1998. *Men Doing Feminism*. New York and London: Routledge.

Gerson, Kathleen. 1993. *No Man's Land: Men's Changing Commitments to Family and Work*. New York: Basic Books.

Hearn, Jeff. 1987. *The Gender of Oppression: Men, Masculinity and the Critique of Marxism*. New York: St. Martin's Press.

Hearn, Jeff, and David Morgan (eds.). 1990. *Men, Masculinities and Social Theory*. London: Unwin Hyman.

Herdt, Gilbert. 1981. *Guardians of the Flutes: Idioms of Masculinity*. New York: McGraw-Hill.

Kimmel, Michael S. (ed.). 1991. *Men Confront Pornography*. New York: Meridian.

———. 1996. *Manhood in America: A Cultural History.* New York: Free Press.

Klein, Alan. 1993. *Little Big Men: Body-Building Subculture and Gender Construction.* Albany: State University of New York Press.

Lefkowitz, Bernard. 1997. *Our Guys: The Glen Ridge Rape and the Secret Life of the Perfect Suburb.* Berkeley: University of California Press.

Majors, Richard, and Janet Mancini Billson. 1992. *Cool Pose: The Dilemmas of Black Manhood in America.* New York: Lexington Books.

May, Larry, and Robert A. Strikwerda (eds). 1992. *Rethinking Masculinity: Philosophical Explorations in the Light of Feminism.* Lanham, MD: Rowman and Littlefield.

Messner, Michael A. 1992. *Power at Play: Sports and the Problem of Masculinity.* Boston: Beacon Press.

———. 1997. *Politics of Masculinities: Men in Movements.* Newbury Park, CA: Sage.

Messner, Michael A., and Donald F. Sabo (eds.). 1990. *Sport, Men, and the Gender Order: Critical Feminist Perspectives.* Champaign, IL: Human Kinetics.

Plummer, Kenneth (ed.). 1981. *The Making of the Modern Homosexual.* London: Hutchinson.

Porter, David (ed.). 1992. *Between Men and Feminism.* New York and London: Routledge.

Putnam, Michael. Forthcoming. *Private I's: Investigating Men's Experiences of Pornographies.* Ph.D. dissertation, City University of New York.

Rowan, John. 1987. *The Horned God: Feminism and Men as Wounding and Healing.* New York and London: Routledge.

Sabo, Don, and David Frederick Gordon (eds.). 1995. *Men's Health and Illness: Gender, Power and the Body.* Newbury Park, CA: Sage.

Sanday, Peggy Reeves. 1990. *Fraternity Gang Rape: Sex, Brotherhood, and Privilege on Campus.* New York: New York University Press.

Schwalbe, Michael. 1996. *Unlocking the Iron Cage: The Men's Movement, Gender Politics, and American Culture.* New York: Oxford University Press.

Scully, Diana. 1990. *Understanding Sexual Violence: A Study of Convicted Rapists.* Boston: Unwin Hyman.

Segal, Lynne. 1990. *Slow Motion: Changing Masculinities, Changing Men.* New Brunswick, NJ: Rutgers University Press.

Seidler, Victor J. 1991. *Recreating Sexual Politics: Men, Feminism and Politics.* New York and London: Routledge.

———. 1994. *Unreasonable Men: Masculinity and Social Theory.* New York and London: Routledge.

Staples, Robert. 1982. *Black Masculinity: The Black Male's Roles in American Society.* San Francisco, CA: Black Scholar Press.

Stoltenberg, John. 1990. *Refusing to Be a Man: Essays on Sex and Justice*. New York: Meridian.

——. 1993. *The End of Manhood: A Book for Men of Conscience*. New York: Plume.

Williams, Christine L. 1995. *Still a Man's World: Men Who Do Women's Work*. Berkeley: University of California Press. ✦

Chapter Ten

Social Construction Feminism

Sources of Gender Inequality

- Social construction of gender differences in everyday life.
- Constant re-creation of the boundaries between the genders.
- Gendering of work organizations and the family.

Remedies

- Make the processes of gender construction visible.
- Challenge gender boundaries in everyday life.
- Restructure work and family roles so they are not based on a gendered division of labor.

Contributions

- A theory of gender that connects face-to-face interaction with institutional structures.
- Analysis of the social construction of sexuality and its social control.
- Making the gendered assumptions of the social order visible and changeable.

While multicultural feminism focuses on how women suffer from the effects of a system of racial and ethnic disadvantage, and men's feminism focuses on the hierarchical relationships of men to other men and to women, social construction feminism looks at the structure of the gendered social order as a whole and at the processes that construct and maintain it. Social construction feminism sees gender as a society-wide institution that is built into all the major social organizations of society. As a social institution, gender determines the distribution of power, privileges, and economic resources. Through parenting, the schools, and the mass media, gendered norms and expectations get built into boys' and girls' sense of self as a certain kind of human being. By the time people get to be adults, alternative ways of acting and arranging work and family life are literally unthinkable.

The social construction of gender not only produces the differences between men's and women's characteristics and behavior, it also produces gender inequality by building dominance and subordination into gendered relationships. Yet we cannot stop "doing gender" because it is part of our basic identity. In a social order based on gender divisions, everyone always "does gender" almost all the time. The following excerpt is from an article by Candace West and Don Zimmerman that has become a classic of social construction feminism. It lays out the interconnections between "doing gender" in the course of everyday life and the build-up of both gendered self-identity and gendered social structures.

Doing Gender

Candace West and Don H. Zimmerman

. . . Our purpose in this article is to propose an ethnomethodologically informed, and therefore distinctively sociological, understanding of gender as a routine, methodical, and recurring accomplishment. We contend that the "doing" of gender is undertaken by women and men whose competence as members of society is hostage to its production. Doing gender involves a complex of socially guided perceptual, interactional, and micropolitical activities that cast particular pursuits as expressions of masculine and feminine "natures."

When we view gender as an accomplishment, an achieved property of situated conduct, our attention shifts from matters internal to the individual and focuses on interactional and, ultimately, institutional arenas. In one sense, of course, it is individuals who "do" gender. But it is a situated doing, carried out in the virtual or real presence of others who are presumed to be oriented to its production. Rather than as a property of individuals, we conceive of gender as an emergent feature of social situations: both as an outcome of and a rationale for various social arrangements and as a means of legitimating one of the most fundamental divisions of society.

To advance our argument, we undertake a critical examination of what sociologists have meant by *gender*, including its treatment as a role enactment in the conventional sense and as a "display" in Goffman's (1976) terminology. Both *gender role* and *gender display* focus on behavioral aspects of being a woman or a man (as opposed, for example, to biological differences between the two). However, we contend that the notion of gender as a role obscures the work that is involved in producing gender in everyday activities, while the notion of gender as a display relegates it to the periphery of interaction. We argue instead that participants in interaction organize their various and manifold activities to reflect or express gender, and they are disposed to perceive the behavior of others in a similar light.

To elaborate our proposal, we suggest at the outset that important but often overlooked distinctions be observed among *sex, sex category*, and *gender*. *Sex* is a determination made through the application of socially agreed upon biological criteria for classifying persons as females or males. The criteria for classification can be genitalia at birth or chromosomal typing before birth, and they do not necessarily agree with one another. Placement in a *sex category* is achieved through application of the sex criteria, but in everyday life, categorization is established and sustained by the socially required identificatory displays that proclaim one's membership in one or the other category. In this sense, one's sex category presumes one's sex and stands as proxy for it in many situations, but sex and sex category can vary independently; that is, it is possible to claim membership in a sex category even when the sex criteria are lacking. *Gender*, in contrast, is the activity of managing situated conduct in light of normative conceptions of attitudes and activities appropriate for one's sex category. Gender activities emerge from and bolster claims to membership in a sex category.

We contend that recognition of the analytical independence of sex, sex category, and gender is essential for understanding the relationships among these elements and the interactional work involved in "being" a gendered person in society. . . .

Garfinkel's (1967, pp. 118–40) case study of Agnes, a transsexual raised as a boy who adopted a female identity at age 17 and underwent a sex reassignment operation several years later, demonstrates how gender is created through interaction and at the same time structures interaction. Agnes, whom Garfinkel characterized as a "practical methodologist," developed a number of procedures for passing as a "normal, natural female" both prior to and after her surgery. She had the practical task of managing the fact that she possessed male genitalia and that she lacked the social resources a girl's biography would presumably provide in everyday interaction. In short, she needed to display herself as a woman, simultaneously learning what it was to be a woman. Of necessity, this full-time pursuit took place at a time when most people's gender would be well-accredited and routinized. Agnes had to consciously contrive what the vast majority of women do without thinking. She was not "faking" what "real" women do naturally. She was obliged to analyze and figure out how to act within socially structured circumstances and conceptions of femininity that women born with appropriate biological credentials come to take for granted early on. As in the case of others who must "pass," such as transvestites, Kabuki actors, or Dustin Hoffman's "Tootsie," Agnes's case makes visible what culture has made invisible—the accomplishment of gender. . . .

Doing gender means creating differences between girls and boys and women and men, differences that are not natural, essential, or biological. Once the differences have been constructed, they are used to reinforce the "essentialness" of gender. In a delightful account of the "arrangement between the sexes," Goffman (1977) observes the creation of a variety of institutionalized frameworks through which our "natural, normal sexedness" can be enacted. The physical features of social setting provide one obvious resource for the expression of our "essential" differences. For example, the sex segregation of North American public bathrooms distinguishes "ladies" from "gentlemen" in matters held to be fundamentally biological, even though both "are somewhat similar in the question of waste products and their elimination" (Goffman 1977, p. 315). These settings are furnished with dimorphic equipment (such as urinals for men or elaborate grooming facilities for women), even though both sexes may achieve the same ends through the same means (and apparently do so in the privacy of their own homes). . . .

Can we avoid doing gender? Earlier, we proposed that insofar as sex category is used as a fundamental criterion for differentiation, doing gender is unavoidable. It is unavoidable because of the social consequences of sex-category membership: the allocation of power and resources not only in the domestic, economic, and political domains but also in the broad arena of interpersonal relations. In virtually any situation, one's sex category can be relevant, and one's performance as an incumbent of that category (i.e., gender) can be subjected to evaluation. Maintaining such pervasive and faithful assignment of lifetime status requires legitimation.

But doing gender also renders the social arrangements based on sex category accountable as normal and natural, that is, legitimate ways of organizing social life. Differences between women and men that are created by this process can then be portrayed as fundamental and enduring dispositions. In this light, the institutional arrangements of a society can be seen as responsive to the differences—the social order being merely an accommodation to the natural order. Thus if, in doing gender, men are also doing dominance and women are doing deference (cf. Goffman 1967, pp. 47–95), the resultant social order, which supposedly reflects "natural differences," is a powerful reinforcer and legitimator of hierarchical arrangements. Frye observes:

> For efficient subordination, what's wanted is that the structure not appear to be a cultural artifact kept in place by human decision or custom, but that it appear *natural*—that it appear to be quite a direct consequence of facts about the beast which are beyond the scope of human manipulation. . . . That we are trained to behave so differently as women and men, and to behave so differently toward women and men, itself contributes mightily to the appearance of extreme dimorphism, but also, the *ways* we act as women and men, and the ways we act toward women and men, mold our bodies and our minds to the shape of subordination and dominance. We do become what we practice being. (1983, 34)

If we do gender appropriately, we simultaneously sustain, reproduce, and render legitimate the institutional arrangements that are based on sex category. If we fail to do gender appropriately, we as individuals—not the institutional arrangements—may be called to account (for our character, motives, and predispositions).

Social movements such as feminism can provide the ideology and impetus to question existing arrangements, and the social support for individuals to explore alternatives to them. Legislative changes, such as that proposed by the Equal Rights Amendment, can also weaken the accountability of conduct to sex category, thereby affording the possibility of more widespread loosening of accountability in general. To be sure, equality under the law does not guarantee equality in other arenas. As Lorber (1986, 577) points out, assurance of "scrupulous equality of categories of people considered essentially different needs constant monitoring." What such proposed changes *can* do is provide the warrant for asking why, if we wish to treat women and men as equals, there needs to be two sex categories at all (see Lorber 1986, 577).

The sex category/gender relationship links the institutional and interactional levels, a coupling that legitimates social arrangements based on sex category and reproduces their asymmetry in face-to-face interaction. Doing gender furnishes the interactional scaffolding of social structure, along with a built-in mechanism of social control. In appreciating the institutional forces that maintain distinctions between women and men, we must not lose sight of the interactional validation of those distinctions that confers upon them their sense of "naturalness" and "rightness."

Social change, then, must be pursued both at the institutional and cultural level of sex category and at the interactional level of gender. Such a conclusion is hardly novel. Nevertheless, we suggest that it is important to recognize that the analytical distinction between institutional and interactional spheres does not pose an either/or choice when it comes to the question of effecting social change. Reconceptualizing gender not as a simple property of individuals but as an integral dynamic of social orders implies a new perspective on the entire network of gender relations:

> [t]he social subordination of women, and the cultural practices which help sustain it; the politics of sexual object-choice, and particularly the oppression of homosexual people; the sexual division of labor, the formation of character and motive, so far as they are organized as femininity and masculinity; the role of the body in social relations, especially the politics of childbirth; and the nature of strategies of sexual liberation movements. (Connell 1985, 261)

Gender is a powerful ideological device, which produces, reproduces, and legitimates the choices and limits that are predicated on sex category. An understanding of how gender is produced in social situations will afford clarification of the interactional scaffolding of social structure and the social control processes that sustain it.

References

Connell, R. W. 1985. "Theorizing Gender." *Sociology* 19:260–72.

Frye, Marilyn. 1983. *The Politics of Reality: Essays in Feminist Theory.* Trumans-burg, NY: The Crossing Press.

Garfinkel, Harold. 1967. *Studies in Ethnomethodology.* Englewood Cliffs, NJ: Prentice-Hall.

Goffman, Erving. [1956] 1967. "The Nature of Deference and Demeanor." Pp. 47–95 in *Interaction Ritual.* New York: Anchor/Doubleday.

——. 1976. "Gender Display." *Studies in the Anthropology of Visual Communication* 3:69–77.

——. 1977. "The Arrangement Between the Sexes." *Theory and Society* 4:301–31.

Lorber, Judith. 1986. "Dismantling Noah's Ark." *Sex Roles* 14:567–80.

The family is a prime site for the maintenance of gender differences. In dual-earner families, women do more housework than the men they live with even if they work longer hours and make more money. In most households, women do most of the daily cooking, cleaning, and laundry. Men's jobs around the house are usually outdoor work, repairs, and car maintenance. Keeping your house neat, dressing your children in clean clothes, and feeding your family means you are a good woman. Work for the family not only maintains the household, it also reinforces gender distinctions.

Similarly, whether the husband or the wife is the main economic support of the household, the husband is considered the breadwinner and the wife the "extra" earner. A good man supports his family. His income is allocated to what are considered the necessities—paying the rent or mortgage, paying electric and heating bills, making car payments, buying basic furniture and the groceries. The wife's income goes to the extras the family often cannot do without—school tuition, clothing, bed linens and window curtains—as well as the supposed luxuries like vacations and babysitters. The gendered division of financial responsibility for the family fits neatly into the gendered salary scales in the job market—bosses can justify paying women less because everyone considers a married woman's husband to be the breadwinner. Women who are the sole support of their household and married men who are poor earners particularly suffer from these inequities.

The organization of work reflects these gendered assumptions. The "worker" in a factory or in a bureaucracy is socially a man—someone who does not have daily responsibility for the maintenance of a home or care of children. The structure of work—hours, overtime, travel—as well as pay scales and promotion ladders reflect the assumption that the ideal worker is a man and not a woman. Countries with paid parental leave, such as Sweden and Norway, have had to deliberately allocate "daddy days" that the father must take or they are forfeited in order to ensure that at least some of the parental responsibility is undertaken by men and that men will not be penalized by their employers for taking time off to be with their children.

Authority and political power are highly gendered. Although there have been women heads of state, the very concept of the boss, manager, and commander-in-chief are masculine, so that women in the top positions of authority often become "honorary men." Women who are not so high on the power scale do not have the "status shield" of women presidents, prime ministers, and cabinet members. They have a harder time maintaining their authority. People's behavior in face-to-face interaction constantly constructs and reinforces these gendered beliefs about leadership ability. When people are evaluated highly, the others in their social situation take what they have to say seriously, follow their suggestions, and defer to their judgment. Those who have low status in the eyes of the others are not listened to, their advice is ignored, and their bids for leadership are simply not acknowledged. Status superiors are granted the benefit of the doubt if they make a mistake; status inferiors have to prove their competence over and over again. In order to be an effective leader, people have to follow you. Men are much more likely to have followers than women. That is how gender inequality gets built into the social production of prestige and power. In social construction feminist theory, inequality is the core of gender itself: Women and men are socially differentiated in order to justify treating them unequally. Thus, although gender is intertwined with other unequal statuses, remedying the gendered part of these structures of inequality may be the most difficult, because gendering is so pervasive. Indeed, it is this pervasiveness that leads so many people to believe that gendering is biological, and therefore "natural."

One of the reasons that gender differences seem so natural is that infants are gendered from a very early age. Experimental studies have shown that adults respond differently to an infant depending on whether they are told it is a "girl" or a "boy" (regardless of the actual sex). They offer the child what they think are gender-appropriate toys and are more gentle with "girls" and more likely to rough-house with "boys." Although elementary school teachers today are attuned to the dangers of treating boys and girls differently, they still separate them in class teams and do not encourage their playing together in games or sports. Children who behave in gender-appropriate ways are considered normal; anything else (girls insulting, threatening, and physically fighting boys and other girls; boys who do not like sports and who cry a lot) is considered "gender deviance."

At the end of her influential book on gendered behavior in schools, Barrie Thorne, a sociologist, has a chapter on how adults can deliberately minimize the social construction of gender differences in the classroom and on the playground. This excerpt is taken from that chapter.

Gender Lessons for Adults

Barrie Thorne

One of the most hopeful lessons I have drawn from research on schooling is that gender-related patterns, such as boys participating more actively and receiving more teacher attention than girls in classroom settings, are, at the most, a matter of statistical difference. There is wide individual variation in patterns like readiness to talk in class, and classrooms vary in patterns of teacher-student interaction. Comparing kids' gender relations in different kindergartens, Goodenough found that informal interactions in some classrooms were far less male dominated than in others.[1] *Understanding that gender relations are not fixed and invariant but vary by context can help teachers and aides reflect on their practices and extend those that seem to promote equitable interactions.*

Only one of the teachers whose practices I observed was explicitly concerned about sexism. Mrs. Smith, the Ashton kindergarten teacher, told me that several years before when she was teaching at another school, she had students line up by gender because it was "convenient," but the other kindergarten teacher told her she should discontinue the practice because of Title IX. Soon after, Mrs. Smith attended a Title IX workshop and gave more thought to grouping practices. She shifted to having students form single lines or sort themselves according to criteria like what they liked to eat or the color of their shoes, which, she observed, was a useful way to teach classification. Mrs. Smith occasionally talked to her colleagues about their practices. For example, as they were preparing for the opening of school, she noticed that another teacher was making pink name tags for girls and blue name tags for boys. "That's sexist," she told her colleague, who reflected on it and then shifted to yellow for everyone.[2] Mrs. Johnson, the Ashton second-grade teacher, was unconcerned about and somewhat dismissive of gender issues. "They're just kids," she said when I first met her and she learned of my interest in gender. But her practices were far from neutral. The graphics on her walls were quite stereotyped, and she verbally separated girls and boys with repeated admonitions like "you girls should get busy." On the other hand, although I doubt this was her intent, some of Mrs. Johnson's practices did lessen the salience of gender. For example, she organized permanent classroom seating according to principles like "hearing, sight, height" and thereby increased communication between girls and boys. In contrast, Miss Bailey, the Oceanside fourth-fifth–grade teacher, let her students choose their own seating, which resulted in almost total gender separation. And she ratified the gender divide by pitting boys against girls in math and spelling contests. But when she formed reading groups based on ability and organized lines according to the principle of "hot lunch versus cold lunch," her practices drew girls and boys together.

By setting up contests that pitted boys against girls, Miss Bailey tried to harness gender rivalry as a motivation for learning. The resulting group antagonism sometimes spilled beyond the academic purposes at hand. When kids defined "the girls" and "the boys" as separate and antagonistic groups, primarily in the lunchrooms and on the playgrounds where they were freer to shape the grounds of interaction, they created pockets of trouble for adults intent on maintaining order. In both schools a few noontime aides were responsible for a large number of students. These were part-time, working-class women employees, some of them mothers or aunts of the students. Students called the aides by their first names and were more familiar and informal with them than with most teachers. The aides often had to respond to the combustible, angry feelings and the yelling, taunting, and complaining that accompanied scenes of cross-gender chasing and invasion. Several Ashton aides tried to solve problems of cross-gender hassling by keeping boys and girls totally apart from one another, for example, by banning boys to the grassy playing fields and telling girls to stay near the building. Ironically, efforts to maintain order by separating girls and boys perpetuate the very polarization, the sense of being opposite and antagonistic sides, that sets spirals of hostility into motion in the first place. After a particularly difficult lunch period when a small number of boys continually raised a ruckus, Betty, an Ashton aide, told all the second-grade boys that for the rest of the week they had to sit at a separate table so she could "keep an eye on" them. Talking above the noisy eaters, Betty loudly said to me, "This is my boys' table. I made them sit here. They're wild, but I love every one." When I went over to the girls' table, formed by default when the aide pulled out all the boys, one of the girls volunteered, "The boys have to sit over there; they're naughty." "Yeah, boys are naughty," echoed several other girls with self-righteous tones.

Separating all boys from all girls perpetuates an image of dichotomous difference (all boys as "naughty" and "wild"; all girls as better behaved) and encourages psychological splitting. Pressed by cultural ideals to display themselves as "good" and "nice," girls may displace anger and conflict onto boys, defining them as "naughty." Boys, in turn, may project forbidden feelings of vulnerability and dependence when they taunt girls as "crybabies" and "tattletales."[3] More cross-gender interaction, of the relaxed rather than borderworking kind, would undermine these cycles of projection. When girls and boys are separated, it is easier to objectify and stereotype the other gender.

A few researchers have examined the gender-related practices, and thinking, of teachers, aides, and principals, including the ways in which they think about interactions among gender, race/ethnicity, social class, and age.[4] Clearly the same individual may engage in contradictory actions, and beliefs and actual practices do not always coincide. Within one school, as at Ashton and Oceanside, there will no doubt be an array of beliefs and practices.[5] For example, compared with staff who work mostly in classrooms, playground aides may deal with a different sort of gender imagery, with more emphasis on the physical, such as connections between sports and dominant forms of masculinity. Overall, however, school staff may be less likely to engage in practices that polarize boys and girls if they question the notion of "natural" and dichotomized gender differences (the empirical evidence overwhelmingly counters that notion) and become aware of alternative ways of grouping and interacting with students.

Notes

1. Wilkinson and Marrett, ed., *Gender Influences in Classroom Interaction*; Klein, ed., *Handbook for Achieving Sex Equity Through Education*; and Goodenough, "Small Group Culture and the Emergence of Sexist Behavior."

2. This incident raises a topic that needs more extensive research: how teachers and staff influence one another's gender practices. Feminist teachers report

collegial experiences ranging from acceptance to hostility. See Sara Delamont, *Sex Roles and the School*; R. W. Connell, *Teachers' Work*; and Kathleen Weiler, *Women Teaching for Change: Gender, Class, and Power.*

3. Drawing on research in schools in England, Walkerdine (*Schoolgirl Fictions*) describes this process, She also observed that teachers tended to adulate boys more than girls, "reading" boys as independent, intelligent, and rational as well as, and through displays of, "naughty." In contrast, she found that teachers downplayed the good performance of girls by calling them "hardworking," "boring," and "not brilliant."

4. In *Women Teaching for Change,* Weiler provides a detailed account of the backgrounds, experiences, and daily practices of feminist teachers in public high schools, including the contradictions they face, for example, as White middle-class women teaching Black working-class boys. Also see Connell, *Teachers' Work*, and Delamont, *Sex Roles and the School.*

5. Patricia S. Griffin compares the techniques of three teachers of physical education in the same middle school. Two used practices that assumed that boys and girls are groups with separate and nonoverlapping interests, talents, and physical characteristics. For example, these teachers had all girls use nerf or rubber footballs, while all boys used regular footballs, and they instituted a rule that "a girl must touch the ball before a shot on goal is taken." Some girls, in fact, were bigger and played better than some boys. The third teacher, who had attended a gender equity workshop, used inclusive language (e.g., changing "defenseman" to "defense person"), grouped students by ability or randomly rather than by gender, deliberately chose both girls and boys for leadership positions, and interrupted sexist student interactions. See Griffin, "Teachers' Perceptions of and Responses to Sex Equity Problems in a Middle School Physical Education Program."

References

Delamont, Sara. 1990. *Sex Roles and the School.* Second Edition. New York and London: Routledge.

Goodenough, Ruth G. 1987. "Small Group Culture and the Emergence of Sexist Behavior: A Comparative Study of Four Children's Groups." In *Interpretive Ethnography of Communication,* ed. George Spindler and Louise Spindler, 409–445. Hillsdale, NJ: Lawrence Erlbaum.

Griffin, Patricia S. 1985. "Teachers' Perceptions of and Responses to Sex Equity Problems in a Middle School Physical Education Program." *Research Quarterly for Exercise and Sport* 56: 103–110.

Klein, Susan S. (ed.). 1985. *Handbook for Achieving Sex Equity through Education.* Baltimore: Johns Hopkins University Press.

Walkerdine, Valerie. 1990. *Schoolgirl Fictions.* New York: Verso.

Weiler, Kathleen. 1988. *Women Teaching for Change: Gender, Class, and Power.* South Hadley, MA: Bergin and Garvey.

Wilkinson, Louise Cherry and Cora B. Marrett (eds.). 1985. *Gender Influences in Classroom Interaction.* New York: Academic Press.

Social construction feminism has paid as much attention to how society shapes sexuality as it has to how society creates gendered patterns of behavior. Indeed, from a social construction feminist perspective, sexuality is gendered. Sexual "scripts" differ for women and for men whether they are heterosexual, homosexual, bisexual, transsexual, or transvestite. Linking the experience of physical sex and gendered social prescriptions for sexual feelings, fantasies, and actions are individual bodies, desires, and patterns of sexual behavior, which coalesce into gendered sexual identities. These identities, however various and individualized, are categorized and patterned into socially recognized gendered sexual statuses—heterosexual man, heterosexual woman, homosexual man, lesbian woman, bisexual man, bisexual woman. The relationships and sexual practices expected of women and men in each sexual category differ—you cannot speak of gender-neutral heterosexuals, homosexuals, or bisexuals. In the social construction perspective, the reaction to deviations from established norms of gender and sexuality are manifestations of power and social control. Religion, the law, and medicine reinforce the boundary lines between women and men. Gender rebellion is made sinful, illegal, or insane. However, most people voluntarily go along with their society's prescriptions because the norms and expectations get built into their individual sense of worth and identity. Even transvestites (males who dress in women's clothes and females who dress in men's clothes) and transsexuals (people who have sex-change surgery) try to pass as "normal" men and women. Male cross-dressers tend to wear very feminine-looking clothing, and male transsexuals use hormones to grow breasts. Because contemporary Western men's clothing is acceptable for women to wear, woman have an easier time "passing."

The power of social construction is evident not only in the re-gendering of the bodies and dress of "transgenders," but in what happens to them in work and family roles. Male-to-female transgenders find that the jobs they are hired for as women pay less than those they had as men. Female-to-male transgenders benefit from the "patriarchal dividend"—men's superior social status. Permanent transgenders have to change all of their identity papers, from birth certificates to passports, to be legally recognized in their new gender. If they are married, they have to get divorced. Changing gender is changing one's basic social status.

In the social construction feminist view, long-lasting change of this deeply gendered social order would have to mean a conscious reordering of the gendered division of labor in the family and at work, and at the same time, undermining the assumptions about the capabilities of women and men that justify the status quo. Such change is unlikely to come about unless the pervasiveness of the social institution of gender and its social construction are openly challenged. Since the processes of gendering end up making them invisible, where are we to start? With individual awareness and attitude change, or with restructuring social institutions and behavioral change? Certainly, both individuals and institutions need to be altered to achieve gender equality, but it may be impossible to do both at once.

Critique. Social construction feminism is faced with a political dilemma. Getting people to understand the constrictions of gender norms and expectations and encouraging resistance to them in daily life will not necessarily change social structures. Couples who have set up egalitarian households and who scrupulously share parenting run into work scheduling problems. Men are still supposed to put work before family, and women, family before work. Conversely, getting work organizations to hire men for women's jobs and women for men's jobs has not changed gender norms. Women bosses are criticized for being too assertive, while men teachers, social workers, and nurses are quickly pushed ahead into administration.

The dilemma of structure and action is built into the theory of social construction. Socially patterned individual actions and institutional structures construct and reinforce each other. People constantly re-create and maintain the gender norms and expectations and patterns of behavior that are built into work and family structures. They may resist or rebel, but the main patterns of the gendered social order are very slow to change.

Summary

Social construction feminism focuses on the processes that both create gender differences and render the construction of gender invisible.

The common social processes that encourage us to see gender differences and to ignore overlaps are the gendered division of labor in the home that allocates child care and housework to women; the consensus that only the man is the breadwinner of a family; gender segregation and gender typing of occupations so that women and men do not do the same kind of work; regendering (as when an occupation goes from men's work to women's work and is justified both ways by "natural" masculine and feminine characteristics); selective comparisons that ignore similarities; and containment, suppression, and erasure of gender-inappropriate behaviors and appearances.

Deviations from what is considered normal for boys and girls are subject to disapproval and punishment by parents, teachers, and peers. In adults, attempts at gender rebellion are controlled by laws, religions, and psychiatry.

For the most part, people act in approved-of ways because the whole gendered social order is set up for men and women to feel different and act differently. Even when social institutions change, as when girls are admitted to an all-boys' school or men are hired for a "woman's" job such as nurse, gender boundaries are not erased. Ways are found for the girls to be distinguishable from the boys (skirts, longer hair), and for the men to do more masculine work (nursing men patients, becoming administrators).

The gendered social order constructs not only differences but gender inequality. Appropriately gendered behavior builds up masculine dominance and feminine subordination. The gendered structure of family work puts more of the burden of housework and childcare on the wife, even if she is a high earner in a prestigious career. The gendered division of the labor market reserves better paying jobs and positions of authority for men. All this has been well documented by earlier feminisms. What social construction feminism reveals is how we all collude in maintaining the unequal gendered social order, most of the time without even realizing we are "doing gender." In addition, social construction feminism has analyzed the multiple ways that gender is built into the social structure of all the institutions in a society.

Suggested Readings in Social Construction Feminism

Acker, Joan. 1990. "Hierarchies, Jobs, and Bodies: A Theory of Gendered Organizations." *Gender & Society* 4:139–58.

Berk, Sarah Fenstermaker. 1985. *The Gender Factory: The Apportionment of Work in American Households.* New York: Plenum.

DeVault, Marjorie L. 1991. *Feeding the Family: The Social Organization of Caring as Gender Work.* Chicago: University of Chicago Press.

Fineman, Martha Albertson. 1995. *The Neutered Mother, the Sexual Family and Other Twentieth Century Tragedies.* New York and London: Routledge.

Foucault, Michel. 1978. *The History of Sexuality: An Introduction.* (Trans. by Robert Hurley). New York: Pantheon.

Gagnon, John, and William Simon. 1973. *Sexual Conduct: The Social Sources of Human Sexuality.* Chicago: Aldine.

Goffman, Erving. 1976. *Gender Advertisements.* New York: Harper Colophon.

Greenberg, David F. 1988. *The Construction of Homosexuality.* Chicago: University of Chicago Press.

Kessler, Suzanne J. and Wendy McKenna. 1978. *Gender: An Ethnomethodological Approach.* Chicago: University of Chicago Press.

Kitzinger, Celia. 1987. *The Social Construction of Lesbianism.* Newbury Park, CA: Sage.

Laws, Judith Long, and Pepper Schwartz. 1977. *Sexual Scripts: The Social Construction of Female Sexuality.* New York: Holt, Rinehart and Winston.

Ortner, Sherry B., and Harriet Whitehead (eds.). 1981. *Sexual Meanings: The Cultural Construction of Gender and Sexuality.* Cambridge, UK: Cambridge University Press.

Potuchek, Jean L. 1997. *Who Supports the Family? Gender and Breadwinning in Dual-Earner Marriages.* Stanford, CA: Stanford University Press.

Richardson, Diane (ed.). 1996. *Theorizing Heterosexuality: Telling It Straight.* Buckingham, Gt. Britain: Open University Press.

Risman, Barbara. 1997. *Gender Vertigo: Toward a Post-Gender Family.* New Haven, CT: Yale University Press.

Rubin, Gayle. 1975. "The Traffic in Women: Notes on the Political Economy of Sex." In *Toward an Anthropology of Women,* edited by Rayna R. [Rapp] Reiter, pp. 157–210. New York: Monthly Review Press.

——. 1984. "Thinking Sex: Notes for a Radical Theory of the Politics of Sexuality." In *Pleasure and Danger: Exploring Female Sexuality,* edited by Carole S. Vance, pp. 267–319. Boston: Routledge & Kegan Paul.

Thorne, Barrie. 1993. *Gender Play: Girls and Boys at School.* New Brunswick, NJ: Rutgers University Press.

West, Candace, and Sarah Fenstermaker. 1995. "Doing Difference," *Gender & Society* 9:8–37.

West, Candace, and Don Zimmerman. 1987. "Doing Gender," *Gender & Society* 1:125–151. ✦

Chapter Eleven

Postmodern Feminism and Queer Theory

Sources of Gender Inequality

- The binary division of the social world into privileged and unprivileged gender and sexual categories.
- The taken-for-grantedness of heterosexuality.
- Cultural and individual replication of normative gender.

Remedies

- Deliberately blurring gender and sexual boundaries.
- Constant questioning of what is normal.
- Popular culture that creates "queer" bodies, sexualities, and genders.

Contributions

- The concepts of gender "performativity" and "queerness."
- Making visible the gender and sexual symbolism in mass culture that supports beliefs about what is normal and natural through a method called "deconstruction."
- Making a place for homosexuality, bisexuality, transvestism, and transsexuality to be openly part of Western culture.

Postmodern feminism and queer theory go the furthest in challenging gender categories as dual, oppositional, and fixed. They argue that sexuality and gender are shifting, fluid, multiple categories. They criticize a politics based on a universal category, Woman, and present instead a more subversive view that undermines the solidity of a social order built on two sexes, two sexualities, and two genders. Equality will come, they say, when there are so many recognized sexes, sexualities, and genders that one cannot be played against the other.

Postmodern feminism questions what we think we know about gender, as shown by the following excerpt from a paper originally presented in 1984 at the German Association for American Studies in Berlin. Jane Flax is a political theorist at Howard University and a psychotherapist who writes on feminist theory. This excerpt can be read as summary and critique of many of the previous feminist theories. It takes us to the point at which feminism was when the theories of instability raised by postmodernism seemed to create more questions than answers.

Postmodernism and Gender Relations

Jane Flax

. . . The fundamental purpose of feminist theory is to analyze how we think, or do not think, or avoid thinking about gender. Obviously, then, to understand the goals of feminist theory we must consider its central subject—gender.

Here, however, we immediately plunge into a complicated and controversial morass. For among feminist theorists there is by no means consensus on such (apparently) elementary questions as: What is gender? How is it related to anatomical sexual differences? How are gender relations constituted and sustained (in one person's lifetime and, more generally, as a social experience over time)? How do gender relations relate to other sorts of social relations such as class or race? Do gender relations have a history (or many)? What causes gender relations to change over time? What are the relationships between gender relations, sexuality, and a sense of individual identity? What are the relationships between heterosexuality, homosexuality, and gender relations? Are there only two genders? What are the relationships between forms of male dominance and gender relations? Could/would gender relations wither away in egalitarian societies? Is there anything distinctively male or female in modes of thought and

social relations? If there is, are these distinctions innate or socially constituted? Are gendered distinctions socially useful or necessary? If so, what
are the consequences for the feminist goal of attaining gender justice?

Confronted with such a bewildering set of questions, it is easy to over-
look the fact that a fundamental transformation in social theory has
occurred. The single most important advance in feminist theory is that the
existence of gender relations has been problematized. Gender can no
longer be treated as a simple, natural fact. The assumption that gender
relations are natural arose from two coinciding circumstances: the unex-
amined identification and confusion of (anatomical) sexual differences
with gender relations, and the absence of active feminist movements. . . .

Contemporary feminist movements are in part rooted in transformations in social experience that challenge widely shared categories of social
meaning and explanation. In the United States, such transformations
include changes in the structure of the economy, the family, the place of
the United States in the world system, the declining authority of previously
powerful social institutions, and the emergence of political groups that
have increasingly more divergent ideas and demands concerning justice,
equality, social legislation, and the proper role of the state. In such a
decentered and unstable universe it seems plausible to question one of
the most natural facets of human existence—gender relations. . . .

"Gender relations" is a category meant to capture a complex set of
social processes. Gender, both as an analytic category and a social process,
is relational. That is, gender relations are complex and unstable processes
(or temporary totalities in the language of dialectics) constituted by and
through interrelated parts. These parts are interdependent, that is, each
part can have no meaning or existence without the others.

Gender relations are differentiated and (so far) asymmetric divisions
and attributions of human traits and capacities. Through gender relations
two types of persons are created: man and woman. Man and woman are
posited as exclusionary categories. One can be only one gender, never the
other or both. The actual content of being a man or woman and the rigid-
ity of the categories themselves are highly variable across cultures and
time. Nevertheless, gender relations so far as we have been able to understand them have been (more or less) relations of domination. That is, gender relations have been (more) defined and (imperfectly) controlled by one
of their interrelated aspects—the man.

These relations of domination and the existence of gender relations
themselves have been concealed in a variety of ways, including defining
women as a "question" or the "sex" or the "other" and men as the uni-

versal (or at least without gender). In a wide variety of cultures and discourses, men tend to be seen as free from or as not determined by gender relations. Thus, for example, academics do not explicitly study the psychology of men or men's history. Male academics do not worry about how being men may distort their intellectual work, while women who study gender relations are considered suspect (of triviality, if not bias). Only recently have scholars begun to consider the possibility that there may be at least three histories in every culture—his, hers, and ours. *His* and *ours* are generally assumed to be equivalents, although in contemporary work there might be some recognition of the existence of that deviant— woman (e.g., women's history). However, it is still rare for scholars to search for the pervasive effects of gender relations on all aspects of a culture in the way that they feel obligated to investigate the impact of relations of power or the organization of production.

To the extent that feminist discourse defines its problematic as "woman," it, too, ironically privileges the man as unproblematic or exempted from determination by gender relations. From the perspective of social relations, men and women are both prisoners of gender, although in highly differentiated but interrelated ways. That men appear to be and (in many cases) are the wardens, or at least the trustees within a social whole, should not blind us to the extent to which they, too, are governed by the rules of gender. (This is not to deny that it matters a great deal—to individual men, to the women and children sometimes connected to them and to those concerned about justice—where men as well as women are distributed within social hierarchies.) . . .

One important barrier to our comprehension of gender relations has been the difficulty of understanding the relationship between *gender* and *sex*. In this context, *sex* means the anatomical differences between male and female. Historically (at least since Aristotle), these anatomical differences have been assigned to the class of natural facts or biology. In turn, biology has been equated with the pre- or nonsocial. Gender relations then become conceptualized as if they are constituted by two opposite terms or distinct types of being—man and woman. Since man and woman seem to be opposites or fundamentally distinct types of being, gender cannot be relational. If gender is as natural and as intrinsically a part of us as the genitals we are born with, it follows that it would be foolish (or even harmful) to attempt either to change gender arrangements or not to take them into account as a delimitation on human activities.

Even though a major focus of feminist theory has been to denaturalize gender, feminists as well as nonfeminists seem to have trouble thinking through the meanings we assign to and the uses we make of the concept "natural." What, after all, is the natural in the context of the human world? There are many aspects of our embodiedness or biology that we might see as given limits to human action which Western medicine and science do not hesitate to challenge. . . .

Thus, in order to understand gender as a social relation, feminist theorists need to deconstruct further the meanings we attach to biology/sex/gender/nature. This process of deconstruction is far from complete and certainly is not easy. Initially, some feminists thought we could merely separate the terms *sex* and *gender*. As we became more sensitive to the social histories of concepts, it became clear that such an (apparent) disjunction, while politically necessary, rested upon problematic and culture-specific oppositions, for example, the one between nature and culture or body and mind. As some feminists began to rethink these oppositions, new questions emerged: Does anatomy (body) have no relation to mind? What difference does it make in the constitution of my social experiences that I have a specifically female body?

Despite the increasing complexity of our questions, most feminists would still insist that gender relations are not (or are not only) equivalent to or a consequence of anatomy. Everyone will agree that there are anatomical differences between men and women. These anatomical differences seem to be primarily located in or are the consequence of the differentiated contributions men and woman make to a common biological necessity—the physical reproduction of our species.

However, the mere existence of such anatomical differentiation is a descriptive fact, one of many observations we might make about the physical characteristics of humans. Part of the problem in deconstruction of the meaning of biology/sex/gender/nature is that sex/gender has been one of the few areas in which (usually female) embodiment can be discussed at all in (nonscientific) Western discourses. There are many other aspects of our embodiedness that seem equally remarkable and interesting, for example, the incredible complexity of the structure and functioning of our brains, the extreme and relatively prolonged physical helplessness of the human neonate as compared to that of other (even related) species, or the fact that every one of us will die.

It is also the case that physically male and female humans resemble each other in many more ways than we differ. Our similarities are even more striking if we compare humans to, say, toads or trees. So why ought the anatomical differences between male and female humans assume such significance in our sense of ourselves as persons? Why ought such complex human social meanings and structures be based on or justified by a relatively narrow range of anatomical differences?

One possible answer to these questions is that the anatomical differences between males and females are connected to and are partially a consequence of one of the most important functions of the species—its physical reproduction. Thus, we might argue, because reproduction is such an important aspect of our species life, characteristics associated with it will be much more salient to us than, say, hair color or height.

Another possible answer to these questions might be that in order for humans physically to reproduce the species, we have to have sexual intercourse. Our anatomical differences make possible (and necessary for physical reproduction) a certain fitting together of distinctively male and female organs. For some humans this "fitting together" is also highly desirable and pleasurable. Hence, our anatomical differences seem to be inextricably connected to (and in some sense even causative of) sexuality.

Thus, there seems to be a complex of relations that have associated, given meanings: penis or clitoris, vagina, and breasts (read distinctively male or female bodies), sexuality (read reproduction—birth and babies), sense of self as a distinct, differentiated gender—as either (and only) male or female person (read gender relations as a natural exclusionary category). That is, we believe there are only two types of humans, and each of us can be only one of them.

A problem with all these apparently obvious associations is that they may assume precisely what requires explanation—that is, gender relations. We live in a world in which gender is a constituting social relation and in which gender is also a relation of domination. Therefore, both men's and women's understanding of anatomy, biology, embodiedness, sexuality, and reproduction is partially rooted in, reflects, and must justify (or challenge) preexisting gender relations. In turn, the existence of gender relations helps us to order and understand the facts of human existence. In other words, gender can become a metaphor for biology just as biology can become a metaphor for gender.

Prisoners of Gender

The apparent connections between gender relations and such important aspects of human existence as birth, reproduction, and sexuality make possible both a conflating of the natural and the social and an overly radical distinction between the two. In modern Western culture and sometimes even in feminist theories, the words *natural* and *social* become conflated in our understanding of "woman." In nonfeminist and some feminist writings about women, a radical disjunction is frequently made between the natural and the social. Women often stand for/symbolize the body, "difference," the concrete. These qualities are also said by some feminist as well as nonfeminist writers to suffuse/define the activities most associated with women: nurturing, mothering, taking care of and being in relation with others, preserving. Women's minds are also often seen as reflecting the qualities of our stereotypically female activities and bodies. Even feminists sometimes say women reason and write differently and have different interests and motives than men. Men are said to have more interest in utilizing the power of abstract reason (mind), to want mastery over nature (including bodies), and to be aggressive and militaristic.

The reemergence of such claims even among some feminists needs further analysis. Is this the beginning of a genuine transvaluation of values or a retreat into traditional gendered ways of understanding the world? In our attempts to correct arbitrary (and gendered) distinctions, feminists often end up reproducing them. Feminist discourse is full of contradictory and irreconcilable conceptions of the nature of our social relations, of men and women and the worth and character of stereotypically masculine and feminine activities. The positing of these conceptions such that only one perspective can be correct (or properly feminist) reveals, among other things, the embeddedness of feminist theory in the very social processes we are trying to critique and our need for more systematic and self-conscious theoretical practice. . . .

The enterprise of feminist theory is fraught with temptations and pitfalls. Insofar as women have been part of all societies, our thinking cannot be free from culture-bound modes of self-understanding. We as well as men internalize the dominant gender's conceptions of masculinity and femininity. Unless we see gender as a social relation rather than as an opposition of inherently different beings, we will not be able to identify the varieties and limitations of different women's (or men's) powers and oppressions within particular societies. Feminist theorists are faced with a fourfold task. We need to (1) articulate feminist viewpoints of/within the social worlds in which we live; (2) think about how we are affected by these worlds; (3) consider the ways in which how we think about them may be implicated in existing power/knowledge relationships; and (4) imagine ways in which these worlds ought to and can be transformed.

Since within contemporary Western societies gender relations have been ones of domination, feminist theories should have a compensatory as well as a critical aspect. That is, we need to recover and explore the aspects of social relations that have been suppressed, unarticulated, or denied within dominant (male) viewpoints. We need to recover and write the histories of women and our activities into the accounts and stories that cultures tell about themselves. Yet, we also need to think about how so-called women's activities are partially constituted by and through their location within the web of social relations that make up any society. That is, we need to know how these activities are affected but also how they effect, enable, or compensate for the consequences of men's activities, as well as their implication in class or race relations.

There should also be a transvaluation of values—a rethinking of our ideas about what is humanly excellent, worthy of praise, or moral. In such a transvaluation, we need to be careful not to assert merely the superiority of the opposite. For example, sometimes feminist theorists tend to oppose autonomy to being-in-relations. Such an opposition does not account for adult forms of being-in-relations that can be claustrophobic without autonomy—an autonomy that, without being-in-relations, can easily degenerate into mastery. Our upbringing as women in this culture often encourages us to deny the many subtle forms of aggression that intimate relations with others can evoke and entail. For example, much of the discussion of mothering and the distinctively female tends to avoid discussing women's anger and aggression—how we internalize them and express them, for example, in relation to children or our own internal selves. Perhaps women are not any less aggressive than men; we may just express our aggression in different, culturally sanctioned (and partially disguised or denied) ways.

Since we live in a society in which men have more power than women, it makes sense to assume that what is considered to be more worthy of praise may be those qualities associated with men. As feminists, we have the right to suspect that even praise of the female may be (at least in part) motivated by a wish to keep women in a restricted (and restrictive) place. Indeed, we need to search into all aspects of a society (the feminist critique included) for the expressions and consequences of relations of domination. We should insist that all such relations are social, that is, they are not the result of the differentiated possession of natural and unequal properties among types of persons.

However, in insisting upon the existence and power of such relations of domination, we should avoid seeing women/ourselves as totally innocent, passive beings. Such a view prevents us from seeing the areas of life in which women have had an effect, in which we are less determined by the will of the other(s), and in which some of us have and do exert power over others (e.g., the differential privileges of race, class, sexual preference, age, or location in the world system).

Any feminist standpoint will necessarily be partial. Thinking about women may illuminate some aspects of a society that have been previously suppressed within the dominant view. But none of us can speak for "woman" because no such person exists except within a specific set of (already gendered) relations—to "man" and to many concrete and different women. . . .

Feminist theories, like other forms of postmodernism, should encourage us to tolerate and interpret ambivalence, ambiguity, and multiplicity as well as to expose the roots of our needs for imposing order and structure no matter how arbitrary and oppressive these needs may be.

If we do our work well, reality will appear even more unstable, complex, and disorderly than it does now. In this sense, perhaps Freud was right when he declared that women are the enemies of civilization.

Reprinted from: Jane Flax, "Postmodernism and Gender Relations in Feminist Theory," in *Signs* 12:626–27, 641–43. Copyright © 1987 by The University of Chicago Press. Reprinted by permission.

Postmodern feminism and queer theory examine the ways societies create beliefs about gender at any time (now and in the past) with *discourses* embedded in cultural representations or *texts*. Not just art, literature, and the mass media, but anything produced by a social group, including newspapers, political pronouncements, and religious liturgy, is a *text*. A text's *discourse* is what it says, does not say, and hints at (sometimes called a *subtext*). The historical and social context and the material conditions under which a text is produced become part of the text's discourse. If a movie or newspaper is produced in a time of conservative values or under a repressive political regime, its discourse is going to be different from what is produced during times of openness or social change. Who provides the money, who does the creative work, and who oversees the managerial side all influence what a text conveys to its audience. The projected audience also shapes any text, although the actual audience may read quite different meanings from those intended by the producers. *Deconstruction* is the process of teasing out all these aspects of a text.

The concepts of deconstruction and texts derived from cultural studies may sound quite esoteric, but we are all familiar with these processes. The coverage of Princess Diana's death and funeral created discourses about her—as wife, mother, divorcée, and benefactor. The days before the funeral were full of discourses on the meaning of royalty. Her funeral became a public ritual with a subtext on the proper expression of grief. As spectators, we read ourselves into the text of her life, using parallels with our own lives or fantasies about how we would like to live.

Soap operas and romance novels are "read" by women the way Diana's life was; action films and war novels are the stuff of men's spectatorship. Postmodern feminism deconstructs cultural representations of gender, as seen in movies, videos, TV, popular music, advertising—whether aimed at adults, teenagers, or children—as well as paintings, operas, theater productions, and ballet. All these media have discourses that overtly and subliminally tell us something about female and male bodies, sexual desire, and gender roles. A romantic song about the man who got away glorifies heterosexuality; a tragedy deploring the death of a salesman tells us that men's hard work should pay off. These discourses influence the way we think about our world, without questioning the underlying assumptions about gender and sexuality. They encourage approved-of choices about work, marriage, and having children by showing them as normal and rewarding and by showing what is disapproved of as leading to a "bad end." By unpacking the covert as well as more obvious meanings of texts, postmodern deconstruction reveals their messages. We can then accept or reject them, or use them for our own purposes.

Queer theory goes beyond cultural productions to examine the discourses of gender and sexuality in everyday life. In queer theory, gender and sexuality are *performances*—identities or selves we create as we display ourselves to others. What we wear and how we use our bodies are signs of gender and sexual orientation. Gender and sexuality can be masked, parodied, flaunted, played with, and mixed up any way we want. Recently, in the audience at an academic lecture was a young man with a conventional haircut but with orange hair, one long earring, dark red lipstick, blue nail polish on fingers and toes, a unisex black T-shirt, a yellow sarong skirt of the kind worn by men and women in tropical resorts, and clunky open-toed sandals. Queer theorists have explored whether such mixed gender displays create a freer social space.

Cross-dressing for "drag" performances, costume parties, Mardi Gras, and gay pride parades are displays of queerness, deliberately playing with gender and sexuality. But when a male transvestite or transsexual wants to be "read" as woman, he wears a demure dress, stockings, and high-heeled shoes. Someone whose looks are unconventionally gendered and who does not want to be forced to conform is in a painfully ambiguous status. The lady with a beard is stared at openly on the street and can find work only in a circus.

Is the circus, night club, or theater the only place gender can be defied? Or can we be gender rebels or *queers* in everyday life? The following excerpt is by one of the chief proponents of queer theory. Eve Kosofsky Sedgwick is a literary critic and poet who has written about ambiguities and "closets" in literature and in recent history. Here, she shows how normative social reality is created, and how questioning the linked binary components of gender and sexuality subverts, or queers, that reality.

What's Queer?

Eve Kosofsky Sedgwick

What's "queer"? Here's one train of thought about it. The depressing thing about the Christmas season—isn't it?—is that it's the time when all the institutions are speaking with one voice. The Church says what the Church says. But the State says the same thing: maybe not (in some ways it hardly matters) in the language of theology, but in the language the State talks: legal holidays, long school hiatus, special postage stamps, and all. And the language of commerce more than chimes in, as consumer purchasing is organized ever more narrowly around the final weeks of the calendar year, the Dow Jones aquiver over Americans' "holiday mood." The media, in turn, fall in triumphally behind the Christmas phalanx: ad-swollen magazines have oozing turkeys on the cover, while for the news industry every question turns into the Christmas question—Will hostages be free *for Christmas?* What did that flash flood or mass murder (umpty-ump people killed and maimed) do to those families' *Christmas?* And meanwhile, the pairing "families/Christmas" becomes increasingly tautological, as families more and more constitute themselves according to the schedule, and in the endlessly iterated image, of the holiday itself constituted in the image of "the" family.

The thing hasn't, finally, so much to do with propaganda for Christianity as with propaganda for Christmas itself. They all—religion, state, capital, ideology, domesticity, the discourses of power and legitimacy—line up with each other so neatly once a year, and the monolith so created is a thing one can come to view with unhappy eyes. What if instead there were a practice of valuing the ways in which meanings and institutions can be at loose ends with each other? What if the richest junctures weren't the ones where *everything means the same thing?* Think of that entity "the family," an impacted social space in which all of the following are meant to line up perfectly with each other:

a surname

a sexual dyad

a legal unit based on state-regulated marriage

a circuit of blood relationships

a system of companionship and succor

a building

a proscenium between "private" and "public"

an economic unit of earning and taxation

the prime site of economic consumption

the prime site of cultural consumption

a mechanism to produce, care for, and acculturate children

a mechanism for accumulating material goods over several generations

a daily routine

a unit in a community of worship

a site of patriotic formation

And of course the list could go on. Looking at my own life, I see that—probably like most people—I have valued and pursued these various elements of family identity to quite differing degrees (e.g., no use at all for worship, much need of companionship). But what's been consistent in this particular life is an interest in not letting very many of these dimensions line up directly with each other at one time. I see it's been a ruling intuition for me that the most productive strategy (intellectually, emotionally) might be, whenever possible, to *dis*articulate them one from another, to *dis*engage them—the bonds of blood, of law, of habitation, of privacy, of companionship and succor—from the lockstep of their unanimity in the system called "family."

Or think of all the elements that are condensed in the notion of sexual identity, something that the common sense of our time presents as a unitary category. Yet, exerting any pressure at all on "sexual identity," you see that its elements include your biological (e.g., chromosomal) sex, male or female;

your self-perceived gender assignment, male or female (supposed to be the same as your biological sex).

the preponderance of your traits of personality and appearance, masculine or feminine (supposed to correspond to your sex and gender);

the biological sex of your preferred partner;

the gender assignment of your preferred partner (supposed to be the same as her/his biological sex);

the masculinity or femininity of your preferred partner (supposed to be the opposite* of your own);

your self-perception as gay or straight (supposed to correspond to whether your preferred partner is your sex or the opposite);

your preferred partner's self-perception as gay or straight (supposed to be the same as yours);

your procreative choice (supposed to be yes if straight, no if gay);

your preferred sexual act(s) (supposed to be insertive if you are male or masculine, receptive if you are female or feminine);

your most eroticized sexual organs (supposed to correspond to the procreative capabilities of your sex, and to your insertive/receptive assignment);

your sexual fantasies (supposed to be highly congruent with your sexual practice, but stronger in intensity);

your main locus of emotional bonds (supposed to reside in your preferred sexual partner);

your enjoyment of power in sexual relations (supposed to be low if you are female or feminine, high if male or masculine);

the people from whom you learn about your own gender and sex (supposed to correspond to yourself in both respects);

your community of cultural and political identification (supposed to correspond to your own identity);

---

* The binary calculus I'm describing here depends on the notion that the male and female sexes are each other's "opposites," but I do want to register a specific demurral against that bit of easy common sense. Under no matter what cultural construction, women and men are more like each other than chalk is like cheese, than ratiocination is like raisins, than up is like down, or than one is like zero. The biological, psychological, and cognitive attributes of men overlap with those of women by vastly more than they differ from them.

And—again—many more. Even this list is remarkable for the silent presumptions it has to make about a given person's sexuality, presumptions that are true only to varying degrees, and for many people not true at all: that everyone "has a sexuality," for instance, and that it is implicated with each person's sense of overall identity in similar ways; that each person's most characteristic erotic expression will be oriented toward another person and not autoerotic; that if it is alloerotic, it will be oriented toward a single partner or kind of partner at a time; that its orientation will not change over time. Normatively, as the parenthetical prescriptions in the list above suggest, it should be possible to deduce anybody's entire set of specs from the initial datum of biological sex alone—if one adds only the normative assumption that "the biological sex of your preferred partner" will be the opposite of one's own. With or without that heterosexist assumption, though, what's striking is the number and *difference* of the dimensions that "sexual identity" is supposed to organize into a seamless and univocal whole.

And if it doesn't?

That's one of the things that "queer" can refer to: the open mesh of possibilities, gaps, overlaps, dissonances and resonances, lapses and excesses of meaning when the constituent elements of anyone's gender, of anyone's sexuality aren't made (or *can't be* made) to signify monolithically. The experimental linguistic, epistemological, representational, political adventures attaching to the very many of us who may at times be moved to describe ourselves as (among many other possibilities) pushy femmes, radical faeries, fantasists, drags, clones, leatherfolk, ladies in tuxedoes, feminist women or feminist men, masturbators, bulldaggers, divas, Snap! queens, butch bottoms, storytellers, transsexuals, aunties, wannabes, lesbian-identified men or lesbians who sleep with men, or . . . people able to relish, learn from, or identify with such.

Again, "queer" can mean something different: a lot of the way I have used it so far in this dossier is to denote, almost simply, same-sex sexual object choice, lesbian or gay, whether or not it is organized around multiple criss-crossings of definitional lines. And given the historical and contemporary force of the prohibitions against *every* same-sex sexual expression, for anyone to disavow those meanings, or to displace them from the term's definitional center, would be to dematerialize any possibility of queerness itself.

At the same time, a lot of the most exciting recent work around "queer" spins the term outward along dimensions that can't be subsumed under gender and sexuality at all: the ways that race, ethnicity,

postcolonial nationality crisscross with these *and other* identity-constitut-
ing, identity-fracturing discourses, for example. Intellectuals and artists of
color whose sexual self-definition includes "queer"—I think of an Isaac
Julien, a Gloria Anzaldúa, a Richard Fung—are using the leverage of
"queer" to do a new kind of justice to the fractal intricacies of language,
skin, migration, state. Thereby, the gravity (I mean the *gravitas*, the meaning, but also the *center* of gravity) of the term "queer" itself deepens and
shifts. . . .

Critique. If social construction feminism puts too much emphasis on
institutions and structures and not enough on individual actions or
agency, postmodern feminism and queer theory have just the opposite
problem. In queer theory, all the emphasis is on agency, impression
management, and presentation of the self in the guise and costume most
likely to produce or parody conformity. Postmodern feminism is mainly
concerned with deconstructing cultural productions, neglecting the more
iron-bound and controlling discourses embedded in organizational,
legal, religious, and political texts.

Social construction feminism's analyses of the institutional and organizational practices that maintain the gender order could be combined
with postmodern feminist and queer theory's deconstruction of how
individuals do and undo gender. Social construction feminism argues
that the gendered social order is constantly restabilized by individual
action, but queer theory has shown how individuals can consciously and
purposefully create disorder and gender instability, opening the way to
social change. However, the underlying gendered social order is stub-
bornly persistent. A postmodern feminism called *materialist feminism*
combines marxist analysis of patriarchal and capitalist institutions with
deconstruction of the symbolic, cultural superstructure that idealizes,
masks, and justifies the underlying and controlling structures of gender
and heterosexuality. For example, elaborate traditional weddings are cultural displays that reinforce romantic heterosexuality. They mask the
economics as well as the patriarchal expectations of traditional families.
When gay men and lesbians have similarly elaborate weddings, queer
theorists point out that they unmask and subvert their "heterogendered"
meanings.

Summary

Postmodern feminism and queer theory question all the conventional assumptions about gender and sexuality, arguing that the categories of "man," "woman," "heterosexual," "homosexual," "male," "female" are performances and displays. Like social construction feminism, postmodern feminism claims that gender is created in the doing—the way we dress, use our bodies, talk, behave. But postmodern feminists do not focus on the social structures that are built up out of repeated gender performances. They argue that gender and sexuality are always in flux, never fixed. There are no permanent identities, making identity politics questionable.

Politically, postmodern feminists are interested in deconstructing the messages we get about gender and sexuality in the mass media, popular culture, and the arts. These messages or texts are subliminal sermons on how to be a man, a woman, and how each should be heterosexually sexy. If we can see through these messages, we can, if we want, reject or modify them.

Queer theory advocates going even further in destabilizing gender and sexuality. Queer theorists parody and play with gender and sexuality. A drag queen, who parodies femininity, and Marilyn Monroe and Madonna, who exaggerate their sexuality, are equally queer examples of female impersonators. Queer politics disturbs what we think is normal and natural. In queer theory, a body can be female and male at the same time, as when a preoperative transsexual uses hormones to grow breasts but still has a penis. Bisexuality upsets the heterosexual-homosexual division. And genders can be as numerous as the imagination can dream up.

Postmodern feminism and queer theory are playful but have the serious intent of making us think about what we take for granted—that men and women, homosexuals and heterosexuals, males and females are totally different creatures, and that we can't make and remake ourselves.

Suggested Readings in Postmodern Feminism and Queer Theory

Beemyn, Brett, and Mickey Eliason (eds.). 1996. *Queer Studies: A Lesbian, Gay, Bisexual, and Transgender Anthology*. New York: New York University Press.

Bornstein, Kate. 1994. *Gender Outlaw: On Men, Women, and the Rest of Us*. New York: Vintage.

Butler, Judith. 1990. *Gender Trouble: Feminism and the Subversion of Identity.* New York and London: Routledge.

DeLauretis, Teresa. 1984. *Alice Doesn't: Feminism, Semiotics, Cinema.* Bloomington: Indiana University Press.

Epstein, Julia, and Kristina Straub. 1991. *Body Guards: The Cultural Politics of Gender Ambiguity.* New York and London: Routledge.

Feinberg, Leslie. 1996. *Transgender Warriors: Making History from Joan of Arc to Dennis Rodman.* Boston: Beacon Press.

Flax, Jane. 1990. *Thinking Fragments: Psychoanalysis, Feminism, and Postmodernism in the Contemporary West.* Berkeley: University of California Press.

Garber, Marjorie. 1992. *Vested Interests: Cross-Dressing and Cultural Anxiety.* New York and London: Routledge.

———. 1995. *Vice Versa: Bisexuality and the Eroticism of Everyday Life.* New York: Simon and Schuster.

———. 1998. *Symptoms of Culture.* New York and London: Routledge.

Hennessey, Rosemary. 1993. *Materialist Feminism and the Politics of Discourse.* New York and London: Routledge.

Herdt, Gilbert (ed.). 1994. *Third Sex, Third Gender: Beyond Sexual Dimorphism in Culture and History.* New York: Zone Books.

Ingraham, Chrys. 1999. *White Weddings: Romancing Heterosexuality in Popular Culture.* New York and London: Routledge.

Jacobs, Sue-Ellen, Wesley Thomas, and Sabine Lang. 1997. *Two-Spirit People: Native American Gender Identity, Sexuality, and Spirituality.* Urbana: University of Illinois Press.

Kates, Gary. 1995. *Monsieur d'Eon Is a Woman: A Tale of Political Intrigue and Sexual Masquerade.* New York: Basic Books.

Mann, Patricia S. 1994. *Micro-Politics: Agency in a Post-Feminist Era.* Minneapolis: University of Minnesota Press.

Nicholson, Linda J. (ed.). 1990. *Feminism/Postmodernism.* New York and London: Routledge.

Sedgwick, Eve Kosofsky. 1990. *Epistemology of the Closet.* Berkeley: University of California Press.

———. 1993. *Tendencies.* Durham, NC: Duke University Press.

Seidman, Steven. 1997. *Difference Troubles: Queering Social Theory and Sexual Politics.* Cambridge, UK: Cambridge University Press.

Walters, Suzanna Danuta. 1995. *Material Girls: Making Sense of Feminist Cultural Theory.* Berkeley: University of California Press.

Warner, Michael (ed.). 1993. *Fear of a Queer Planet: Queer Politics and Social Theory.* Ann Arbor: University of Michigan Press.

Whisman, Vera. 1996. *Queer by Choice: Lesbians, Gay Men and the Politics of Difference.* New York and London: Routledge.

Woodhouse, Annie. 1989. *Fantastic Women: Sex, Gender, and Transvestism.* New Brunswick, NJ: Rutgers University Press. ✦

Part V

Feminist Theories of the Body

The New Nature-Nurture Debates

A constant thread in modern feminist theory has been the question of the source and stability of sex differences. If they are "natural," it is felt that there is not much to be done about altering them, but a lot could be done to make sure that the differences are not the legitimation for unequal legal rights or oppressive practices. The politics of difference, however, ends up in attempts to determine what treatment is equitable, given what seems to be a substantially wide and unbridgeable gap between male and female "natures." As Catharine MacKinnon says,

> Socially one tells a woman from a man by their difference from each other, but a woman is discriminated against on the basis of sex only when she can first be said to be the same as man. A built-in tension exists between this concept of equality, which presupposes sameness, and this concept of sex, which presupposes difference. Sex equality becomes a contradiction in terms, something of an oxymoron. (1990, 215)

To get out of this bind, many feminists argued that women and men aren't all that different naturally but are made so by social pressures; therefore, they should be treated equally. The most famous "nurture"

213

statement is Simone De Beauvoir's "One is not born, but rather becomes, a woman" (1953, 267). Social constructionist feminists have invoked as proofs that gender is made by society the ability of transsexuals to change their whole gendered persona from woman to man or man to woman, the successful gender development of intersexuals with ambiguous genitalia who grow up in assigned gender identities that do not match their chromosomes (XXs living as men, XYs living as women), the way transvestites with normal genitalia can pass for much of their lives as members of the "opposite sex," and the multiple genders in non-Western societies (Herdt 1994). A conceptual distinction has been made between physical genitals and "cultural genitals" (the assumed body beneath feminine or masculine clothing). Professional sports and the Olympics were also cited as proof of how men's and women's bodies are shaped by cultural values, training regimens, and opportunities for competition (Hargreaves 1994). In so-called "normals," gender has also been seen as a performance that establishes and reinforces identity (Butler 1990).

But more recently, these social constructions of gender seemed to crumble. Transsexuals once again began to insist that if their bodies did not dictate their gender, their brains did, and intersexuals want their gender identities to match their genes rather than their surgically constructed genitalia (Gagné and Tewksbury 1998, Turner 1999). Transvestism has turned into drag—performances of masculinity and femininity that do not deny but use female and male bodies as a counterpoint to opposite-gender costumes (Ekins 1997). The feminist contention that women's sports performances were gradually catching up with men's and might even surpass them has been tempered by a closer statistical analysis, which contends that women's rapid record-breaking in running and swimming is likely to level off soon and never surpass men's speeds (Wainer, Nju, and Palmer 2000).

The case of the male child who was gender-reassigned and raised as a girl after a botched circumcision destroyed his penis, who then chose to become a boy when he became a teenager, seems to clinch the argument that biology trumps socialization (Colapinto 1997). Money and Ehrhardt (1972) claimed that this case was a natural experiment in whether one could raise a male as a girl because the child in question had an identical twin, who was being raised as a boy. But this case can be read as the rejection of a devalued gender status as much as it can the inevitable emergence of bodily and psychological hard-wiring.

The child chose to reject the reassigned sex status on reaching puberty, when hormones and further genital surgery were prescribed by doctors to create additional feminization. According to the original account of the case, the mother said early on that her gender-reassigned daughter was a tomboy (Money and Ehrhardt 1972, 118–123). But the mother had also been a tomboy, and she acknowledged that the behavior she was imposing on her daughter was more restrictive than what she demanded of her son. Femininity never had any appeal for "Joan." Colapinto (1997, 68) quotes Joan's identical twin brother as saying,

> "When I say there was nothing feminine about Joan," Kevin laughs, "I mean there was nothing feminine. She walked like a guy. She talked about guy things, didn't give a crap about cleaning house, getting married, wearing makeup. . . . We both wanted to play with guys, build forts and have snowball fights and play army."

Enrolled in Girl Scouts, Joan was miserable:

> I remember making daisy chains and thinking, "If this is the most exciting thing in Girl Scouts, forget it," Joan says. "I kept thinking of the fun stuff my brother was doing in Cubs."

Is this rejection of conventional "girl things" the result of internal masculinization or the gender resistance of a rebellious child? Being a man is a preferred status in many societies, so it is not surprising for those with ambiguous genitalia to prefer that gender identity (Herdt and Davidson 1988). More research needs to be done on the life histories of intersexed adolescents and adults in today's less gender-fixed climate to see to what extent they have chosen to go against their sex assignment as infants and how their lives compare to transsexuals who opt to have genital surgery to change their sex.

Theories of the Sources of Sex Differences

The sources of bodily and behavioral differences between females and males are no longer thought to be just chromosomes, hormones, or even genes, because these can all produce ambiguously sexed bodies. Scientists sought for a different source for the clear-cut gender identities of "normals," as well as for the people with normal genitalia and hormone production who insisted that the feeling that their gender identity did not match their bodies started very early in life. This same source might also explain why some homosexuals argue that their sexual orientation had so early an onset and was so deep-seated that it couldn't be the result of life experiences.

Currently, the biological source of gender identity and gendered behavior is believed to be brain organization. Organization theory, which goes back to 1959, argues that the male brain is organized or "hard-wired" for masculinity by prenatal androgens produced by the fetal testicles. The female brain is organized for subsequent feminine behavior by maternal and fetal estrogen input. Organization theory was widely adopted by psychologists and neuroendocrinologists and became textbook knowledge by the 1960s. Yet since the 1930s, there has been evidence that human development in males and females depends on both estrogens and androgens. Furthermore, in the 1970s, it was found that "male" hormones had to be converted to "female" hormones before "masculinizing" the brain. Information about the hormonal "mixed bag" hit the newspapers as new knowledge in the 1990s, concurrent with now-accepted ideas of the overlap of masculinity and femininity.

Organization theory was popular with animal researchers because it provided a method for showing the effects of prenatal hormones on mature sexual behavior. Pregnant rats were administered large doses of testosterone or estrogen, which resulted in altered sexual behavior in the offspring—mounting in females and sexual receptivity in males. These results were extrapolated to human sexuality, as a theory of the origin of homosexuality, and by extension to stereotypical gendered behavior, including skills and career choice. The theory of "brain sex" suppressed evidence of male-female behavioral overlaps in humans and in animals, and did not allow for social factors in the gendering of human behavior. In fact, there was a great deal of effort to separate out the biological from the social causes of masculinity and femininity in the search for "bedrock" origins. Interactive models and bio-social perspectives did not emerge until the 1980s. They were, in part, a reflection of the work done by a developing sociology of the body, which argued for a loop-back interchange of bodily, behavioral, environmental, and social structural factors.

Another theoretical source of inbred gendered behavior, this time expressed through genetic inheritance, is evolutionary adaptation going back hundreds of thousands of years to when humans lived in gathering and hunting tribes. Evolutionary psychology theory argues that the behavior prehistoric humans needed to survive is still ingrained in our genes. These survival adaptations are supposedly expressed even today in men's roaming, predatoriness, and sexual promiscuity and in women's nesting, nurturing, and sexual loyalty.

There are three problems with this argument that today's gendered behavior is the product of yesterday's evolution. First, haven't humans continued to evolve? Haven't women and men had to adapt to changing technologies, environments, and social structures? Second, humans don't behave instinctively, but think through how they will act in different situations and in encounters with different people. Third, much of the received wisdom about prehistoric adaptations is biased by gender stereotypes and by data based only on male subjects.

For example, a recent study of responses to stress found that adult women don't have a "fight-or-flight" response, but rather a "tend-and-befriend" reaction (Taylor et al. 2000). In situations provoking fear or anxiety, men tend to stand and defend themselves physically, or run away to protect themselves. Women often seek out support from other people, or they protectively look after their children. Since most of the subjects of research on stress responses were men, this alternative behavior was virtually unknown. The biological source of stress responses in men is testosterone; in women it is oxytocin, the same hormone that induces labor in childbirth and milk let-down in breast-feeding. There is also a social explanation for these sex differences in stress-response behavior. Women usually have children to protect, and so their responses may be psychologically or socially induced, and the high oxytocin levels may be an effect of maternal protectiveness rather than a cause of it—or there may be, more plausibly, a loop-back effect. Similarly, in men, aggression raises testosterone levels and these raised levels in turn produce more aggressiveness.

Body Politics

The debate is thus much more complex than "nature versus nurture." What is "nature" for humans is female and male reproductive systems and secondary sex characteristics, the human genome, the evolution of human bodies, the evolution of human psyches; for you it is your individual body, your genetic package, your brain. What is "nurture" is your life experiences, the social milieu of similarly located people, the culture of your society at a specific point in time, and the physical environment in which you live most of your life. What we are as material bodies is the result of all the "natural" and "nurtured" input working together and affecting each other.

The politics surrounding the "nature versus nurture" debates is similarly complex. If there is not a simple or single answer to the question of whether sex differences are genetic, hormonal, long-term evolutionary adaptations, or recently learned behavior, then there isn't a simple or single way of determining how much or how little can be changed by new social patterns. Rather than accepting whatever the status quo is for their time and place as natural and unchangeable, feminists have pushed for social changes and have shown that women's and men's bodies and behaviors are indeed natural—but quite changeable.

To say the body is socially constructed is not to deny its material reality or universality. Bodies are born and bodies die. Testicles produce sperm and ovaries produce eggs. Female mammals gestate and give birth; male mammals do not. Male bodies usually have less body fat and more muscle than female bodies. But when we ask about the physical capacities of human men and women, we are asking questions about social practices and judgments that vary by culture and ethnicity, time and place, and are different for the rich and the poor. Our bodies are socially constructed in material and cultural worlds, in nourishing and in depriving physical environments, under conditions of freedom and constraint. As R.W. Connell says,

> Body-reflexive practices . . . are not internal to the individual. They involve social relations and symbolism; they may well involve large-scale institutions. Particular versions of masculinity [and femininity] are constituted in their circuits as meaningful bodies and embodied meanings. Through body-reflexive practices, more than individual lives are formed: a social world is formed. (1995, 64)

What Do Bodies "Mean"?

Bodies have different meanings in different cultures. In some cultures, no man wants a thin bride—fat shows health, wealth, and fertility. Looking at the different sports in the Olympics, we can see many different body types produced by selection, training, and, unfortunately, the use of muscle-enhancing drugs. These diverse bodies are the result of the requirements of various sports and override gender—burly women and men shot-putters look a lot the same, and both look quite different from women and men gymnasts. Nonathletes, too, come in many different sizes and shapes, many of them self-constructed. The popularity of gyms and home exercise equipment reflects our culture's preoccupation with the "perfect body." That preoccupation is not surprising, because people whose bodies look like what is admired are themselves admirable for having stayed thin and gotten toned. By judging, rewarding, and shaming people of different body sizes, shapes, weights, and musculature, members of a social group persuade and coerce each other to construct socially acceptable bodies.

Gender is one of the most significant factors in the transformation of physical bodies into social bodies. In Western culture, dieting, breast enhancement, and face lifts are ways that women have changed their appearance to fit ideals of feminine beauty, while men lift weights, get hair transplants, and undergo cosmetic surgery to mold their bodies and faces to a masculine ideal. These practices may lead to illnesses, such as eating disorders, infections, and systemic damage from drug use or leaking silicone implants, but by themselves, they are not considered abnormal because they are responses to culturally idealized views of how women's and men's bodies should look.

In the following excerpt from the Introduction to a book of readings called *Embodied Practices*, Kathy Davis, a sociologist who has written a book about how women use cosmetic surgery to make themselves look "normal," discusses these issues of power and domination, agency and resistance, and cultural meanings in social practices that shape bodies. She advises feminists to remember that bodies are not abstractions, but the site of experiences and practices that locate us in a culturally nuanced physical world.

Embody-ing Theory

Kathy Davis

Feminist scholarship on the body invariably links women's embodied experience with practices of power. From the sexualization of the female body in advertising to the mass rape of women in wartime, women's bodies have been subjected to processes of exploitation, inferiorization, exclusion, control and violence. The female body is symbolically deployed in discourses of power—discourses which justify social inequality and power hierarchies based on gender and other forms of bodily difference.

Although power is standard fare for any feminist perspective on the body, these perspectives vary, depending on how the body is conceptualized (as material entity, as text or as negotiated practice) or the kind of theoretical framework which is used to account for the social, cultural and symbolic conditions of feminine embodiment (Davis 1995).

Initially, feminist scholars regarded power as a fairly straightforward matter of male domination and female subordination in a patriarchal social order (Davis et al. 1991). Feminist scholarship focused on how women's bodies have been regulated, colonized, mutilated or violated. Women were viewed as the victims of oppression and all women were oppressed in and through their bodies. The female body in all its materiality was regarded as the primary object through which masculinist power operated. A feminist body/politics was advocated which attacked all oppressive body practices and ideologies. The aim was, ultimately, to provide directions for collective forms of resistance. A set of specifically feminist aesthetics or empowering alternatives to the patriarchal body regimes was proposed to help individual women to develop more "authentic" and empowering relationships to their bodies.

In the wake of the "linguistic turn," the focus in feminist theory on the body shifted from women's experience of oppression to how images of the female body were implicated in power relations. Drawing upon Foucauldian notions on power, the female body became a text which could be read as a cultural statement about gender/power relations. The concern for commonality in women's bodily practices was replaced by a preoccupation with the multiplicity of cultural meanings which could be attributed to the female body, notably through scientific texts, the popular media or everyday common sense. Emphasis shifted from power as exploitation, coercion or manipulation to the subtle, pervasive and ambiguous processes of discipline and normalization through cultural representations. Given our 'embeddedness' in cultural discourses which define the female body as inferior and in need of constant surveillance, it was not surprising that the focus became collusion and compliance rather than collective forms of (feminist) protest.

Susan Bordo (1993) provides one of the most thorough and powerful cultural readings of how domination is enacted upon and through female bodies. She explores how cultural constructions of femininity intersect with the Cartesian legacy of mind-over-matter and contemporary body discourses of control and mastery to produce a normalizing politics of the body. Caught between the tensions of consumer culture, the cultural ambivalence toward female appetites and the backlash against women's power, women in Western culture believe that by controlling or containing their bodies and their appetites, they can escape the pernicious cycle of insufficiency, of never being good enough. They can take on "male" power—power-as-self-mastery—and, paradoxically, feel empowered or liberated by the very bodily norms and practices which constrain or enslave them. While Bordo acknowledges women's possibilities for resistance, she is deeply skeptical about using notions like choice, freedom or agency to describe women's interactions with their bodies. Ostensibly liberatory practices are constantly in danger of being "reabsorbed" in the dominant cultural discourse of liberal individualism. While Bordo admits that the "old" oppressor/oppressed model of power needs to be replaced with a more sophisticated understanding of power, she warns feminists to keep their sights firmly fixed on the systematic, pervasive and repressive nature of modern body cultures. In our present "culture of mystification"—a culture which constantly entices us with false promises of power and pleasure—we need to be concerned with domination rather than freedom and with constraint rather than choice.

Female Agents and Subversive Bodies

While domination has been the primary theoretical focus of feminist perspectives on the body, it is not without its drawbacks. Some feminists have argued that a one-sided attention to the constraints of the body culture obscures women's active and—at least to some extent—knowledgeable engagement with their bodies. Others have claimed that the symbolic possibilities for a transgressive body politics have been given short shrift within feminist body theory. Taken together, these critiques have introduced the notions of agency and subversion into feminist scholarship on the body.

The first strand of scholarship has attempted to redress the imbalance in feminist theory on the body by producing a wealth of empirical studies which explore the active role individuals play in contemporary body regimes. . . .

At a theoretical level, attempts have been made to conceptualize agency and the female body. Dorothy Smith (1990) has, for example, posited the notion of women as "secret agent" behind the gendered discourses of femininity. When women confront cultural discourses which instruct them that their bodies are inferior, a gap is created between the body as deficient and the body as an object to be remedied. Dissatisfaction becomes an active process, whereby women engage with their bodies as an object of work, for "doing femininity." The notion of biographical agency has been elaborated in Davis (1995). By exploring women's struggles with cultural discourses of feminine beauty and their ambivalence in deciding to have their bodies altered surgically, a framework is developed for understanding bodily practices like cosmetic surgery as both an expression of the objectification of the female body and an opportunity to become an embodied subject.

In the second strand of thought, attention has shifted from agency and the mundane embodied practices of individuals to symbolic possibilities of subverting cultural gender norms through the body. It is argued that practices like cross-dressing, "gender bending" or transsexuality disrupt or subvert the homogenizing cultural norms of gender. The example of Madonna, the female body builder or the male transvestite are potential sources of "gender trouble" (Butler, 1989), precisely because they upset our normative conceptions of the appropriate female or male body and provide inspiration for a transgressive body politics (Epstein and Straub 1991; Garber 1992; Halberstam and Livingstone 1995). While these practices may themselves shore up stereotypical notions of femininity (the drag queen being a case in point) and are not necessarily empowering for the individuals who engage in them, they do create symbolic space. It is the possibility for experimenting with alternative identities which has fired the imagination of many feminist scholars, providing the theoretical impetus for a (post)feminist perspective on the body. . . .

Embodied Theory

Feminists can now, together with critical male academics, create a truly embodied science—a science which takes account of the body in everyday life as well as in social theory.

Unfortunately, a second look shows that such relief on the part of feminists would be premature. The body may be back, but the new body theory is just as masculinist and disembodied as it ever was. While it acknowledges the importance of feminism in helping to make the body a topic, actual feminist scholarship on the body is notably absent from much of the literature within the "new body theory." . . .

Feminist theory on the body provides an essential corrective to the masculinist character of much of the "new" body theory precisely because it takes difference, domination and subversion as starting points for understanding the conditions and experiences of embodiment in contemporary culture. Bodies are not generic but bear the markers of culturally constructed difference. Understanding what embodiment means to individuals depends upon being able to sort out how sexual, "racial" and other differences intersect and give meaning to their interactions with their bodies and through their bodies with the world around them. Conditions of embodiment are organized by systemic patterns of domination and subordination, making it impossible to grasp individual body practices, body regimes and discourses about the body without taking power into account. By assuming that the theorist is also embodied, feminist theory opens up possibilities for exploring new ways of doing theory—ways which use embodiment as a theoretical resource for an explicitly corporeal epistemology or ethics (Braidotti 1994; Grosz 1994; Gatens 1996).

This raises the question whether feminist scholarship, which—in contrast to (male-)stream body theory—introduced gender/power relations to the analysis of the body, has also created theoretical frameworks which are embodied. . . . [There are] two problems which in my view stand in the way of developing embodied theories on the body.

The first problem concerns the grounding of theories on the body in the concrete embodied experiences and practices of individuals in the social world. While there has been a wealth of feminist scholarship devoted to exploring the particularities of embodiment, recent feminist theory on the body has displayed a marked ambivalence towards the material body and a tendency to privilege the body as metaphor. Priority is given to the deconstructive project—that is, to dismantling the mind/body split in Western philosophy or debunking gendered symbols and dichotomies rather than to attending to individuals' actual material bodies or their everyday interactions with their bodies and through their bodies with the world around them.

Bodies are not simply abstractions, however, but are embedded in the immediacies of everyday, lived experience. Embodied theory requires interaction between theories about the body and analyses of the particularities of embodied experiences and practices. It needs to explicitly tackle the relationship between the symbolic and the material, between representations of the body and embodiment as experience or social practice in concrete social, cultural and historical contexts.

The second problem concerns the reflexivity of theorizing the body. As topic, the body evokes a range of emotions among feminist scholars, ranging from unease and ambivalence to passion and fascination. Like any theory on the body, feminist theory is entangled in a set of irresolvable tensions which emerge in the wake of contradictions between modernist and postmodernist projects (Frank 1990). It is essential, for example, to deconstruct the body as bedrock of sexual difference, but also to validate difference in order to do justice to individuals' embodied experiences. It is necessary to focus on the systematic features of domination as enacted through the female body (Bordo 1993), but also to uncover the myriad ways that women engage in subversion, in and through their bodies. And, it is mandatory that feminist scholarship takes an explicitly political stance, but also avoids being moralistic or overly political, thereby ignoring the aesthetic features of contemporary body practices.

It seems to me—and here I agree with Frank—that feminist theory needs to be less concerned with achieving theoretical closure and more interested in exploring the tensions which the body evokes. This would entail using the tensions evoked by the contradictions mentioned above as a resource for further theoretical reflection. It would mean embracing rather than avoiding those aspects of embodiment which disturb and/or fascinate us as part and parcel of our theories on the body. In the process of becoming more self-conscious and reflexive, feminist theory on the body will also become more embodied.

References

Bordo, Susan. 1993. See Suggested Readings.

Braidotti, Rosi. 1994. *Nomadic Subjects: Embodiment and Sexual Difference in Contemporary Feminist Theory.* New York: Columbia University Press.

Davis, Kathy. 1995. See Suggested Readings.

Davis, Kathy, Monique Leijenaar, and Jantine Oldersma. 1991. *The Gender of Power.* London: Sage.

Epstein, Julia and and Kristina Straub (eds.). 1991. *Body Guards: The Cultural Politics of Gender Ambiguity.* New York and London. Routledge.

Frank, Arthur W. 1990. "Bringing Bodies Back In: A Decade Review." *Theory, Culture & Society* 7:131–62.

Garber, Marjorie. 1992. *Vested Interests: Cross-Dressing and Cultural Anxiety.* New York: Routledge, Chapman and Hall.

Gatens, Moira. 1996. See Suggested Readings.

Grosz, Elizabeth. 1994. See Suggested Readings.

Halberstam, Judith, and Ira Livingstone (eds.). 1995. *Posthuman Bodies.* Bloomington: Indiana University Press.

Smith, Dorothy. 1990. *Texts, Facts and Femininity. Exploring the Relations of Ruling.* London and New York: Routledge.

How Bodies Change

We cannot talk about "the" female or male body, because bodies change over a lifetime. Not just aging, but physical and social experiences are absorbed by our bodies and our brains and these in turn change our bodies and our brains.

Anne Fausto-Sterling is a biologist who has been an important influence on feminist thinking about the body through her 1985 book, *Myths of Gender*. The following excerpt is from her new book, *Sexing the Body*. In it, she critiques the research that uses simplistic definitions of masculinity and femininity to prove that gendered behavior is hard-wired into the brain. But she goes further, developing an argument that led her to postulate five sexes in 1993—male, female, male and female pseudohermaphrodites, and intersexuals. Her contention today is that even those categories are too rigid. She argues now that sex is a continuum, that genitalia come in many sizes and shapes, and that our body's changeability over a lifetime belies the contention that we have a biological unity fixed before birth and determining our lives from then on.

Sexual Anatomy and Reproduction

Anne Fausto-Sterling

During our lives, the brain changes as part of a dynamic developmental system that includes everything from nerve cells to interpersonal interactions. In principle, we can apply similar concepts to gonads and genitals. The gonads and genitals developed during fetal development continue to grow and change shape during childhood, affected by such things as nutrition, health status, and random accidents. At puberty anatomic sex expands to include not only genital differentiation but also secondary sex characteristics, which in turn depend not only on nutrition and general health but also on levels of physical activity. For example, women who train for long-distance events lose body fat, and below a certain fat-to-protein ratio, the menstrual cycle shuts down. Thus, gonadal structure and function respond to exercise and nutrition levels, and of course they also change during the life cycle.

Not only does sexual physiology change with age—so, too, does sexual anatomy. I don't mean that a penis drops off or an ovary dissolves, but that one's physique, one's anatomical function, and how one experiences one's sexual body change over time. We take for granted that the bodies of a new-born, a twenty-year-old, and an eighty-year-old differ. Yet we persist in a static vision of anatomical sex. The changes that occur throughout the life cycle all happen as part of a biocultural system in which cells and culture mutually construct each other. For example, competitive athletics leads both athletes, and a larger public who emulate them, to reshape bodies through a process that is at once natural and artificial. Natural, because changing patterns of diet and exercise change our physiology and anatomy. Artificial, because cultural practices help us decide what look to aim for and how best to achieve it. Furthermore, disease, accident, or surgery—from the transformations undergone by surgical transsexuals, to the array of procedures (applied to secondary sexual characteristics) that include breast reduction or enlargement and penile enlargement—can modify our anatomic sex. We think of anatomy as constant, but it isn't; neither, then, are those aspects of human sexuality that derive from our body's structure, function, and inward and outward image.

Reproduction also changes throughout the life cycle. As we grow, we move from a period of reproductive immaturity into one during which procreation is possible. We may or may not actually have children (or actually be fertile, for that matter), and when and how we choose to do so will profoundly affect the experience. Motherhood at twenty and at forty, in a heterosexual couple, as a single parent, or in a lesbian partnership is not a singular, biological experience. It will differ emotionally and physiologically according to one's age, social circumstance, general health, and financial resources. The body and the circumstances in which it reproduces are not separable entities. Here again something that we often think of as static changes across the life cycle and can be understood only in terms of a biocultural system.[1]

In their book *Rethinking Innateness*, the psychologist Jeffrey Elman and his colleagues ask why animals with complex social lives go through long periods of postnatal immaturity, which would seem to present big dangers: "vulnerability, dependence, consumption of parental and social resources." "Of all primates," they note, "humans take the longest to mature."[2] Their answer: long periods of development allow more time for the environment (historical, cultural, and physical) to shape the developing organism. Indeed, development within a social system is the sine qua non of human sexual complexity. Form and behavior emerge only via a dynamic system of development. Our psyches connect the outside to the inside (and vice versa) because our multi-year development occurs integrated within a social system.[3]

Notes

1. For analyses of embodiment during pregnancy and of the effects of new technologies of fetal visualization on the embodiment of pregnancy, see Young 1990, chapter 9, and Rapp 1997.
2. Elman et al. 1996, pp. 354, 365.
3. Elman and colleagues acknowledge their intellectual debt to other system theorists.

References

Elman, J. L., E. A. Bates et al. 1996. *Rethinking Innateness: A Connectionist Perspective on Development.* Cambridge,MA: MIT Press.

Rapp, R. "Real Time Fetus: The Role of the Sonogram in the Age of Monitored Reproduction." Pp. 31–48 in *Cyborgs and Citadels,* edited by G. L. Downey and J. Dumit. Santa Fe, NM: School of American Research Press.

Young, I. M. 1990. *Throwing Like a Girl and Other Essays in Feminist Philosophy and Social Theory.* Bloomington: Indiana University Press.

Genders and Genitalia

Intersexuals are born with ambiguous genitalia, looking neither clearly male nor female. They also frequently have divergent combinations of chromosomes, hormones, and physiology, whose effects may not show up until puberty. In Western societies, infants with ambiguous genitalia are assigned a sex and usually undergo "clarifying" surgery; they are then brought up in the assigned sex. Current research has shown that for intersexuals, not only is gender socially constructed, but sex is as well.

Suzanne Kessler, a psychologist, interviewed pediatric plastic surgeons working with intersexed infants and found that what sex the child with ambiguous genitalia is assigned depends on the size of the penis/clitoris. According to her research, only if the surgeon feels that he (and it is usually a he) can make an adequate-sized penis will the child be made into a boy; otherwise, the sex assignment will be "female." Kessler points out that this social determination of the sex of the child and its construction through surgery is masked by medical rhetoric. The doctors' message to the parents is that the child has a true sex that is female or male, and that the surgery is needed to make the anomalous genitals match the true sex. In actuality, the sex is socially constructed, because the child usually ends up with a combination of male and female biology but is designated male or female and socialized in the norms of the assigned sex and gender.

In the last few years, there has been an intersex movement that protests against "clarifying" surgery on infants. This movement argues that such surgery is genital mutilation that ruins future sexual pleasure. The following excerpt from Kessler's book, *Lessons from the Intersexed,* discusses alternative ways intersexuality can be perceived that discourage arbitrary sex assignment and surgery to make the external genitals match. She goes on to imagine gender categories that are not based on genitalia, and, going further, doing away with gender categories altogether.

The Future of Intersex

Suzanne J. Kessler

What would it take for larger-than-typical clitorises, absent vaginas, smaller-than-typical penises, off-center urinary openings, and irregularly shaped scrota and labia to become acceptable markers of gender? Where would such a genital reconceptualization start and how would it impact on ideas about gender? In other words, how can what we mean by a female or a male be given more latitude?

Even physicians who manage intersexuality in the traditional way reveal that it might be possible to see and name things otherwise: "Detailed examination [of a two-day-old infant's genitals] showed a structure . . . that *could be perceived as either a clitoris or a micropenis* "[1](my emphasis). If the determination is to assign the infant to the female gender, based on internal reproductive structure (a return to nineteenth-century criteria), the genital would be called a clitoris. If the determination is to assign the infant to the male gender, the genital would be called a penis. In neither case would surgery be required; rhetoric would be.[2]

I propose two very different options for talking about what is now known as "intersexuality." One would be to confront intersexuality directly. Physicians would not be so quick to normalize the condition for parents but would help them acknowledge and deal with having an intersexed child and with prejudices about gender. In support groups conducted by adult intersexuals like those belonging to the Intersex Society of North America (ISNA), parents would be encouraged to explore their often unstated concerns: Will my intersexed daughter be a lesbian if she has a large clitoris or XY chromosomes? Will my intersexed son be a real man if he has a small penis? What does it mean to have a child who is legitimately different from other children?

If one looks, one can find some examples of parents ready to hear a new philosophy. There are the parents of a young girl who, when told about her XY chromosomal pattern, her absent vagina, and her diagnosis of androgen-insensitivity syndrome (AIS), responded: "Wow—how interesting! She's really special. Let's see what we can find out about this."[3] In a sample of boys and men with micropenises, those able to make the best adjustments had parents who thought the appearance of the penis was satisfactory and conveyed this to their sons.[4]

The medical literature, which is sprinkled with words like "trauma" and "tragedy" and cautionary tales of parents failing to abide by medical recommendations, is silent on "the wide variety of (often positive) responses to what one might see as a death sentence."[5] Obviously, in order for physicians to adopt a new stance, they would need to examine their own gender-related assumptions in the context of a major cultural shift in gender beliefs.

The second way of talking differently about intersexuality would involve not seeing it. By this I do not mean that physicians would shelter parents from intersexuality while believing in it themselves. This is how the situation is currently normalized. Rather, I mean that physicians would refuse to give intersexuality credibility, even for themselves. By bracketing the existence of intersexuality, they would be left with only genitals that might not even be noteworthy beyond their initial signal of an underlying medical condition. That it is possible to ignore or reinterpret conventional signs of intersexuality is evidenced by those men with diagnosable but "uncorrected" hypospadias and their sexual partners who were unaware of any penile "deformity."[6]

This second way of managing atypical genitals actually builds upon current medical practices. Physicians know that they have to be careful about the language they use with parents. For example, they refrain from using the terms "hermaphrodite" or "intersex" because the meanings of those terms are so emotionally loaded. To talk in a new way about intersexuality would involve being even more mindful about language. Instead of referring to a girl's clitoris as "masculinized," or her chromosomes as "male," the girl would be described as having a clitoris larger than most, or labia more fused than most, or having XY chromosomes.[7] The doctor would convey expertise by telling parents, "That's not a penis on your daughter. It doesn't have a urethral tube or meatus." Given this script, it is not guaranteed that parents would always decide against surgical alteration, but they could at least make a more measured decision if they were led to see that what was being discussed was a cosmetic issue and not a gender one. Cosmetic issues are issues that lay persons can reasonably have an opinion about and disagree with surgeons about, but gender issues are not, or at least not yet.

Genital variability can continue to be seen as a condition to be remedied or in a new way—as an expansion of what is meant by female and male. Whether the meaning one imparts to genital variability reifies gender or trivializes it has important implications for gender and intersex management. We need to consider different possibilities about how to manage intersexuality, including the possibility of not managing it at all.

The future of intersex is in some sense the future of gender. In whose hands is this future? The parents of intersexed infants have the legal responsibility, but they take their cues from the medical professionals, whose status permits them to define the "real" view of intersexuality, relegating other views, like the political intersexuals', to a fringe perspective.[8] Self-help groups could provide parents with an alternative interpretation of their situation, thus altering their relationship to the medical community and to intersexuality. Viewing their child's "condition" in some of the ways I have been proposing will give parents the strength to authorize as little surgery and as much honesty as necessary. Through more honest discussions of gender, parents may find some common ground with political intersexuals within the transgender movement, a force that has the potential for bending (if not breaking) the gender system.

Any revolution in thinking about gender hinges on understanding that there is no one best way to be a male or a female or any other gender possibility—not even in terms of what is between your legs. . . .

Treating genital formations as innate but malleable, much like hair, would be to take them and gender less seriously. In the acceptance of genital variability and gender variability lies the subversion of both genitals and gender. Dichotomized, idealized, and created by surgeons, genitals mean gender. A belief in two genders encourages talk about "female genitals" and "male genitals" as homogenous types, regardless of how much variability there is within a category.[9] Similarly, the idea of "intersexed" masks the fact that "intersexed genitals" vary from each other as much as they vary from the more idealized forms.

Although it is unlikely that the nontransgender public will embrace an intersexed gender in the near future, as I have shown, people are capable of accepting more genital variation. Accepting more genital variation will maintain, at least temporarily, the two-gender system, but it will begin to unlock gender and genitals. Ultimately, the power of genitals to mark gender will be weakened, and the power of gender to define lives will be blunted.

By subverting genital primacy, gender will be removed from the biological body and placed in the social-interactional one. Even if there are still two genders, male and female, how you "do" male or female, including how you "do" genitals, would be open to interpretation[10]. Physicians teach parents of intersexed infants that the fetus is bipotential, but they talk about gender as being "finished" at sixteen or twenty weeks, just because the genitals are. Gender need not be thought of as finished, not for people who identify as intersexed, nor for any of us. Once we dispense with "sex" and acknowledge gender as located in the social-interactional body, it will be easier to treat it as a work-in-progress.

This is assuming, though, that gender is something worth working on. It may not be. If intersexuality imparts any lesson, it is that gender is a responsibility and a burden—for those being categorized and those categorizing. We rightfully complain about gender oppression in all its social and political manifestations, but we have not seriously grappled with the fact that we afflict ourselves with a need to locate a bodily basis for assertions about gender. We must use whatever means we have to give up on gender. The problems of intersexuality will vanish and we will, in this way, compensate intersexuals for all the lessons they have provided.

Notes

1. Theresa Quattrin, Susan Aronica, and Tom Mazur, "Management of Male Pseudohermaphroditism: A Case Report Spanning Twenty-One Years," *Journal of Pediatric Psychology* 15, no. 6 (1990):701.

2. That surgeries are performed as a way of avoiding speech is illustrated by a group of surgeons who explain that both the clitoral glands and shaft in girls must be reduced because "failure to do so will leave a button of unsightly tissue that requires further explanation at some point by the parent, child, and surgeon" (Stanley Kogan, Paul Smey, and Selwyn B. Levitt, "Reply by Authors," *The Journal of Urology* 130[October 1983]: 748.)

3. *ALIAS* (newsletter of the Androgen Insensitivity Support Group) 1, no. 5 (summer 1996): 4.

4. Reilly, J. M. and C. R. J. Woodhouse, "Small Penis and the Male Sexual Role." *The Journal of Urology* 142 (August 1989): 569–71.

5. *ALIAS* 1, no. 5 (summer 1996): 4.

6. Fichtner, J., et al., "Analysis of Meatal Location in 500 Men: Wide Variation Questions Need for Meatal Advancement in All Pediatric Anterior Hypospadias Cases." *The Journal of Urology* 154 (August 1995): 883–84.

7. Some parents are advised to tell their XY daughters that one of her chromosomes has a short arm. Although this is an inventive, nongendered way of describing her "male-pattern" chromosomes, it is not exactly what I am advocating as a different script, since the physicians and parents both "know" it is XY (really male) and are collaborating in a way to obscure it from the daughter.

8. In cases of intersexuality, it is not guaranteed that parents will follow physicians' interpretations and advice. In one case, a couple was counseled that their fetus was most probably an XX male. Despite medical advice to continue the pregnancy (because physicians expected that the child would be normal, even though sterile), the "distressed" parents decided to terminate the pregnancy. Bernard LeFiblec, Author's Reply to "Termination of XX Male Fetus," *The Lancet* 343 (7 May 1994): 1165.

9. One adult (nonintersexed) female, in reflecting upon her genitals, demonstrates that genital variability is available for analysis if we look and ask: "As a child I thought [I had] an unusual looking genital area. . . . [W]hile other little girls seemed to have a neat little crack in front, I had a wider crack and skin (labia) coming out. I was enormously relieved when pubic hair covered up this anomaly. . . . I never discussed this with anyone."

10. Using the verb *do* to emphasize the social-constructed nature of gender was introduced by Candace West and Don H. Zimmerman in the paper "Doing Gender," *Gender and Society* 1 (1987): 125–51.

Disabilities and Gender

Much of the research and theory on social bodies considers only physically able bodies or those whose bodies have been enhanced by athletic training and weight lifting or modified by chosen surgical practices, such as liposuction, breast reduction or implants, and penis enlargement. Consideration of those who are born with physical anomalies or whose bodies are altered by illness or accident has only recently moved from medical and psychological studies to sociological analysis of their *social bodies.*

In a review of research on gendering in people with disabilities, Judith Lorber, who has written on gender and Western medical systems, found that women and men whose disabilities allow similar levels of physical functioning have very different life chances. Women are less likely to find jobs that allow them to be economically independent. They are also less likely to have a lifetime partner, because they need the care and attention that women are expected to give to others. They may be better able to find a life partner or a circle of women caregivers if they are lesbian. Heterosexual women with disabilities, however, may find the fulfillment of traditional wife-mother gender roles beyond reach. The opposite situation occurs for men with disabilities. They are more likely to find a life partner, a woman if they are heterosexual, a man if they are gay. In the traditional husband role, care received is recompensed with economic support, so as long as a man with disabilities can earn an income, he can fulfill his family role obligations. In short, as the following excerpt from "Gender Contradictions and Status Dilemmas in Disability" shows, if you add the dimension of disabled bodiedness to gender and sexuality, you get very different data than if you look only at able-bodied women and men.

Toward a Continuum of Bodiedness

Judith Lorber

The conventional norms of femininity have locked women with disabilities into a paradoxical situation—as women, it is all right for them to be helpless and dependent, but, because they are disabled, they are unlikely to have a man to take care of them. Feminists have argued that norms of independence and economic self-support provide a better model for all women, and that giving women with disabilities the means to accomplish these goals would go a long way to enhancing their self-esteem and quality of life (Asch and Fine 1988).

For men with disabilities, the change has to come in challenges to conventional masculinity. Men could expand their options by having different kinds of relationships rather than overburdening one caregiving woman. Both women and men might welcome group living, but it would have to be autonomous and without restrictions on sexual coupling and children.

Gender expectations and assumptions are harder to change than the physical environment and job requirements. If social groups parcel out roles on the basis of gender, then identity as a woman and a man are tied to being able to fulfill these gender-appropriate roles. Looking at the problem of masculinity and physical disability in the lives of 10 men, Thomas Gerschick and Adam Stephen Miller (1994) discovered three strategies: reliance on conventional norms and expectations of manhood, reformulation of these norms, and creation of new norms. The men who relied on the predominant ideals of masculinity felt they had to demonstrate physical strength, athleticism, sexual prowess and independence. Their self-image was tied to heroics and risk-taking, but they often felt inadequate and incomplete because they couldn't do what they wanted or go where they wanted. The men who reformulated these norms defined their ways of coping with their physical limitations as demonstrations of strength and independence. For example, two quadriplegics who needed round-the-clock personal care assistants did not feel they were dependent on others, but had hired helpers whom they directed and controlled. The men who rejected the standard version of masculinity put more emphasis on relationships than on individual accomplishments, were comfortable with varieties of sexuality, and felt they were nonconformists.

To erase the status dilemmas of women and men with physical disabilities, conventional norms about bodies, functions, beauty and sexuality need to be re-examined (Asch and Fine 1988; Wendell 1992). Making the experiences of women and people of color visible forced a reconsideration of stereotypes of normality and otherness; similarly, because "physically disabled people have experiences which are not available to the able-bodied, they are in a better position to transcend cultural mythologies about the body" (Wendell 1992, 77). Few people are as beautiful as movie stars or as muscular as body builders. A woman without arms or legs claimed the statue of Venus de Milo as her model of beauty (Frank 1988). Orgasms can be felt in many parts of the body other than the genitals. Races can be run in wheelchairs as well as on foot, on horses, on bicycles and in cars.

Bodies matter to the person with pain, limited mobility and sensory difficulties, but the way they matter is also a social phenomenon (Butler 1993; Wendell 1992). One answer to the status contradictions imposed on people with disabilities is to discard the concept of "other." A study of nondisabled people who had long-term relationships with people with extremely severe disabilities found that the "partnership" was based on a sense of essential humanity and full integration into each other's social space (Bogdan and Taylor 1989). Ability and disability, bodily integrity and bodily dysfunction and standards of beauty are all relative. The variety of bodies and social environments make all of us part of a complex continuum of able-bodiness, just as the variety of women and men calls into question gender stereotypes.

References

Asch, A., and M. Fine. 1988. "Introduction: Beyond Pedestals." In *Women with Disabilities: Essays in Psychology, Culture, and Politics,* edited by M. Fine and A. Asch. Philadelphia: Temple University Press.

Frank, G. 1988. "On Embodiment: A Case Study of Congenital Limb Deficiency in American Culture." In *Women with Disabilities: Essays in Psychology, Culture, and Politics,* edited by M. Fine and A. Asch. Philadelphia: Temple University Press.

Gerschick, T. J., and A. S. Miller. 1994. "Gender Identities at the Crossroads of Masculinity and Physical Disability." *Masculinities* 2: 34–55.

Wendell, S. 1992. "Toward a Feminist Theory of Disability." In *Feminist Perspectives in Medical Ethics,* edited by H. B. Holmes and L. M. Purdy. Bloomington, IN: University Press.

Mothering and Evolution

The theory of evolution is that bodies and behavior must be adaptive if a species is to survive. Success in survival involves living long enough to pass on one's genes, which will replicate the successfully adapted bodies and behavior. Sara Blaffer Hrdy, an anthropologist who has studied primates and written about human evolution, claims that this story downplays purposeful action on the part of mothers that is necessarily varied because human environments vary. In *Mother Nature,* Blaffer Hrdy argues that prehistorically, historically, and in the present, "every female who becomes a mother does it her way" (p. 79). A mother's goal is not so much to get the best man's genes to pass on as to ensure the survival of her "best" children—the healthiest, liveliest, and fattest—those with the best chance of living to adulthood. To do so, she may abandon, kill, or fail to feed sickly children, twins, or deformed infants. She will certainly recruit *alloparents* to help her care for and raise her children— older children, other women in her kin group and community, and fathers. In the following excerpt, Blaffer Hrdy describes these and other maternal strategies.

The Effects of Maternal Decisions

Sarah Blaffer Hrdy

Mothers have always had to make the most of resources at hand while coping with the sliding scale of paternal and alloparental help available. Mothers make tradeoffs compatible with their own subsistence, the needs of different children, and their own future reproductive prospects. These tradeoffs are made in a world of constantly shifting constraints and options. In foraging societies, for example, suckling infants are far more costly than older children, who are at least mobile. Not so in our own increasingly technological society, where costs of child-rearing (for example, college tuition) go up—not down—with the child's age.[1]

Some mothers encounter completely novel options—like breast milk for hire in the eighteenth century, or new birth technologies in the twentieth—that allow women forty-five and older to give birth. A woman who postponed reproduction in the Pleistocene was probably waiting out a famine, or looking forward to a situation with more stable allomaternal assistance. In the twenty-first century, career women will count on amniocentesis, in vitro fertilization, and procedures combining the DNA in their own eggs with cytoplasmic material from a younger woman's eggs to keep reproducing beyond their prime reproductive years. Such techniques will reduce risks to a woman from delaying reproduction (allowing her to achieve a desired professional or social status prior to bearing children), but are likely to introduce other risks or tradeoffs yet unknown.

No social creature, even the most independent woman, makes such decisions in a vacuum. In addition to laws, technologies, and protection from environmental hazards, there are today, as in the past, people both more and less powerful than the mother herself who shape the reproductive options available to her. Now, as in the past, mothers do not live in any one type of family arrangement. Nor is there any one species-typical level of maternal commitment to infants. Without question, historical context matters a great deal. But to interpret variation in the way mothers respond to infants as meaning that somehow a woman's biology is irrelevant to her emotions, or that there are no evolved maternal responses, is to misread both the human record and a vast amount of evidence for other animals.

No one suggests that the hundreds of thousands of mothers in eighteenth-century Europe who sent babies to wet nurses, or the mothers who abandoned infants outright at foundling homes, were typical of all mothers at all times. In a state of ecological release, in which the costs of caring impinge far less on the mother's health and well-being, mothers can afford the luxury of loving each baby born. This is especially likely to be so when women have the inestimable privilege of consciously planning when births will occur. Nevertheless, the "unnatural" mothers chronicled here can only be the visible tip of an iceberg of maternal ambivalence that left no record.

These nuances of maternal emotions and the many "little decisions" mothers make are rarely measurable. For every mother who abandons her infant outright, there have to be thousands of other mothers who abjured such draconian remedies yet nevertheless fell short of commitment in ways that lowered infant viability.

Legacy of Ambivalence

And what does this degree of ambivalence mean for the notion of "maternal instinct"? So long as we are clear about what we mean, there is no reason not to use the shorthand instinctive to describe the adoration of their babies that mothers feel. Like all primate females, women and girls find babies utterly enticing and attractive, and most are eager to hold and care for them. This is especially likely to be true of a recent mother because of the hormonal changes during pregnancy and birth that lower her threshold for forming an affiliative bond with an especially attractive (in terms of its smell and odd appearance) little stranger, and such bonds intensify during lactation. Virtually all female primates, if they remain in close proximity to a small baby long enough, learn to recognize and form an attachment to that particular baby.

Every human mother's response to her infant is influenced by a composite of biological responses of mammalian, primate, and human origin. These include endocrinal priming during pregnancy; physical changes (including changes in the brain) during and after birth; the complex feedback loops of lactation; and the cognitive mechanisms that enhance the likelihood of recognizing and learning to prefer kin. *But almost none of these biological responses are automatic.* To survive over evolutionary time, all of these systems had to pass through the evolutionary crucible. . . . [of costs versus benefits]. One way or another, whether the cue is fat deposits that influence activation of the ovaries, or signals indicating that social support is forthcoming, probable costs and potential benefits are factored in. In humans, whose infants are so costly, and for whom conscious planning (thanks to the neocortex) is a factor, maternal investment in offspring is complicated by a range of utterly new considerations: cultural expectations, gender roles, sentiments like honor or shame, sex preferences, and the mother's awareness of the future. Such complexities do not erase more ancient predispositions to nurture. All the systems in this messy composite are vetted according to costs, benefits, and genetic relatedness to the infant recipient of altruistic maternal acts. But none of this guarantees perfect synchrony between systems. We should not be surprised that conflicting motivations emerge at both conscious and unconscious levels, in ambivalent maternal emotions psychoanalyst Rozsika Parker sums up as feeling "torn apart."[2]

We are still far from understanding how genetically influenced receptors in the brain, thresholds for responding to different chemical signals, hormone levels, and feelings of anxiety or contentment interact to produce the myriad "decisions" that continuously affect maternal commitment. Yet this fact remains: human infants are so vulnerable and dependent for so long a time, that the level of commitment to them by the close relative on the spot at birth, primed to care, and lactating, is the single most important component of infant well-being.

Throughout human evolution, the mother has been her infant's niche. Physical and social circumstances affect the baby as they affect her. Whether or not an infant ingests colostrum, nurses for five months or five years, whether a mother keeps her infant nearby or turns him over to an allomother, each represents a maternal decision with implications for infant survival. Demographically and statistically, multiple, small maternal decisions about how much to invest, and for how long, in any given infant add up to life-or-death outcomes for human offspring.

Other ape neonates cling for dear life to the mother's hair. For human babies survival is more complicated. There is no environmental hazard more omnipresent or immediate in its impact than a retrenchment in maternal care. Consequences of "little maternal decisions" are far more perilous in some habitats than others. Maintaining maternal commitment was once as important for an infant's survival as oxygen, and often it still is. Yet there is little in the routine ethnographic or historical descriptions of mothers to suggest that maintaining adequate maternal commitment was a problem. Is this because it was not? Or is it, as I believe, because an idealized view of maternal commitment has been taken for granted for so long, and because decisions leading to small retrenchments are so unremarkable?

As birth intervals grew shorter through the course of human evolution and recent human history, pressure on mothers to delegate caretaking to others became even more intense. Whenever they safely could, or when they had little choice, mothers handed babies over to fathers or allo-parents, weaned them early, or swaddled them and hung them from doors. At the psychological level, these decisions differ little from those a contemporary mother makes everyday when she asks her neighbor to baby-sit or contracts for more or less adequate daycare. She is playing the odds, and evaluating her priorities. Hence I am dumbfounded when I hear contemporary politicians lament "the breakdown of the family" in the modern world.

Hominid fathers have been choosing between investing in the children they already have and finding new mates with whom to sire more for as long as there has been a division of labor between hunters and gatherers and a practice of hominid males sharing food with immatures. World-wide, such tensions have far more to do with the prevalence of female-headed households than feminism possibly could. Approximately one-third to one-half of all households in the world are female-headed, most of these in countries too poor to have been touched by a social movement that is less than two centuries old and so far primarily a luxury that only educated Western women have been able to afford.[3]

Over the millennia, mothers have factored into their decisions information about the effects a particular birth would have on older children; the probable response of father or stepfather; the infant's own prospects for survival; and the prospect of translating efforts into subsequent reproductive success. Unlike other primates, women possess the capacity to foresee outcomes. Being born to a wise and foresightful mother would seem like good fortune to most of us. But it would be a blessing that brought with it peculiar hazards.

This is why the human infant, though born especially helpless, has had to become psychologically sophisticated in specialized ways, attuning himself to the task of assessing and extracting commitment from those closest to him, especially his mother. Infancy and childhood comprise the first perilous bottleneck every contributor to the human gene pool must pass through. Small downward adjustments of maternal priorities regarding a given infant, which cumulatively amount to life-or-death decisions, have had an enormous impact on the direction of human evolution. Degree of maternal commitment was itself a selection pressure impinging on each newborn. What, then, were the evolutionary consequences on the bodies, minds, and temperaments of human infants?

Notes

1. Kaplan, H. 1997. "The Evolution of the Human Life Course." Pp. 175–211 in *Between Zeus and the Salmon: The Biodemography of Longevity,* edited by K. Wacher and C. Finch. Washington, DC: National Academy Press.
2. Parker, R. 1995. *Mother Love/Mother Hate: The Power of Maternal Ambivalence.* New York: Basic Books.
3. Figures on female-headed households from Judith Bruce at the Population Council, New York, and Bruce, J. 1989. "Homes Divided." *World Development* 17:979–81.

Genes, Souls, and the Human Community

The mapping of the human genome has been much in the news as a major achievement of modern science. Many positive predictions have been made as to the way it will transform the detection and treatment of diseases, but there have also been warnings of the dangers of genetically engineering babies in the hopes of creating "perfect" children. A recent movie, *Gattaca,* showed a whole society divided into "valids" who had been produced with good genes, "invalids" in whom the engineering didn't quite work, and "god-children," whose parents didn't avail themselves of the new technology. The plot concerns two men. One is an "invalid" who desperately wants to become an astronaut but is assigned a janitor's job in a space-rocket launch station. The other man is a high-level "valid" with paralyzed legs as the result of a failed suicide attempt. He tried to commit suicide because he came in second in a sports competition. The newly invalid "valid" becomes the housemate of the "invalid," who uses his ward's blood, urine, hair, eyesight, height, and identity to achieve his dream of space flight. As he is leaving, both men realize that paralyzed legs would not matter in weightless space, where everyone floats.

Barbara Katz Rothman, a sociologist who has written on the tragic responses to prenatal testing for genetic defects and the commodification of motherhood, writes in *Genetic Maps and Human Imaginations* about how little thought of the consequences in human lives and societies goes into scientific priorities and programs. She recounts the costs of the human eugenics movement, an early-twentieth-century attempt to create perfect humans through selective breeding. She lays out the dangers of current "microeugenics," that allows parents to test fetuses for certain deformities and defects—and for sex—and encourages selective abortion. In her discussion of the genetics of illness, she notes that much less effort has gone into mapping detrimental physical environmental conditions than into the search for genetic causes.

In the following excerpt, Katz Rothman raises ethical and philosophical issues of community and personhood—the social and interactive ("nurture") part of human nature that makes us truly human.

In Search of Imagination

Barbara Katz Rothman

Genetics is offering us a way of reading the past, of reading history, in sweeps of time broader than we can imagine. Genetics is teaching us to read the connections, the ties, the relationships between all the forms of life on earth. We share genetic structures not just with chimpanzees or even dogs and cows, but with such simple life forms as yeast. I knead the bread and the cells in my hand and the cells in the yeast are written in the same language, with even, here and there, a recognizable fragment of a word, a DNA sequence, in common. But while some of us are left staring into the bread bowl pondering the wondrousness of life, others among us are running around the planet looking for "uniqueness," that which marks each individual and that which separates the various peoples of the earth from one another.

As science, the Human Genome Project, this attempt to map all of the genes, and the new genetic determinist thinking that has been accompanying it, is a lot like the man-on-the-moon project of a generation ago. It pulls together a lot of the scientific community, gives a finite goal, and inspires much talk about human control. But as I think about the Human Genome Project, the words of a Leonard Cohen song keep running through my mind: "No, they'll never, they'll never reach the moon now. At least not the one we were after."

They wanted to understand our place in the cosmos. They found some interesting rocks. They want to understand the meaning of life. They're finding some interesting proteins. We're always trying to find the meaning of life and our place in the cosmos. The meaning of life is no more to be found in the genetic code than in the composition of rocks.

The problem is that genetic thinking is reductionist: it breaks things up, reduces them to the smallest possible parts—adenine, thymine, cytosine and guanine, the ATCG of the genetic code. Those letters are seen as forming words, creating a code for the construction of life. But the map of life they're drawing is without context: it stands alone. "Shy" genes don't blush; gay genes don't go off to gay bars; smart genes don't do math. These "genes for" have no meaning without a context: the context is the person and the intersecting communities in which that person lives. When I think of this map without a context, this environmentless listing of code, I want to write in the borders, "Beyond here there be dragons."

The dragons, some friendly and some not, are what they still cannot imagine: that which gives place and meaning to the map of the individual. People are more than their cells, and to understand that we have to look within the person to what we sometimes call the "soul," and we have to look beyond the person to the community, to the social world in which that soul comes into being.

What genetic thinking—what all reductionist thinking—lacks is an imagination, the leap of the mind that takes us beyond the pieces to see the whole. And that may be as close as we're going to get to understanding the meaning of life: the whole is greater than the sum of its parts. That is what defines life. Something is there, something that is more than the constitutive molecules, and that something is life. The "problem" of life, the thing that needs explaining, is, what is that "something"? In the language of physics, the problem of life is that it defies the second law of thermodynamics: life is not subject to the law of entropy. It does not dissolve into nothingness, but lives. Erwin Schroedinger was the "father of quantum mechanics," a physicist and a philosopher, and someone who predicted the essential structure of DNA, what it had to be in order to work. Evelyn Fox Keller[1] tells us how in 1943, as an older man, struggling to keep himself going while in exile from his German homeland, he answered the question "When is a piece of matter said to be active?" "When it goes on 'doing something,' moving, exchanging material with its environment, and so forth, and that for a much longer period than we would expect an inanimate piece of matter to 'keep going'under similar circumstances."

Molecules themselves are just molecules: a living being does something. Not only *does* it keep on "doing something," an activity Fox Keller reminds us that an older man would surely value, but—with the eyes of a mother—life makes more of itself, it creates and recreates itself.

Trying to reduce life to DNA confronts this problem: DNA is not "alive." It is inert. It just sits there. DNA doesn't create life: life creates DNA. Robert Pollack, the biologist who told us that "children are assembled as a collection of discrete, randomly assorted, stable, dominant and recessive ancestral alleles," tells us that life is just DNA's way of making more DNA, something he calls a depressing, reductionist summary of natural selection. "To those of us who choose to make it so, life is more than that, but we cannot call on biological justifications for our choice." But is that all life is, even biologically?

We can get caught in this circle forever: does life make DNA or does DNA make life? What we must remember is that life itself is not DNA. It is not reducible to DNA. Life, whatever it is and whatever it means, is something more than the sum of its parts.

That is true at the level of the cell; true at the level of the person; true at the level of the society. Reductionism does not work: the cell isn't just a bunch or even a code of molecules; the person isn't just a mass or even an organization of cells; and the society isn't just a collection of people. In the organization itself, in the whole, exists something that was not there in the parts.

The map that they're creating is supposed to be a map of the person, blueprints for the individual. It is a map that represents the individual as DNA, as code. The metaphors are well and truly mixed: maps, blueprints, codes. What they share is their reductionism: they take the whole, the person, and reduce it to adenine, thymine, cytosine and guanine, arranged in base pairs, twisting up a spiral staircase, trying to find life.

The genes do not just unfold themselves, produce proteins, grow into a body, become a person, organize a social world. The social world does not unfold from the genes, life as a product of gene action. Like a bread, life happens *somewhere*, and if it doesn't happen somewhere, some specific place, in its own history and place and time, it just doesn't happen at all.

The ability to speak is surely "genetic." But, just as surely, genes do not produce speech. Once upon a time, some kings were arguing about which kingdom had the real, true, natural human language. They could see that there were similarities in their languages, and they argued about which was the original, and which were the corruptions of the true tongue. So they raised a baby in total isolation from speech: no one ever said a word to that child. And they waited to hear what language the baby would speak.

Every way of thinking about the social world has, implicitly, a way of thinking about the individual; and every way of thinking about the individual has an implicit way of thinking about the social world. The kings thought of the individual as something preformed, complete, divine, and so they thought of society as something that could corrupt. Since nothing more could be added, society could only take away from the divine perfection of the individual person. The geneticists start with the letters A, T, C, G and build up to the social world. Genetic thinking, because it sees the individual person as dictated by genes, sees the society as an inevitable playing out of "human nature." If there is war, there must be "aggression genes" to account for it; if there's great disparity in wealth, there must be great disparity in genetic attributes, and so on. The social order is explained by looking at the characteristics of individuals, characteristics themselves explained by genes.

It sounds like a natural alliance with the political right: arguing from human nature to the social order is a conservative stance. But in its early days, genetic thinking as it played out in the eugenics movement attracted some very progressive, left-wing thinkers. Genetic thinking does hold out hope for making a better world: you just have to make better people. The older eugenics involved clumsy attempts to control "breeding," encouraging more children among the better types, and discouraging, one way or the other, children of the lesser types. Contemporary approaches offer a far more sophisticated technology. But both are hopelessly mired in the reductionist thinking that fails to imagine the whole as something more.

This isn't the first time that sociology confronted reductionism and determinism and tried to point a way out. The philosophy of George Herbert Mead,[2] the underpinning of the symbolic interactionist approach to sociology, grew in response to the reductionist and determinist interpretations of Freud and of Marx, and out of the biological determinism of the 1920s and 1930s. Mead put the person back in, the person as an actor, a person, we might say, with a soul.

Rather than reducing the person to a set of structures—genes, or ids and egos, or IQ, or attitudes, or any other set of things—the interactionists view the person as a process. Mind is a process by which people deal with the world, an ongoing activity. Judgments, perceptions, concepts, ideas—these are actions we engage in, things we do. We organize the world we live in, we make sense of it, we think about it. We're not just Pavlov's dog: between the stimulus and the response is a mind.

The self is a product of the mind, one of the things we have ideas about. But the self—who I feel I am, who you feel you are—is more than just a product; it too is a process. I am a process, I am what I am doing, but I am also something more. I see that, as we all see that in ourselves. We know ourselves, we see ourselves, we recognize ourselves. And we know, see and recognize others, and ourselves in them. We see others as people like us, and in interaction, we create a social world, an ongoing process. We exist in each other's minds, we grow and come to being in social life, communally, and our minds are in a sense fragments of the larger social mind: each mind is just a fraction, a prism, through which one sees the mind, the consciousness, the social world. We construct the world, and the world constructs us, in endless, constant process.

The self, the person, the being—who you are and who I am—is not just the location where determinist forces intersect. We are, each of us, more than that, more than the sum of those parts. Sometimes we talk about that process of acquiring a sense of self, of becoming our own true selves, as if it happens more or less on its own: "The child develops." I think about that process as a sociologist, but also as a mother. Children do not just develop. A baby not nurtured dies. Even if fed and kept warm, if it is not nurtured, if it is not mothered, it dies. The individual without a context, the blueprint sitting there by itself, cannot become, cannot be. Life ends, and entropy does take over. . . .

What then is a person? When does it start? If it isn't the object written by DNA, there in the plans, then what is it? At this time the question of personhood has been so taken over by the abortion debate that we are hard put to see it in any other terms. But the question of what makes a person is one that every society wrestles with, and in so doing, defines itself.

One of the ways of talking about personhood is to talk about ensoulment.[3] Genetic thinking has so become the coin of the realm that it now seems almost self-evident that conception, the moment when genetic identity is laid down, would be the moment of ensoulment. But people had ideas about the soul long before they had ideas about conception as we now understand it, conception as the joining of egg and sperm to produce the genetic code.

In patriarchal thinking, the life force resides in sperm; it is planted in the body of the woman. But semen isn't people: it's hard to imagine baptisms or last rites for seed spilled, however innocently or guiltily. So when did the seed become a person? For the Catholic Church, from the beginning of the twelfth century when the question came up, through the nineteenth century, a distinction was made between an "unformed embryo" and a person. The journey of the soul to the fetus, a process they called "hominization," did not occur until 40 days after conception for a male fetus, and 80 days for a female. There was, actually, some question about whether the female ever acquired a soul: the Council of Trent debated the existence of women's souls in 1545, finally tabling the issue.

In the 1860s—the same time that Virchow discovered the cell, that Gregor Mendel observed genetics in action, when the American Civil War was being fought without a position on slavery being taken by the Catholic Church, a time when in many ways the understanding of the person was changing—the Church decided that hominization was not to be the basis of decision-making in abortion. With conception, they declared, there was a potential human being, and that potential was itself to be valued as a person—the beginning of genetic thinking.

Other traditions have placed that moment of personhood at "quickening," the moment when the baby makes itself felt. The word "quicken" refers to life, but it also refers to the first time the mother feels the baby move inside of her. Life is an act of communication. The baby reaches out and touches the mother, makes her feel its presence, and the mother gives the world a person. She declares that a new human being is among us.

Still others have waited for birth, for the appearance of the baby before the eyes of the community. Some use the moment of birth itself, and some opt for an occasion a few days later, to offer a ritual welcoming to those babies that made the passage safely.

And at the end of life too, we mark the passing of a person, and in so doing, recognize what constitutes a person. The anthropologists use the presence of ritual burial sites as proof of the humanness of a group: humans mark death. And in marking death, what we are marking is life, a particular life. Something is gone from the world when a person dies, and the rituals of death mark that passing, acknowledging as well the life that was.

Other advances in biotechnology, not just genetics, have forced on us this question of what makes a person. The discussion of brain death was about just this: at what point does a body stop being a person and become "the remains," just a body? How much life does there have to be for personhood?

And at the intersection of life and death, a discussion has opened up about the uses of anencephalic babies as organ donors for other babies. In this context we must ask, is it a baby the woman has given birth to, or the body of a baby? If it is a baby, then it has to be cared for as a baby for as long as it lives. If it is not a baby, not a human person, but only the body of one, then not only do we owe it none of the loving nurturance we owe a baby, even a doomed baby, but we are free to look at that body as we look at other bodies: as a thing, and sometimes even as a potential resource.

The person is never just a body, or just its actions, or just the time and space it takes up in the world: there is always that something else, that indefinable something that is life, that makes the whole greater than the sum of its parts. That person, that self, is not just the working of the genes, or the location where various determinist forces intersect. The whole is something more. Because every vision of the social world rests on an understanding of the self, of personhood, we need a way of thinking about the person that lets us create a good world. What can we call that something more, how shall we imagine it? What about the idea of a soul?. . .

The soul is itself a creation of the social world, made and formed and brought into being in a social way, between people. And our ideas about the soul, what it is and what it means, are also social ideas, ideas we share.

The leap of imagination we need is to see that soul, that self, that individual, is made not just from the letters of a code, but also from other people. That which is holy and precious and unique about each of us is also that which is shared between all of us.

Notes

1. Keller, Evelyn Fox. 1995. *Refiguring Life: Metaphors of Twentieth-Century Biology.* New York: Columbia University Press.

2. Mead, George Herbert. 1934. *Mind, Self and Society.* Chicago: University of Chicago Press.

3. There are many discussions of the history of ensoulment as a concept, including Beverly Wildung Harrison, *Our Right to Choose: Toward a New Ethic of Abortion* (Boston: Beacon Press, 1983); see especially chapter 5, "The History

of Christian Teaching on Abortion Reconceived," pp. 122–24 and 130–32. See also Paul Ramsey, "The Morality of Abortion," in *Life or Death, Ethics and Options,* ed. Daniel Laddy (Seattle: University of Washington Press, 1971). And there is an interesting discussion of the nuances of a debate of competing theories of preformation in the seventeenth and eighteenth centuries, between those who believed that the embryo unfolded from the sperm and those who believed it unfolded from the ovary. See Clara Pinto-Correia, *The Ovary of Eve: Egg and Sperm and Preformation* (Chicago: University of Chicago Press, 1997).

Reprinted from Barbara Katz Rothman, *Genetic Maps and Human Imaginations: The Limits of Science in Understanding Who We Are,* pp. 221–29, 231. Copyright © 1998 by Barbara Katz Rothman. Used by permission of W. W. Norton & Company, Inc.

Toward a Feminist Perspective on the Body

Feminists have critiqued the research on sex/gender differences for its underlying assumptions about the universality and immutability of masculine and feminine behavior, and particularly for its legitimation of men's dominance of women. The reasoning is that if the same behavior is found throughout the world and throughout human history and prehistory, the source must be biological. But the behavior of women and men is not the same throughout the world. Any introductory cultural anthropology text has descriptions of assertive women and passive men, of men weaving and women building houses, of women heads of families, and of kinship structures where children belong to the mother's tribe, not the father's. The dominant status of men varies today and has varied throughout history. Scandinavian countries are much more egalitarian when it comes to gender than fundamentalist Islamic countries, yet their women and men presumably have the same kinds of genes, chromosomes, hormones, brains, and evolutionary history.

Much of the research on the biological sources of gendered behavior compares genetically identified females and males (sex differences) to explain social behavior (gender differences). In biology, the hypothesized source of sex differences has been XX and XY chromosomes, then testosterone and estrogen, and now it is the prenatal "hardwiring" of the brain through genetic and/or hormonal input. Thus, a girl's choice of a career in elementary school teaching and a boy's selection of engineering is attributed to genes, chromosomes, hormones, brain organization, or prehistoric human evolution. Socialization, family and peer pressure, the advice of school counselors, and the gender-typing of jobs are omitted from the picture.

Even though there has been experimental evidence since the 1930s that the so-called male and female hormones are equally important to the development of both sexes, and we know from sex testing at sports competitions that people with XY chromosomes can have female anatomy and physiology, all of the research efforts in the twentieth century have been geared to finding clear male-female differences, preferably with an easily identifiable physiological source. Before the intensive criticism of feminist scientists and social scientists, there was very little effort to document the social sources of masculinity and femininity in Western societies.

A feminist synthesis would argue that genes and hormones have a loop-back effect with physical environments and individual life experiences. There is agency and intention in how we shape our bodies, whether we conform to, resist, or rebel against conventional models of how female and male bodies should look and function, how men and women should behave.

Because our bodies are socially constructed in deeply gendered societies, they will of necessity be gendered, because a gender-neutral or androgynous or "unisex" body is an anathema in a world where people must know quickly and precisely where to place others they encounter for the first time or in short, face-to-face interactions. How you look to the other person (masculine or feminine) is tied to who you are (woman or man). Your social identity is a gendered identity, and all your identity papers and bureaucratic records document your gender over and over again. Who you are is therefore gendered. We'll never know how much of this gendering is biology and how much social construction unless we have a degendered society, one that doesn't produce or exaggerate differences through markedly different treatment and expectations of boys and girls.

A feminist perspective on the body rests on the evidence that in humans, the neural pathways in the brain are not completed prenatally; the interplay between the body and the brain and the physical and social environment create a loop-back effect; and the outcome is a much more varied physiological mixture than our culture and sciences can accept at present. But social changes produce new views of what is natural, and our adaptive bodies and brains change as well. Fausto-Sterling makes this prediction:

> Gender systems change. As they transform, they produce different accounts of nature. Now, at the dawn of a new century, it is possible to witness such change in the making. We are moving from an era of sexual

dimorphism to one of variety beyond the number two. We inhabit a moment in history when we have the theoretical understanding and practical power to ask a question unheard of before in our culture: "Should there be only two sexes?" (2000, 77)

References

Butler, Judith. 1990. *Gender Trouble: Feminism and the Subversion of Identity.* New York and London: Routledge.

Colapinto, John. 1997. "The True Story of John/Joan." *Rolling Stone,* Dec. 11, pp. 54–97.

——. 2000. *As Nature Made Him: The Boy Who Was Raised as a Girl.* New York: HarperCollins.

Connell, R.W. 1995. *Masculinities.* Berkeley: University of California Press.

de Beauvoir, Simone. [1949] 1953. *The Second Sex.* (Trans. by H. M. Parshley.) New York: Knopf.

Ekins, Richard. 1997. *Male Femaling: A Grounded Theory Approach to Cross-dressing and Sex-changing.* New York and London: Routledge.

Gagné, Patricia, and Richard Tewksbury. 1998. "Rethinking Binary Conceptions and Social Constructions: Transgender Experiences of Gender and Sexuality." Pp. 73–102 in *Advances in Gender Research,* vol.3, edited by Marcia Texler Segal and Vasilikie Demos. Greenwich, CT: JAI.

Hargreaves, Jennie. 1994. See Suggested Readings.

Herdt, Gilbert (ed.). 1994. See Suggested Readings.

Herdt, Gilbert, and Julian Davidson. 1988. "The Sambia 'Turnim-Man': Sociocultural and Clinical Aspects of Gender Formation in Male Pseudo Hermaphrodites with 5alpha-Reductase Deficiency in Papua, New Guinea." *Archives of Sexual Behavior* 17:33–56.

MacKinnon, Catharine A. 1990. "Legal Perspectives on Sexual Difference." Pp. 213–24 in *Theoretical Perspectives on Sexual Difference,* edited by Deborah L. Rhode, New Haven, CT: Yale University Press.

Money, John, and Anke A. Ehrhardt. 1972. *Man & Woman, Boy & Girl.* Baltimore, MD: Johns Hopkins University Press.

Taylor, Shelley E., Laura Cousino Klein, Brian P. Lewis, Tara L. Gruenewald et al. 2000. "Biobehavioral Responses to Stress in Females: Tend-and-Befriend, Not Fight-or-Flight." *Psychological Review* 107:411–429.

Turner, Stephanie S. 1999. "Intersex Identities: Locating New Intersections of Sex and Gender." *Gender & Society* 13:457–79.

Wainer, Howard, Catherine Nju, and Samuel Palmer. 2000. "Assessing Time Trends in Sex Differences in Swimming and Running." *Chance* 13:10–17.

Suggested Readings in Feminist Theories of the Body

Birke, Lynda. 2000. *Feminism and the Biological Body.* New Brunswick, NJ: Rutgers University Press.

Bordo, Susan R. 1993. *Unbearable Weight: Feminism, Western Culture, and the Body.* Berkeley: University of California Press.

Brownworth, Victoria, and Susan Raffo. 1999. *Restricted Access: Lesbians on Disability.* Seattle, WA: Seal Press.

Butler, Judith. 1993. *Bodies That Matter: On the Discursive Limits of "Sex."* New York and London: Routledge.

Davis, Kathy. 1995. *Reshaping the Female Body: The Dilemma of Cosmetic Surgery.* New York and London: Routledge.

Davis, Kathy (ed.). 1997. *Embodied Practices.* London: Sage.

Deegan, Mary Jo, and Nancy A. Brooks (eds.). 1985. *Women and Disability: The Double Handicap.* New Brunswick, NJ: Transaction Books.

Donchin, Anne, and Laura Purdy (eds.). 1999. *Embodying Bioethics: Recent Feminist Advances.* Savage, MD: Rowman & Littlefield.

Dreger, Alice Domurat. 1998. *Hermaphrodites and the Medical Invention of Sex.* Cambridge, MA: Harvard University Press.

Fausto-Sterling, Anne. 1985. *Myths of Gender: Biological Theories About Women and Men.* New York: Basic Books.

——. 2000. *Sexing the Body: Gender Politics and the Construction of Sexuality.* New York: Basic Books.

Fine, Michelle, and Adrienne Asch (eds.). 1988. *Women with Disabilities: Essays in Psychology, Culture, and Politics.* Philadelphia: Temple University Press.

Gallagher, Catherine, and Thomas Laqueur (eds.). 1987. *The Making of the Modern Body.* Berkeley: University of California Press.

Gatens, Moira. 1996. *Imaginary Bodies: Essays on Corporeality, Power and Ethics.* New York and London: Routledge.

Gowaty, Patricia Adair (ed.). 1996. *Feminism and Evolutionary Biology: Boundaries, Intersections and Frontiers.* New York: Chapman and Hall.

Grosz, Elizabeth. 1994. *Volatile Bodies: Toward a Corporeal Feminism.* Bloomington: Indiana University Press.

——. 1996. *Space, Time and Perversion: Essays on the Politics of the Body.* New York and London: Routledge.

Halberstam, Judith. 1998. *Female Masculinity.* Durham, NC: Duke University Press.

Hargreaves, Jennifer A. (ed.). 1994. *Sporting Females: Critical Issues in the History and Sociology of Women's Sports.* New York and London: Routledge.

Herdt, Gilbert (ed.). 1994. *Third Sex Third Gender: Beyond Sexual Dimorphism in Culture and History.* New York: Zone Books.

Hillyer, Barbara. 1993. *Feminism and Disability.* Norman: University of Oklahoma Press.

Hrdy, Sarah Blaffer. [1981] 1999. *The Woman That Never Evolved.* Cambridge, MA: Harvard University Press.

——. 1999. *Mother Nature: A History of Mothers, Infants, and Natural Selection.* New York: Pantheon.

Hubbard, Ruth. 1990. *The Politics of Women's Biology.* New Brunswick, NJ: Rutgers University Press.

Jacobus, Mary, Evelyn Fox Keller, and Sally Shuttleworth (eds.). 1990. *Body/ Politics: Women and the Discourses of Science.* New York and London: Routledge.

Jordanova, Ludmilla. 1989. *Sexual Visions: Images of Gender in Science and Medicine Between the Eighteenth and Twentieth Centuries.* Madison, WI: University of Wisconsin Press.

Kessler, Suzanne J. 1998. *Lessons from the Intersexed.* New Brunswick, NJ: Rutgers University Press.

Laqueur, Thomas. 1990. *Making Sex: Body and Gender from the Greeks to Freud.* Cambridge, MA: Harvard University Press.

Lonsdale, Susan. 1990. *Women and Disability.* New York: St. Martin's Press.

Lorber, Judith. 1993. "Believing Is Seeing: Biology as Ideology." *Gender & Society* 7:568–81.

——. 1997. *Gender and the Social Construction of Illness.* Thousand Oaks, CA: Sage.

Lorber, Judith, and Patricia Yancey Martin. 1997. "The Socially Constructed Body: Insights from Feminist Theory." In *Illuminating Social Life: Classical and Contemporary Theory Revisited,* edited by Peter Kivisto, pp. 183–206. Thousand Oaks, CA: Pine Forge Press.

Mairs, Nancy. 1986. *Plaintext.* Tucson: University of Arizona Press.

Price, Janet, and Margrit Shildrick (eds.). 1999. *Feminist Theory and the Body.* New York and London: Routledge.

Raymond, Janice G. 1979. *The Transsexual Empire: The Making of the She-male.* Boston: Beacon.

Rossi, Alice S. 1977. "A Biosocial Perspective on Parenting." *Daedalus* 106:1–31.

Rothman, Barbara Katz. 1998. *Genetic Maps and Human Imaginations: The Limits of Science in Understanding Who We Are.* New York: Norton. (To be reissued as *The Book of Life.* Boston: Beacon, 2001.)

Sayers, Janet. 1982. *Biological Politics: Feminist and Anti-feminist Perspectives.* London and New York: Tavistock.

Sered, Susan. 2000. *What Makes Women Sick? Maternity, Modesty, and Militarism in Israeli Society.* Hanover, NH: University Press of New England.

Tong, Rosemarie, Gwen Anderson, and Aida Santos (eds.). 2000. *Globalizing Feminist Bioethics: Women's Health Concerns Worldwide.* Boulder, CO: Westview.

Van den Wijngaard, Marianne. 1997. *Reinventing the Sexes: The Biomedical Construction of Femininity and Masculinity.* Bloomington: Indiana University Press.

Vertinsky, Patricia. 1990. *The Eternally Wounded Woman: Women, Doctors and Exercise in the Late Nineteenth Century.* Manchester, UK: Manchester University Press.

Weiss, Meira. 1994. *Conditional Love: Parents' Attitudes Toward Handicapped Children.* Westport, CT: Bergin & Garvey.

Weitz, Rose (ed.). 1998. *The Politics of Women's Bodies: Sexuality, Appearance and Behavior.* New York: Oxford University Press.

Wendell, Susan. 1996. *The Rejected Body: Feminist Philosophical Reflections on Disability.* New York and London: Routledge. ✦

Part VI

Feminist Politics for the Twenty-First Century

In the past 150 years, women's status in the Western world has improved enormously (Jackson 1998), but the revolution (or evolution) that would make women and men truly equal has not yet occurred. The question that puzzles me is why, with regard to gender inequality, the more things change, the more they stay the same. The answer, I suggest, is that the structure of modern society is built on gender divisions. From a social constructionist gender perspective, it is the division of people into two unequally valued categories that is at the heart of gender inequality. I argue that it is this gendering that needs to be challenged by feminists, with the long-term goal of not just minimizing, but doing away with binary gender divisions completely. To this end, I call for a feminist degendering movement.

Gender divisions are so common in our daily life and, for most people, so "natural," that it is only the rare gender rebel who challenges them. While racial, ethnic, class, and sexual divisions have been significantly challenged, the belief that gender divisions are normal and natural is still an underlying frame for modern social life. Most feminists who seek change in the structure and value system of gendered social orders rarely challenge the binary divisions. As Christine Delphy says, "Feminists seem to want to abolish hierarchy and even sex roles, but not difference itself" (1993, 6). That is, while feminists want women and men to be equal, few talk now about doing away with gender divisions altogether. One who does is Sandra Bem, who advocates "a vision of utopia in which gender polarization . . . has been so completely dismantled that— except in narrowly biological contexts like reproduction—the distinction between male and female no longer organizes the culture and the psyche" (1993, 192).

Eradicating the social divide between females and males is hardly a new idea for feminists. In 1971, Shulamith Firestone said,

> the end goal of feminist revolution must be . . . not just the elimination of male *privilege* but of the sex *distinction* itself: genital differences between human beings would no longer matter culturally. (p. 11)

In 1972, Lois Gould's classic tale of degendering, "X: A Fabulous Child's Story" was published in *Ms. Magazine* (Gould 1972). In 1980, Monique Wittig challenged lesbians and gay men to deny the divisive power of heterosexuality by refusing to think of themselves as women and men. More recently, postmodernists and queer theorists have questioned the two-fold divisions of gender, sexuality, and even sex, undermining the solidity of a world built on men/women, heterosexuals/homosexuals, and male/female (see chapter 11).

But feminism as a movement has lost sight of Firestone's revolutionary goal in the fight for equal treatment within the present gender structure. The feminist drive for equality has settled for minimizing gender divisions, yet these divisions continue to reproduce inequality. The distinctions between women and men may be deceptive, as Cynthia Fuchs Epstein (1988) argues, but they are unlikely to wither away by themselves. Women and men more and more do similar work, but the work world continues to replicate occupational gender segregation even as women move into jobs formerly considered men's work (Jacobs 1989). During the 1970s and 1980s, women who went into occupations where the employees were predominantly men soon found that their coworkers became predominantly women because the men left (Reskin and Roos 1990). In fact, it was because the men were leaving increasingly unattractive work sectors that positions opened for women. The underlying gender structure of the work world remained intact.

As feminists, we need a gender perspective to make this structure visible. But we also need to think beyond gender to the possibilities of a nongendered social order. In *Paradoxes of Gender,* I suggested two thought experiments that render gender irrelevant (Lorber 1994, 292–302; also see Lorber 1986). In the first, an imaginary society divided into two genders treats them strictly equally, with half of all jobs held by men and half by women, family work done half by women and half by men, alternating men and women as head of governments, and equal numbers of women and men in the officer corps and ranks of armed forces, on sports teams, in cultural productions, and so on throughout society. In the second imaginary society, all work is equally valued and recompensed, regardless of who does it, and families and work groups are structured for equality of control of resources and decisions. Either path would render gender irrelevant—strict parity by the interchangeability of women and men, and strict equality by making no category of people more valuable than any other. Strict parity would make it pointless to construct and maintain gender differences; strict equality would contradict the purpose of gender divisions by undercutting the subordination of women by men. Christine Delphy says,

> If we define men within a gender framework, they are first and foremost dominants with characteristics which enable them to remain dominants. To be like them would be also to be dominants, but this is a contradiction in terms. . . . [T]o be dominant one must have someone to dominate. (1993, 8)

Without denying the importance of continuing to fight for gender equality, for an end to sexual exploitation and violence, and for women's freedom from men's domination, I believe that feminism needs a long-term strategy to undermine the overall gendered structure of the societies in which most of us live. Feminism has long battled against the content and rationale of women's devaluation and subordinate status. We now need a feminist degendering movement that would rebel against the division of the social world into two basic categories—the very structure of women's inequality.

Gender as a Structure of Inequality

Gender is a social creation, a product of human inventiveness adopted for its usefulness in allocating reciprocal rights and responsibilities, work tasks, and the physical and social reproduction of new members of any society. The gendered division of work in early societies did not separate subsistence labor and child care—women did both—and many of these societies were egalitarian or possibly even woman-dominated, given women's important contribution to the food supply and their evident role in the procreation of valued children. Accidentally or deliberately, but in any case probably quite gradually, gender got inextricably built into stratification and inequality, producing a subordinate group, "women," whose labor, sexuality, and childbearing could be exploited.

The unequal distribution of power, property, and prestige between women and men is now part of the structure of modern societies. As a result, gender statuses today are inherently unequal, and gendering continues to produce inequality. Subordination of women is an intrinsic part of the modern social order, not because men are naturally superior or dominant (if they were, there would be no subordinate men) or because women bear children (if that were true, no mother would ever be a leader in her society). The subordination of women persists because it produces a group that can be exploited as workers, sexual partners, childbearers, and emotional nurturers, in the marketplace and in the household. Policies that could establish true gender equality are not seriously implemented because they would erode the exploitation of women's labor, sexuality, and emotions. Societies and communities that have tried to establish egalitarianism rarely give as much attention to gender inequality as they do to economic inequality.

Since the gendered social order is at present a system of power and dominance mostly favoring men, redressing the imbalance would mean giving women some of men's privileges, such as freedom from housework, and men some of women's responsibilities, such as taking care of infants. Instead, men have gotten women's privileges, such as limits on the number of hours a day a paid worker can be required to work, and women have gotten men's responsibilities, such as economic support of their families (Stacey 1991, 259). Lesbians and homosexual men are able to break the microsystem of domination and subordination, since personal power differentials are not gendered in their families and their communities, but they participate in the gendered macrosystem, especially in the world of work, as women and men.

A truly radical goal for feminism would be a society without gender. Of course, we would want a society without economic inequities, racial distinctions, or sexual exploitation. These are inequalities as well, and they are also all implicated in the social production of gender inequality. We have tried to make women and men equal in every sphere of life, but we also have to undermine the construction and maintenance of gender distinctions and the constant divisions of so many aspects of life by gender. The resultant degendered social order would not be a society of indistinguishable clones—individuality and cross-cutting groupings would produce much more variety than two genders (Lorber 1996).

As pervasive as gender is, because it is constructed and maintained through daily interaction, it can be resisted and reshaped by gender trouble-makers (Butler 1990). The social construction perspective argues that people create their social realities and identities, including their gender, through their actions with others—their families, friends, colleagues. Gender is a constant performance, but its enactment is hemmed in by the general rules of social life, cultural expectations, workplace norms, and laws. These social restraints are also amenable to change, but not easily, because the social order is structured for stability (Giddens 1984). Many aspects of gender have been changed through individual agency, group pressure, and social movements.[1] But the underlying structure has not.

Feminist movements have focused on the inequalities and exploitations, especially in the gendered work world and domestic division of labor, but have found that as one set of gendered practices is eliminated, others rise to take their place. To keep women down, differences from men must be maintained and used as a rationale for women's inferior status (Reskin 1988). Feminists have either minimized these differences, to little effect, or maximized and valorized them, also to little effect. The problem is that the focus has been on differences between women and men as individuals or as social actors. These differences are a means to an end—legitimation and justification of gendered social orders. Feminist social scientists have mapped out the effects of gendering on daily lives and on social institutions and have produced reams of data on how these processes maintain inequality between women and men (see Lorber 1994). I suggest that it is now time to find ways to undercut the first principle of the gendered social order, the division into "men" and "women."

Feminist Change

Like feminists of the past, we are faced with the dilemma of gender-neutral equality versus gender-marked equity. Arguing for gender equality, we claim that women and men are virtually interchangeable. Taking the stance of gender equity, we recognize the physiological and procreative sex differences between females and males and look for ways to make them socially equivalent. The dilemma, or what Joan Wallach Scott calls the inevitable feminist paradox, is that the fight to erase the effects of sex differences invokes them:

> To the extent that it acted for "women," feminism produced the "sexual difference" it sought to eliminate. This paradox—the need both to accept and to refuse "sexual difference"—was the constitutive condition of feminism as a political movement throughout its history. (1996, 3–4)

The gendered social orders of modern Western societies themselves reflect this ambiguity, shifting like pendulums between values and practices that emphasize sex differences and those that emphasize gender equality. Today, housework and childrearing are considered work and given due value in divorce settlements. At the same time, no one demands that a married woman spend her whole life cooking, cleaning, and taking care of children. But most men living in households with adult women do not share equally in domestic work, so women now routinely have a double work shift (Hochschild 1989), or they hire to do "their" work another woman from the supply of those disadvantaged by poor education or immigrant status (Glenn 1992). Not much has changed in the work-family structure for women, except that married mothers with good educations now have social approval for the life-long, full-time pursuit of prestigious careers as well as the freedom to quit "for the sake of their family."

For most women in postindustrial societies whose households are not totally economically dependent on them, the work-family combination remains what it has been since the industrial revolution took the production of goods and services out of the home and into factories and offices—their paid work is fitted around the care of children and the maintenance of households. Most European countries and Israel have policies of maternal leave and subsidized child care that encourage women with small children to stay in the paid work force, but because they have the organizational and emotional responsibility for their families, they are discouraged from competing with men for high-level, better-paid, full-time positions (Izraeli 1992). Since there has been little restructuring of either the workplace or family life, many women in European countries are having one child or none at all (Specter 1998). In the

United States, the "brave new families" sharing resources, children, and domestic labor seem to be as much the fall-out from divorce and step-parenting as the outcome of deliberate attempts to live and love as equals (Stacey 1991).

A gender perspective can account for these paradoxical inequalities buried in what have seemed like successes in the fight for women's equality—full-time jobs, subsidized child care, opening up of the professions and politics. Women's seeming always to "come home" is the outcome of a gendered division of labor that consistently discourages and does not reward their total immersion in public life (Rantalaiho and Heiskanen 1997). Women do not choose families over careers because of their biologically based nurturant and relational characteristics but because they are socially rewarded when they do so.

An unequally structured gender order needs to be addressed directly, through a feminist degendering movement, rather than through a woman's movement. We need to undermine the current structure of gender politically and institutionally, develop strategies for dismantling the gendered division of labor in the family and workplaces, and wherever possible, degender everyday interaction.

A Feminist Degendering Movement

The legitimacy of the gendered social order can be subverted at the level of its underlying discourse—its biological assumptions, its binarism, and its socially constructed gender differences. It can be openly challenged by nongendered practices in ordinary interaction, in families, child-rearing, language, and organization of space. And to the extent that feminists have control over organizations, they can be organized in nongendered ways.

On the level of discourse, we need to frame research questions and political issues so that they are not based on the standardized categories of "men" vs. "women," and "boys" vs. "girls" and on the taken-for-granted assumptions that their characteristics are uniform and universal, and thus somehow related to procreation and parenting. At the very least, we can start with the work already done by multicultural feminists on the intersections of gender, social class, and racial ethnic categories; by researchers of multiple masculinities; and by the ongoing studies of sexualities and transgenders.

These multiviewed perspectives can be translated into praxis by seeking solutions to problems in ways that question conventional categories and conventional assumptions. When we ask "What is the problem?" we need to challenge "deeply held cultural assumptions, given specific historical, economic and cultural locations" (Bacchi 1999, 205). When faced with a political solution to a social problem, we can ask if gender categorization and separation are necessary and what the latent consequences are likely to be of different treatment of women and men. To this end, we must dissect the layers of power embedded in the gendered "relations of ruling" (D. E. Smith 1990).

We can try to blur gender boundaries in our everyday lives and undermine the built-in gender divisions in our work worlds. Whenever we can, we should encourage the degendering of instrumental tasks, physical labor, athletic prowess, emotional sustenance, and physical spaces. Every time a man changes a baby's diapers, it's a small rebellion; if he can do it in a gender-neutral public baby station, it's a social transformation.[2] As Christine Delphy says:

> We do not know what the values, individual personality traits, and culture of a nonhierarchical society would be like, and we have great difficulty in imagining it. But to imagine it we must think that it is possible. Practices produce values; other practices produce other values. (1993, 8)

As examples of some attempts to undermine one aspect of the gendered social order, child care, consider the following efforts at degendering parenting.

In many European countries, child care help and subsidized parental leave for either parent has changed mothering from a full-time occupation to something that can be combined with paid work out of the home and so can be participated in by both parents. To encourage the active involvement of fathers, Sweden has allocated leave time in the first year of a newborn's life that the father must take or it is forfeited—"daddy days." But without programs geared to new fathers and social encouragement of their fuller participation in infant care, most men use only the minimum postbirth two weeks (Swedin 1995). Changed values and attitudes regarding the importance of hands-on infant care by fathers and their capacity for nurturant behavior have yet to be institutionalized by changes in the gendered structure of work and family.

Some people have structured their families to be gender-equal on every level—domestic work, child care, and financial contribution to the household (Bem 1998; Deutsch 1999; Risman 1998; Schwartz 1994). However, as long as work is structured for a married-man-with-wife career pattern, and men's work is paid better than women's work, gender-equal families will be very hard to attain for the majority of people. Other heterosexual couples have reversed roles—the woman is the breadwinner and the man the child-carer and housekeeper (Wheelock 1990). One study reported that the domestic world is so gendered that male househusbands suffered from ostracism and isolation, and also from a suspicion of homosexuality (C. D. Smith 1998). Oddly, lesbian and gay couples who have reared children in a variety of family arrangements have blended more easily into hetero-coupled social worlds, at least in some communities (Weston 1991). Corporate and government policies that offer health insurance and other benefits to any couple in a long-term household arrangement have helped to restructure family life in ways that do not assume heterogendered partnering; allocating benefits universally to individuals rather than to couples through the "head of household" would undermine the idea of gendered families even more (Robson 1994).

At the other end of the spectrum is the deepening of the gendered divisions of work in the global economy. Financed by capital from developed countries, work organizations around the world exploit the labor of poor, young, unmarried women under sweatshop-like conditions, while reserving better-paid jobs and support for entrepreneurship to middle-class men (Mies et al. 1988; Moghadam 1996). The policies of the International Monetary Fund and other financial restructuring agencies do not include gender desegregation or encouraging women's education and access to health resources that would allow them to break into men's occupations (Sparr 1994; Ward 1990). In many developing countries, violence and sexual exploitation, as well as the spread of AIDS heterosexually, seriously undermine efforts to upgrade the lives of women and girls (United Nations 2000). Feminist work here has all it can do to prevent women's lives from worsening. A gender perspective is needed to influence the programs of development agencies to be attentive to possible deleterious effects on women and girls of seemingly gender-neutral policies. Degendering would be counterproductive until women attain some measures of equality with men.

So I am not suggesting that a movement to eradicate gender divisions is universally useful. It would be most effective where women have achieved a high measure of equality. Tracing the rise in women's status in the United States in the last 150 years, Jackson (1998) argues that thanks to increasing bureaucratization and rationalization of many areas of modern life, women have substantial equality with men in jobs, legal rights, education, and voting power. However, despite these marks of formal equality, what he calls "residual inequalities" remain to be tackled—the rarity of women in high political office and at the top levels of prestigious and lucrative professions, the widespread imbalance in domestic labor, greater costs to women in divorce or staying unpartnered, sexual harassment, rape, physical violence, and the persistent belief that women and men are inherently different (p. 8). A feminist degendering movement that pushed for gender neutrality at the informal levels of interaction in the work world and in the family would enhance the social forces of rationality and objectivity that have given women in the Western world their formal equality with men in laws, jobs, and voting power. It would not do much good in directly combating sexual harassment, rape, and physical violence, but it might undercut the legitimation of these harmful manifestations of masculinity. A degendering movement whose goal is greater equality would also have to include pressure for erasure of other invidious divisions, especially those based on racial categories and ethnicity, and for open access to economic resources, educational opportunities, and political power.

What could be lost are the valued qualities of women's lives that difference feminists have valorized—nurturance, relationality, emotionality—if the outcome of degendering is what we have come to see as a masculine world: objective, instrumental, and bureaucratic. But in actuality, the modern world is both formal in organization and informal in practice, rule-based and relational, rational and emotional at one and the same time, and so are the people in it, women and men. Diminishment of gender as an organizing principle of institutions and everyday life would not turn women into men any more than it would turn men into women. It would rather degenderize the best—and the worst—qualities of people.

Toward the End of Gender

In sum, to change modern Western gendered social orders to be less gendered will mean changing everyday gendered behavior, modifying gender-organized attitudes and values—especially about families and children—and, most of all, restructuring the gendered division of work and redressing the gendered power imbalances in the governments of dominant nations. A movement to change the embedded gendered social order needs individual agency, informal social action, and formal political organizations (none of which are separate from each other). Because gender so imbues our lives, a feminist degendering movement will be everywhere and ongoing. If this sounds like the "good old days" of pervasive personal politics, it is—but rather than just fighting sexism or the oppression of women by male-dominated institutions, it includes men and attends as well to other subordinating social statuses. Most of all, it directly targets the processes and practices of gendering and their outcome—gendered people, practices, and power.

Notes

1. For recent research on gender and social movements, see the special issue, "Gender and Social Movements," edited by Verta Taylor and Nancy Whittier, *Gender & Society* Part 1, vol. 12, December 1998; Part 2, vol. 13, February 1999.

2. For me, the success of the degendering movement will be marked by unisex bathrooms. This is not a trivial goal—gender-divided bathrooms replicate the supposed biological base of the gendered social order and the symbolic separation of men's and women's social worlds. They also are constant evidence of gender inequity, since there are never enough ladies' rooms in public spaces (Molotch 1988).

References

Bacchi, Carol Lee. 1999. *Women, Policy and Politics: The Construction of Policy Problems*. Thousand Oaks, CA: Sage.

Bem, Sandra Lipsitz. 1993. *The Lenses of Gender: Transforming the Debate on Sexual Inequality*. New Haven, CT: Yale University Press.

———. 1998. *An Unconventional Family*. New Haven, CT: Yale University Press.

Delphy, Christine. 1993. "Rethinking Sex and Gender." *Women's Studies International Forum* 16:1–9.

Deutsch, Francine M. 1999. *Halving It All: How Equally Shared Parenting Works*. Cambridge, MA: Harvard University Press.

Epstein, Cynthia Fuchs. 1988. *Deceptive Distinctions: Sex, Gender and the Social Order*. New Haven, CT: Yale University Press.

Firestone, Shulamith. 1971. *The Dialectic of Sex: The Case for Feminist Revolution*. New York: Bantam.

Giddens, Anthony. 1984. *The Constitution of Society: Outline of the Theory of Structuration*. Berkeley: University of California Press.

Glenn, Evelyn Nakano. 1992. "From Servitude to Service Work: Historical Continuities in the Racial Division of Paid Reproductive Labor." *Signs* 18:1–43.

Hochschild, Arlie Russell with Anne Machung. 1989. *The Second Shift: Working Parents and the Revolution at Home*. New York: Viking.

Izraeli, Dafina N. 1992. "Culture, Policy, and Women in Dual-Earner Families in Israel." In Susan Lewis, Dafina N. Izraeli, and Helena Hootsmans (eds.), *Dual-Earner Families: International Perspectives*. Thousand Oaks, CA: Sage.

Jackson, Robert Max. 1998. *Destined for Equality: The Inevitable Rise of Women's Status*. Cambridge, MA: Harvard University Press.

Jacobs, Jerry A. 1989. *Revolving Doors: Sex Segregation and Women's Careers*. Stanford, CA: Stanford University Press.

Lorber, Judith. 1986. "Dismantling Noah's Ark," *Sex Roles* 14:567–580.

——. 1994. *Paradoxes of Gender*. New Haven, CT: Yale.

——. 1996. "Beyond the Binaries: Depolarizing the Categories of Sex, Sexuality, and Gender," *Sociological Inquiry* 66:143–159.

Mies, Maria, Veronika Bennholdt-Thomsen, and Claudia von Werlhof. 1988. *Women: The Last Colony*. London: Zed Books.

Moghadam, Valentine M. (ed.). 1996. *Patriarchy and Development: Women's Positions at the End of the Twentieth Century*. Oxford, UK: Clarendon Press.

Molotch, Harvey. 1988. "The Restroom and Equal Opportunity." *Sociological Forum* 3:128–32.

Rantalaiho, Liisa, and Tuula Heiskanen (eds.). 1997. *Gendered Practices in Working Life*. New York: St. Martin's Press.

Reskin, Barbara F. 1988. "Bringing the Men Back In: Sex Differentiation and the Devaluation of Women's Work." *Gender & Society* 2:58–81.

Reskin, Barabara F., and Patricia A. Roos. 1990. *Job Queues, Gender Queues: Explaining Women's Inroads into Male Occupations*. Philadelphia: Temple University Press.

Risman, Barbara J. 1998. *Gender Vertigo: American Families in Transition*. New Haven, CT: Yale University Press.

Robson, Deane R. 1994. "Resisting the Family: Repositioning Lesbians in Legal Theory." *Signs* 19:975–996.

Schwartz, Pepper. 1994. *Love Between Equals: How Peer Marriage Really Works*. New York: Free Press.

Scott, Joan Wallach. 1996. *Only Paradoxes to Offer: French Feminists and the Rights of Man*. Cambridge, MA: Harvard University Press.

Smith, Calvin D. 1998. " 'Men Don't Do This Sort of Thing:' A Case Study of the Social Isolation of Househusbands." *Men and Masculinities* 1:138–172.

Smith, Dorothy E. 1990. *Texts, Facts, and Femininity: Exploring the Relations of Ruling.* New York and London: Routledge.

Sparr, Pam. (ed.). 1994. *Mortgaging Women's Lives: Feminist Critiques of Structural Adjustment.* London: Zed Books.

Specter, Michael. 1998. "Population Implosion Worries a Graying Europe." *New York Times,* July 10, A1,6.

Stacey, Judith 1991. *Brave New Families.* New York: Basic Books.

Swedin, G. 1995. "Modern Swedish Fatherhood." In *Men on Men: Eight Swedish Men's Personal Views on Equality, Masculinity and Parenthood.* Sweden: Ministry of Health and Social Affairs.

United Nations. 2000. *The World's Women 2000: Trends and Statistics.* New York: Department of Economic and Social Affairs.

Ward, Kathryn (ed.). 1990. *Women Workers and Global Restructuring.* Ithaca, NY: ILR Books.

Wheelock, Jane. 1990. *Husbands at Home: The Domestic Economy in a Post-Industrial Society.* New York and London: Routledge.

Wittig, Monique. 1980. "The Straight Mind." *Feminist Issues* 1: 103–111. ✦

Internet Sources for Research on Women, Men, and Gender

Many of these web sites have links to other useful sites.

General Resources

AAUW (Association of American University Women) Research Reports—http://www.aauw.org/2000/research.html

Center for Gender in Organizations—http://artemis.simmons.edu/gsm/cgo

Disabled Peoples' International Women's Committee—http://www.dpi.org/women.html

Disabled women on the web—http://www.disabilityhistory.org

Documents for the Women's Liberation Movement: An On-Line Archival Collection (Duke University)—http://scriptorium.lib.duke.edu/wlm

Feminism—http://www.wwwomen.com/category/femini1.html

Feminist periodicals—http://library.wisc.edu/libraries/WomensStudies

Feminist science fiction—http://www.ninthwonder.com/femspec

Feminist theory—http://www.cddc.vt.edu/feminism

Gender and society (background information and links to other sites)—http://www.trinity.edu/~mkearl/gender.html

Gender studies sources—http://vos.ucsb.edu/shuttle/gender.html

Institute for Research on Women and Gender—http://www.umich.edu/~irwg/index.html

Jewish Women's Archive—http://www.jwa.org/main.html

Murray Research Center—http://www.radcliffe.edu/murray

National Council for Research on Women—http://www.ncrw.org

269

NOEMA: The Collaborative Bibliography of Women in Philosophy— http://billyboy.ius.indiana.edu/WomeninPhilosophy/WomeninPhilo. html

Sociologists for Women in Society—http://www.socwomen.org

Status of women in U.S. (by states) - http://www.iwpr.org/states/ index.html

Syllabi on the Web for Women- and Gender-Related Courses—http:// www.umbc.edu/cwit/syllabi.html

ViVa Women's history database—http://www.iisg.nl~womhist/ vivahome.html

Women of achievement and history—http://www.undelete.org

Women of color—http://www.hsph.harvard.edu/grhf/WoC

Women's issues—http://research.umbc.edu/~korenman/wmst/ links.html

Women's studies—http://www.umbc.edu/wmst/wmsttoc.html

Health and Reproduction

Female Genital Mutilation Education and Networking Project—http:// www.fgmnetwork.org

Global Reproductive Health Forum at Harvard—http:// www.hsph.harvard.edu/grhf

National Women's Health Information Center—http:// www.4woman.gov

Women of Color Health Data Book—http://www.4women.gov/owh/ pub/woc

International

Canadian Women's Movement Archives—http://www.uottawa.ca/ library/cwma.html

Central and Eastern Europe—http://www.ceu.hu/gend/gendir.html

Circular Crossings: Area Studies and Women's Studies—http:// www.womencrossing.org

Comparative international data on women in politics—http://www.ipu.org/iss-e/women.html

European women's issues—http://women-www.uia.ac.be/women

Gender in Development—http://www.undp.org/gender/resources

Global activism—http://www.womenswire.net or http://www.womenswire.org

International Archives of the Second Wave of Feminism—http://www.wennet.net/~celesten/2ndwave.html

Nordic countries—http://www.nikk.uio.no/english-index.html

Study of Global Women: An Annotated Web Bibliography—http://multiweb.lib.calpoly.edu/classes/ws411/index.html

UK Gender Theory Resource Page—http://www.theory.org.uk

UK National Library of Women—http://www.lgu.ac.uk/fawcett

UN Internet Gateway on the Advancement and Empowerment of Women—http://www.un.org/womenwatch

Women's EDGE—http://www.womensedge.org

Women's Environment and Development Organization (WEDO)—http://www.wedo.org

Women and International Development—http://www.isp.msu.edu/WID

Women's International Studies Europe (WISE)—http://uia.ac.be/women/wise

Men's Issues

Men and Masculinities Bibliography—http://www.anu.edu.au/~a112465/mensbiblio/mensbibliomenu.html

Men's issues—http://menshealthnetwork.org

Men's issues—http://www.pscw.uva.nl/SOCIOSITE/TOPICS/Men.html

Men's issues—http://www.vix.com/pub/men/index.html

Men's Rape Prevention Project—http://www.mrpp.org

NOMAS: The National Organization for Men Against Sexism—http://www.nomas.org

Pro-feminism—http://www.profeminist.org

Teaching Men's Lives—http://www.hu.mtu.edu/~jijasken/menslives.html

White Ribbon Campaign (Men against violence against women)—http://www.whiteribbon.ca

Sexuality and Transgender

Intersex Society of North America—http://www.isna.org

Lesbigay scholars directory—http://newark.rutgers.edu/~lcrew/lbg_edir.html

Transgender and feminism—http://www.transfeminism.org

Transgender issues—http://www.ifge.org

Transgender links—http://www.gender.org/resources/links.html

Science and Technology

Center for the Study of Women, Science, & Technology— http://www.wst.gatech.edu

Center for Women and Information Technology—http://www.umbc.edu/cwit

On-Line Journals

AVIVA—http://www.aviva.org

Feminism and Nonviolence Studies—http://www.fnsa.org

Genders—http://www.genders.org

Journal of International Women's Studies—http://www.mcla.mass.edu/academics/sba-womenctr

Women's International Net—http://www.winmagazine.org
Archives—http://winmagazine.org/chrono.htm

XY Magazine—http://www.anu.edu.au/~a112465/XY/reprint.htm ✦